A Thousand Dreams

VANCOUVER'S DOWNTOWN EASTSIDE AND THE FIGHT FOR ITS FUTURE

LARRY CAMPBELL,
NEIL BOYD & LORI CULBERT

A THOUSAND
DREAMS

GREYSTONE BOOKS
D&M PUBLISHERS INC.
Vancouver/Toronto

Greystone Books
An imprint of D&M Publishers Inc.
2323 Quebec Street, Suite 201
Vancouver BC Canada V5T 4S7
www.greystonebooks.com

Library and Archives Canada Cataloguing in Publication
Campbell, Larry
A thousand dreams : Vancouver's Downtown Eastside and the fight for its future / Larry Campbell, Neil Boyd, Lori Culbert.

ISBN 978-1-55365-298-4

1. Downtown-Eastside (Vancouver, B.C.). 2. Downtown-Eastside
(Vancouver, B.C.)—Social conditions. I. Boyd, Neil, 1951–
II. Culbert, Lori, 1967– III. Title.

HN110.V3C34 2009   971.1'33   C2009-904685-7

Editing by Barbara Pulling
Cover and text design by Naomi MacDougall
Cover illustration by Naomi MacDougall
Back cover photos, from left to right: Judy Graves talks to a woman on the streets of Vancouver (Don MacKinnon/Canwest); Lisa Alexson and Andy Desjarlais take in a picnic in Oppenheimer Park (Rob Kruyt/*Vancouver Sun*); a drug user exchanges needles with DEYAS's Ron Graham (Jeff Vinnick/*Vancouver Sun*)
Printed and bound in Canada by Friesens
Printed on acid-free paper that is forest friendly (100% post-consumer recycled paper) and has been processed chlorine free

We gratefully acknowledge the financial support of the Canada Council for the Arts, the British Columbia Arts Council, the Province of British Columbia through the Book Publishing Tax Credit, and the Government of Canada through the Book Publishing Industry Development Program (BPIDP) for our publishing activities.

Mixed Sources
Cert no. SW-COC-001271
© 1996 FSC
FSC

DEDICATED TO the Downtown Eastside,
the resilient and socially committed community
that inspired this book

CONTENTS

Preface

THE DOWNTOWN EASTSIDE WAS ONCE the heart of Vancouver's retail and banking district. People flocked to the neighbourhood to shop at Woodward's, go to the theatre, eat at the many restaurants along Hastings Street, or generally enjoy a night on the town. The hotels were full of labourers on leave from well-paying jobs in B.C.'s thriving resource sector. The area was home to the port for ships sailing into Burrard Inlet; it was the terminus for the cross-country Canadian Pacific Railway and the central destination for streetcars and trams from 1890 to 1950. But then economic conditions changed—retail stores and hotels moved well west of Main Street and to suburban locations. And the streetcars and trams were displaced by the automobile.

As the neighbourhood's economy declined, the once-grand hotels became down-and-out beer parlours, with single-occupancy rooms above housing people with a variety of difficulties. By the 1990s, the Downtown Eastside seemed to be in a kind of free fall. Crack cocaine had been added to the problems of alcohol abuse and the intravenous use of a newly potent heroin;

overdose deaths and HIV infection rates skyrocketed. Mentally ill men and women continued to be released from facilities into the community without the provision of any meaningful resources—and, most importantly, without any kind of supportive housing. In 1993, the federal government had simply stopped funding social housing, as part of its deficit-cutting agenda. All of this combined to produce a perfect storm.

The Downtown Eastside—the neighbourhood that is the subject of this book—is just ten blocks long and about five blocks wide. But the area has produced a community that is remarkably distinct. Take a walk along Hastings Street from Gore to Abbott. There are always dozens of people waiting in lines for food and other kinds of meagre support, and many individuals who might best be described as wounded, some openly buying and selling drugs, others pushing shopping carts, sorting through dumpsters, or trying to guide a needle into their veins in the alleys just east or west of Main Street.

But for all of its vulnerability and despair, this is also a community of hopefulness and resilience. Like the green shoots that arise from the ashes of a devastating forest fire, the seeds of renewal and vitality survive and persist in the Downtown Eastside. The area is full of long-time residents, community activists, and social service workers—hundreds of people who believe passionately in the future of the neighbourhood and are willing to fight for it.

This book is an attempt to describe the history and the current realities of the Downtown Eastside—and an effort to chart a course forward, to provide some relief for the most vulnerable among us. It is also a celebration of the human spirit and of the commitment of the many men and women you will read about in the pages that follow. The book is a collaborative undertaking by three authors from different backgrounds. One of us is a lawyer and academic, one a journalist, and one a person who has navigated his way through the firestorm of the Downtown East-side in a variety of key roles: police officer, chief coroner, mayor of Vancouver, social service agency board member, and Liberal senator. Ours are just three of the many voices you will hear in these pages, however, and for that reason we refer to ourselves in the third person when we appear as part of the story.

Vancouver's Downtown Eastside has seen many positive changes in the first decade of the twenty-first century: municipal and provincial commitments to increased supportive housing, innovative drug treatment and health care, and new partner-ships among police and social service providers. But sustained change can't happen in isolation—the federal government must join others already at the table. And we need more than the voices of politicians. People from all parts of the country and all walks of life need to enter the debate about what will help the Downtown Eastside, and other compromised citizens and com-munities, move towards a brighter future.

Larry Campbell, Neil Boyd, and *Lori Culbert*

1 | The Early Years

VANCOUVER OFFICIALLY BECAME A CITY in April 1886. It burned to the ground two months later: a bush fire whipped up by high winds destroyed nearly all of the infant city's 350 wooden buildings. Out of the ashes, the 2,500 residents constructed a new community of brick and stone buildings on the Pacific Ocean's picturesque Burrard Inlet, with breathtaking views of mountains hugging a northern coastline covered in old-growth trees. The area was part of the traditional territory of the Squamish and Musqueam First Nations. The initial townsite covered six blocks of undulating terrain from Burrard Inlet to Hastings Street, between Cambie and Carrall Streets. Today, a portion of that historic section is called Gastown, and the rest is part of what is known as the Downtown Eastside.

Water Street was lined with warehouses in those early days. Cordova Street was the city's commercial centre, because it was the highest (and therefore the driest) road: shoppers walked on wooden sidewalks to avoid the mud. Rich folks built their mansions at the western end of Hastings, on bluffs that overlooked the wharfs below. The newly completed Canadian Pacific Railway tracks delivered the first passenger train to Burrard Inlet in 1887.

The CPR had made a land deal with the new city, and the company built the initial version of the grandiose Hotel Vancouver on Granville Street. That was the start of businesses moving a few blocks southwest, to today's downtown core. Cordova Street kept its prominence, however, because the first streetcar line was built along it and opened in 1890. By the turn of the century, Vancouver was home to at least sixty hotels, fancy ones patronized by wealthy shoppers and more modest ones frequented by loggers, miners, and fishermen off work for a few days. The Bismarck Café, built in 1904 at Abbott and Hastings, offered multiple private dining rooms, including one just for women, along with an orchestra and an electric fountain. The simpler hotels had barbershops and bath houses in the basement, so that men arriving after weeks in the bush could get themselves cleaned up for a night on the town. One hotel on Cordova had a "horse elevator" to take the animals into basement stalls where they would be kept for the evening— the city's first underground parking lot, says local historian and author John Atkin. It was during the first decade of the twentieth century that many of Vancouver's most prominent buildings were constructed, including the flagship Woodward's department store and the Carnegie Library in 1903. The library was built at Main and Hastings, a key intersection for the growing city—Main was the central artery for cars and trucks. City hall and some banks were already located there, making that corner the financial and political heart of Vancouver. The impressive, three-storey library was named after American philanthropist Andrew Carnegie, who provided $50,000 for the project.

As local historian and author Sandy Cameron has written, this core area was very diverse and, at times, divided. Chinatown and Japantown were created in the late 1800s outside Vancouver's official boundaries. People of Chinese descent, mainly single men working low-paying jobs, settled on swampy land near Carrall and Pender Streets. Japanese families gathered along Powell Street, where they prospered running their own fishing boats. On the evening of September 7, 1907, after a decade of anti-Asiatic sentiment and the formation of British Columbia's Asiatic Exclusion League, about ten thousand Vancouverites converged on city hall. The trouble had been brewing for a long time. British Columbia's labour shortage of the late nineteenth century had been replaced by a labour surplus in the early years of the twentieth century. The Chinese and the Japanese, willing to work for forty per cent of white wages, had originally been welcomed but were now reviled for taking jobs from white workers. Racist cartoons and editorials on the front page of the *Vancouver Province* newspaper expressed concern about the "yellow peril" and the eventual domination of the "bright browed races" by the Chinese and the Japanese. The rally at city hall was sponsored by trade unionists and federal Conservative politicians. After the speeches, the angry crowd poured into the Chinese and Japanese districts, beating people, smashing windows, and, in many instances, completely destroying the businesses of the new immigrants.

The federal government in Ottawa sent Mackenzie King, the young deputy minister of labour, to Vancouver in the fall of 1907 to settle damage claims arising from the riot. The prime minister of the day, Wilfrid Laurier, was originally open to settling only Japanese claims for loss, explaining to King that Japan was an important trading partner; China was not. But King persisted in his view that Chinese merchants should be compensated. He told Laurier that "fear, and not justice" appeared to be motivating the distinction. Laurier relented, and King returned to Vancouver in May 1908 to receive claims from Chinese merchants. In the course of his inquiry, King received two claims from smoking-opium merchants. The Lee Yuen Opium Company was the first to speak to the assembled commission, and King's initial response to their request was reported in the *Vancouver Province* on May 29. He told those present that he would look into the smoking-opium business and expressed the view that Chinese druggists should be licensed in much the same way white druggists were.

Smoking-opium factories had operated in the cities of Vancouver, Victoria, and New Westminster for the previous forty years, selling their product to both whites and Chinese. There had been little concern with the businesses. An 1885 judicial inquiry had concluded that alcohol represented a much more significant social problem in the province than did the use of smoking opium. But in the early days of June 1908, King privately received a deputation of local Chinese merchants and clergymen interested in anti-opium legislation. On June 3, he told the commission, with the media present, "It should be made impossible to manufacture this drug anywhere in the Dominion. We will get some good out of this riot yet."

Upon his return to Ottawa, King submitted a report on the "dire need" to suppress the trade in opium, and within six weeks the minister of labour rose in the House of Commons to propose the first reading of the Opium and Drug Act. It was the beginning of the criminalization in Canada of certain mind-active drugs. Cocaine was declared a prohibited substance in 1911, with marijuana, "the new menace," added in 1923. Opiated tonics, elixirs, and analgesics, the commercial products of a white patent-medicine industry, were not targeted by these new prohibitions, nor were alcohol and tobacco. The prohibition on the sale and manufacture of smoking opium was not premised, either, on a careful weighing of the harms of various psychoactive substances; it was a calculated political response to a racist riot. How else to explain the introduction of the law by Canada's minister of labour?

At the time, the United States and China were moving to secure the global prohibition of opium. The movement was spearheaded by an American missionary with close ties to President Teddy Roosevelt, Bishop Brent of the Philippines. Roosevelt provided his full support for an idea that he believed had a kind of moral imperative. The Chinese, who had had British Indian opium forced on their population in the late 1850s after losing two opium wars, were happy to try to end the trade. Only Britain opposed the move to global prohibition at the International Opium Commission in Shanghai in 1909. The British argued for regulation of the trade, suggesting that criminalization was likely to produce far worse consequences than regulation of access by the medical profession and others. But the British were painted as amoral profiteers, and America succeeded in its mission. A line between legal and illegal drugs was drawn in Shanghai, and the horrific consequences remain with us today.

Once the train of prohibition was sent running down the tracks, it quickly gathered steam. The initial federal legislation prohibited only the manufacture and sale of smoking opium, with maximum penalties of three months' imprisonment, but police lobbied for new offences and increased penalties. They were remarkably successful. The offence of possession of illegal drugs was created in 1911, and by 1929 (after the RCMP had become the enforcement arm of the federal Department of Health), penalties for sale, manufacture, and distribution were increased to a maximum of seven years' imprisonment. That was boosted to fourteen years in 1954 and to life imprisonment in 1961. An industry of illegal drug control had been created.

There was more hardship to come for the Chinese and the Japanese of Vancouver. The entire Japanese population was forced to move to internment camps, mainly located in B.C.'s interior, after the attack on Pearl Harbor in 1941. And the

Chinese community, suffering continued discrimination, fought to improve their basic human rights—one of many forms of resistance displayed by defiant Downtown Eastside residents over the years. The area also had a tradition of union activism. In the Relief Camp Workers general strike of 1935, about 1,700 men left Depression-era camps over working conditions and twenty-cents-a-day pay, says Sandy Cameron in his book *Fighting for Community*. After six fruitless weeks, three hundred of the men occupied the museum on the top floor of the Carnegie Library, and hundreds of others took over the Woodward's food floor, chanting, "When do we eat?" They were supported by other unemployed men who marched up Hastings Street and cheered as the "When do we eat?" banner was unfurled from the Carnegie's window. The occupation ended that evening, after the mayor offered the strikers food and lodging for two days. But seven hundred of the frustrated men boarded a freight train to Ottawa to continue protesting. The dreaded relief camps were abolished in 1936.

The 1930s brought hundreds of men into Vancouver looking for work. When the Depression ended, most able-bodied men returned to their hometowns. But those who had been injured working in rough resource sector jobs, as well as the sick and the elderly, were left behind. It was a phenomenon that occurred in many large North American cities in the 1940s, turning working-class communities into "skid roads." The down-and-outers stayed on in the Downtown Eastside for companionship and acceptance, and they could afford the dollar-per-day rent in the boarding houses on their meagre government-issued cheques. Many passed the day in dark beer parlours. After prohibition ended in 1920, the temperance movement convinced the government that people shouldn't be seen drinking alcohol, so beer parlours were either located in hotel basements or had their windows covered over. Inside, there was no sense of time or much concern about how many ten-cent beers the patrons consumed.

Still, although the neighbourhood had its alcoholics, the streets were largely civilized places. The Downtown Eastside had the highest number of theatre seats in the city, as families and the well-heeled flocked to plays and movies; it also had the most bar seats in Vancouver, mainly filled by those numbing life's challenges with cheap beer, but some occupied by the theatre crowd sipping highballs. Even into the 1950s, John Atkin says, the two extremes were not in conflict: "It could all coexist, because it was somehow in balance. You could still see an area sort of rough around the edges, but very viable."

Among the centrepieces of Skid Road was the Carnegie Library, a place where people attended community functions, socialized, and read books. In the city museum, on the library's top floor, one of the most popular attractions was a mummified child found in an Egyptian tomb. But the much-loved building also had its challenges. A librarian wrote to the medical health officer in 1940, concerned about "chicken lice" that had likely migrated into the Carnegie from the city market next door. Dr. Stewart Murray sent back a rather flippant reply, expressing surprise at the complaint and suggesting the fleas "boost[ed] the number of living things that visit the library." There were plenty of living creatures inside the Carnegie in those days, including rats that chewed through books stored in the library basement.

The future of the fifty-four-year-old building became uncertain in 1957, when the growing city of Vancouver moved its library several blocks southwest, to the burgeoning downtown area of Robson and Burrard Streets. The museum took over all three floors of the Carnegie, which had fallen into disrepair; the building's roof was leaking, and plaster was falling from the walls. There were funding battles and public complaints, and the museum closed ten years later. Mayor Tom Campbell told the *Vancouver Sun* in 1968 that the closure of the museum was essentially a demolition order for the Carnegie. "I can't see any use for a derelict building," Campbell said. "I want to see a modern highrise office building or hotel in its place." The land was so valuable, Campbell argued, that redeveloping it could rejuvenate the neighbourhood.

With more roads being built and cars becoming more common, Vancouver's streetcar line was disabled in 1955. The Interurban rail system for commuters shut down three years later. The Interurban and the streetcars had shared a central station at Hastings and Carrall, which an estimated ten thousand people used every day. The North Shore Ferry halted its service to Columbia Street in the late 1950s, and Union Steamship boats stopped bringing commercial travellers and tourists by water to the city. John Atkin argues that the loss of those commuters and shoppers was another death knell for the area. "All the stores and the coffee shops that relied on the pedestrian traffic closed up in a few years," says Atkin, who today conducts walking tours of historic Vancouver. By the 1960s, the area's hotels had started to change from well-respected nightly rentals to rundown residential buildings.

A city hall profile of Skid Road in January 1965 showed a neighbourhood filled with mainly unmarried, undereducated men. There were about 5,300 residents, thirty per cent of them of British origin, thirty-seven per cent from the continent of Asia, and a small handful of Aboriginal people. Among them were many pensioners, disabled people, and "transients" who worked in the resource industries and collected social assistance in the off-season. The city hall report estimated there were about five hundred unemployable people living in the neighbourhood; twenty-five per cent of them were alcoholics, four per cent were suspected of being sex-trade workers, and four per cent were drug addicts. (Heroin injection was first documented in the Downtown Eastside in the late 1960s, as it was in many urban centres across North America.) The area had two per cent of the city's population but racked up thirty-three per cent of the criminal charges laid by police, though the vast majority of these were for relatively minor offences like public drunkenness and theft.

The 1965 city hall report, simply entitled *Downtown East Side*, said Vancouver's Skid Road had distinguished itself from those of many other cities because its residents had rallied to stop politicians, developers, and bulldozers from levelling the place. "The popular image of skid road is of a depressed area peopled by chronic alcoholics and hopeless derelicts; an area usually regarded as a necessary evil. This image should be dispelled," said the report's introduction, written by the city's director of planning, W.E. Graham. "Many people live here because they have little choice. Some are physically disabled and live solely on welfare assistance; some are pensioners eking out their allowances in the cheapest accommodation they can find. Some, by lack of skills, are practically unemployable, and some live here simply because they enjoy the constant activity of the area. Compared to the rest of the city, few people here have any family ties. Many have acute personal problems—and almost all are poor."

George Chow moved to the Downtown Eastside in 1965, when he was fourteen years old. He was a member of the fourth generation in his family to migrate from China to Canada seeking work: his great-grandfather came in the late 1890s, his grandfather in 1911, and his father in 1955. Chow's mother brought him to join his father a decade later, and the family—two parents and three sons—shared a two-room apartment over a London Drugs store at Union and Main Streets. Chow and his younger brother John slept in bunkbeds in a corner of the main room, which contained the kitchen and a living space, while their parents slept with the baby in the smaller second room. There were communal bathrooms in the building for the tenants. The brothers watched TV in the caretaker's suite, because their family didn't own one. Chow recalls thinking that the apartment building was clean and well kept, and downtown Vancouver vibrant. He and his brother went to "new Canadian classes" at the now-closed Sir William Dawson school, where they spent three months studying English with children who had moved to Vancouver from all parts of the world. The brothers played soccer or rode their bikes in a park that is now home to the Strathcona Community Gardens. "Friday after school we'd walk down Pender Street, and we'd cut down to Pigeon Park and continue our journey to Woodward's. Sometimes we'd venture up to Granville Street," recalls Chow, who would later become a Vancouver city councillor. His family often ate out at Chinatown's many restaurants, including the Ho Ho, the Bamboo Terrace, and Ming's, most of them decorated with dazzling neon signs. Young George and John followed the glittering lights along Hastings at night, passing the lit-up pig outside Save-on-Meats while walking to theatres to see John Wayne and Bruce Lee movies.

In the fall of 1965, Chow entered Britannia high school. His parents insisted he wear pants and a blazer, while the long-time Vancouverites wore jeans and had slicked-back hair. He encountered some racial tension, even from other Chinese kids. "I think we felt like outsiders because Canadian-born Chinese kids called us 'imports,'" Chow remembers. He couldn't play after school with other kids because he had to work evenings and weekends in the family's restaurant, which was across from the Sunrise Market at Powell and Gore (where the jail stands today). His father had opened the "greasy spoon" with a partner, and the two men were both cooks and waiters. Chow's mother worked in a fish cannery on the nearby waterfront. Chow can remember serving a wide variety of clients, including single mothers, retirees, and Aboriginal people, at the unlicensed restaurant. "I got to meet all kinds of clients. There were Japanese Canadians from Japantown, which was thriving then," he recalls. "It was just a community to me."

When the family's first apartment building was expropriated so that the Georgia Street Viaduct could be built, the Chows moved to a more rundown apartment at the corner of Main and Keefer, where they had four small rooms and only one window. The bathrooms were still communal. Their neighbours were a mix of workers, people on welfare, and others struggling to get by. "Alcohol, you would see bottles all over. Drunks staggering. The rooms were patched up because people got into arguments and punched the walls, which had to be repaired," Chow recalls. However, he never remembers being scared while walking alone between the family's apartment and the restaurant in the evenings. "Back in those days, I know there were drunks, but that's about it. They weren't a threat. When we lived there as kids, weapons were unheard of."

The 1965 city hall report indicated the same thing. East of Main Street, Hastings was a residential neighbourhood of mainly low-income families. West of Main Street, Hastings was often empty at night, except for small gatherings outside beer parlours. Five evenings a week people would be walking home from the Industrial League baseball games played at the Powell Street Grounds. During the day, older men, disabled by hard work or alcoholism, dozed in Victory Square or on benches at Pioneer Place. The fancy clothiers and carriage shops of bygone days had been replaced with rooming houses, pool halls, and second-hand stores. "Vancouver's skid road is centred on Carrall and Cordova Streets, once the fashionable heart of the city and now a backwash in the westward drift of downtown," the report said.

There were a handful of services located in Skid Road to help the increasing number of destitute people. The three-hundred-bed Central City Mission, founded in 1910, was the largest temporary shelter at the time in Canada. In 1963, the emergency beds were slept in 98,000 times, at a rate of thirty cents a night or free if men couldn't afford the fee. The mission also served 115,000 free breakfasts and lunches that year to clients who were struggling to find work. The seventy-eight-bed Salvation Army Harbour Light rehabilitation centre for alcoholics and drug addicts was the first of its kind in Canada, and clients could stay for as long as twelve months. Harbour Light served up to one thousand free meals a day, operated a medical clinic staffed by volunteer physicians, and ran an employment bureau. The Salvation Army also operated a separate 208-bed "transient shelter." Other services in the area included a hundred-bed Catholic Charities Hostel offering free breakfasts and suppers, as well as daily breadlines at First United Church and the building housing the Franciscan Sisters of Atonement. B.C. had an Alcoholism Foundation at the time, devoted to preventing young people from becoming drunks, but the city hall report noted the organization was doing nothing to help the vulnerable people on Hastings: "The foundation does not have the resources to spend much of its energies on the chronic drunkenness offender—the habitué of skid road."

The report's conclusions would be echoed many times in the decades to come: the neighbourhood needed more housing, better resources for the ailing, and less polarization among the social service agencies. "Many agencies are working more or less independently tackling a vast problem with limited resources. Most of them enable the alcoholic, the derelict and the transient man to maintain his way of life more easily and safely than in another part of the city. Their chances of doing more than merely keeping pace with the present situation, however, are hindered by limited resources and limited coordination," the report said. "The eventual elimination of skid road depends on prevention. It depends on the education of the young. It depends on the treatment of the victims of alcoholism before they reach the rock bottom of skid road. It depends on the continued increase in pension plans, which can do much to reduce the poverty of old age in the years to come. Perhaps, above all, it depends on the need to provide our young people with sufficient training to find their place in a rapidly changing world, continually demanding higher and higher skills."

Sandy Cameron came to the Downtown Eastside from Ontario, like many men looking for work, in 1965. He initially got a job prospecting for copper in Whistler, which was just a mountain with a few shacks at the time, nothing like the luxury resort it would become. His home base was the Dominion, a single-room occupancy (SRO) hotel charging eight dollars a week for a sunny room with big windows but no kitchen or bathroom. He cooked on a hot plate and ate one meal a day in a local diner. Cameron dabbled in other work as well, and along the way he built a strong bond with his new neighbourhood. "I did connect with this community. I was changing occupations, and this community is a place where people can go when making changes in their lives. This is a very non-judgemental community, where people give each other a lot of support." Cameron was drawn to the retired loggers, miners, fishermen, and construction workers who, over a pint in the beer parlours, would relive their dangerous and exciting working days. They were a cussing, fiery-tempered lot who were proud of their accomplishments in "building this province," recalls Cameron. "They were very independent, feisty, hard-working men. They fought hard for their unions to fight exploitation." Cameron started recording the stories of the Downtown Eastside, because he thought they should be better known.

Despite the economic challenges and hardship for some residents, Cameron remembers the Skid Road of the 1960s as a vibrant place with open stores and friendly faces, where people had enough to get by. He recalls people banding together in 1968 to stop bulldozers from carrying out city hall's plans to redevelop Strathcona, the residential neighbourhood east of Main and Hastings. "There is this long tradition of struggle by all the various groups," says Cameron, to protect what he calls "the soul of Vancouver." The neighbourhood was home to many people like Cameron, who loved its history and inclusiveness. But there were numerous battles to come over the area's health and longevity. The struggle would be prolonged and personal for those who truly believed in the Downtown Eastside.

2 | We Call It the Downtown Eastside

BRUCE ERIKSEN RAN AWAY TO Vancouver's Downtown Eastside when he was fourteen years old, fleeing a horrendous childhood. He worked a series of jobs over the next sixteen years, mostly drinking away his paycheques until he sobered up at age thirty. He got a job as an ironworker but hurt his back building Vancouver's Knight Street Bridge and then turned his attention to fighting to protect the neighbourhood that had been his home since his teenage years. It was early 1973 when the forty-five-year-old Eriksen spotted an advertisement at the welfare office for a job with the People's Aid Project, a new, federally funded group formed to advocate for the rights of Downtown Eastside residents. The project was being organized by Peter Davies, a former British soldier who was a social justice activist with the First United Church on East Hastings. Eriksen was known to be cantankerous, but he was already a vocal champion of the neighbourhood.

People's Aid, with Eriksen on board, held its inaugural meeting in April 1973; forty people gathered to complain about issues such as the failure of governments to enforce liquor laws in beer parlours or housing bylaws in the rundown hotels. On the group's behalf, Eriksen sent a strongly worded letter to Mayor Art Phillips, who had been elected with the municipal party TEAM (The Electors' Action Movement) the year before. The letter said, in part, "The people of Vancouver have heard enough talk from wealthy politicians and jingoistic bureaucrats about decent housing. Now's the time to evict the cockroaches and rats, to turn on the water at hotels where they turn it off at night, to restrain the landlords who give only 5 days' notice of rental increases, to turn on the furnaces and light up the dank hallways. The new City Administration claims to be for people. We'll see."

Eriksen was also an artist, and that summer a twenty-year-old University of British Columbia student named Libby Davies visited him to ask if the fledgling newspaper she worked for, the *Downtown East,* could publish a cartoon he had drawn. Wary of the sharp-tongued Eriksen, her co-workers had sent Davies—the youngest member of the staff and the daughter of Eriksen's boss, Peter Davies—to sweet-talk him. The encounter was memorable: Davies got not only the cartoon but a life partner. The unlikely couple came from very different backgrounds but shared a keen sense of social justice. Davies was in her second summer of work in the Downtown Eastside in 1973. The year before she'd received a federal grant to start a food store inside a health clinic her father was running on Cordova Street. She bought food in bulk, divided it up, and sold it in smaller amounts at discount prices for people cooking on hot plates in SROs. She also collected the soup that hadn't been sold each day from the Woodward's café, rolling it on a trolley to the clinic and serving it up for the needy. Those two summers spent in the Downtown Eastside convinced Davies that's where she wanted to be, and she dropped out of university to work full-time with Eriksen. Together, they transformed the People's Aid Project into the Downtown Eastside Residents' Association (DERA), a militant group that fought for improvements in living conditions.

One of DERA's initial causes was getting provincial liquor laws enforced in hotel beer parlours. Pensioners living in tiny SROS considered the pub downstairs to be their living room, the place where they could socialize and chat with neighbours. But these old men were told by the pub managers that they had to drink to stay in the bar, and they were continually brought more beer than they had ordered. There was a myth about the neighbourhood, Libby Davies says today, that out-of-control residents had turned it into a Skid Road hell hole, but DERA fingered beer parlour managers as the major culprits. It took Bruce Eriksen just a few months to have six beer parlours closed or put on probation and to get the hours limited in cafés where criminals were known to hang out. The owners of those businesses were not happy, and a contract was put on Eriksen's life. Davies recalls the police knocking on their apartment door to warn Eriksen he should leave town for his own safety, which he did for four days. When he returned, he announced publicly that he wouldn't leave again and said if he was killed he hoped it would promote change in the Downtown Eastside.

One evening in 1974, Eriksen and Davies went into the pub in the Patricia Hotel for a drink. Waitress Jean Swanson recognized Eriksen from the TV news; her boss had warned her not to over-serve the customers when Eriksen was in the bar. However, she didn't know the young woman with him and asked her for ID; the two women would later become lifelong allies. That evening, Eriksen took Swanson to task for her bar's over-serving habits, she recalls. The thirty-one-year-old single mother needed the job to support her two young kids; though she knew her employer's policies were turning her vulnerable clients into alcoholics, she had felt powerless to do anything about it. But she was immediately struck by this couple and their cause. A short time later, Swanson saw Eriksen having his regular lunch at the Ovaltine Café and struck up the courage to ask him for a job with DERA. "He asked me if I had any experience, and I said, 'I was editor of the school newspaper in high school,'" Swanson remembers. Six weeks later, Eriksen offered her a job at the *Downtown East*; DERA had taken over the small newspaper. Together, Eriksen, Davies, and Swanson became a formidable force at DERA, making history in the 1970s in the Downtown Eastside.

Homelessness wasn't a problem during that decade, as there were ample rooming houses. But DERA was concerned about the deplorable conditions of some of these homes. After thirteen people died in Downtown Eastside hotel fires in 1973, DERA fought to force SROs to follow fire bylaws by installing sprinklers. Since the installations, no one has died in a hotel fire in the neighbourhood, Libby Davies says today. The following year, DERA battled to open Oppenheimer Lodge, the first purposefully built social housing project for seniors, which had been stalled because electrical workers were on strike. Eriksen discovered that Mayor Art Phillips had been so eager to complete Granville Mall, downtown's high-profile urban renewal project, that city hall had arranged a special deal to have the electrical work done at that site. Eriksen took protesters to Granville Mall, halting the mayor's project and giving Eriksen the leverage he needed. The lodge for seniors was opened later that year.

The Downtown Eastside was a dynamic place to work in those days for one young RCMP officer. In 1973, Larry Campbell joined the Vancouver Street Crew, a team of four Mounties and four city police officers who targeted drug problems. Back then, when the biggest issue was alcohol, the street crew knew every drug dealer and most of the addicts. "There wasn't mayhem. There was no open dealing; there was no open using," Campbell says today. People shot drugs in their rooms, because they had rooms. "There were no shuttered buildings at that time. People moved to the neighbourhood and stayed there. People were raising children and going to work each morning. They might not have had the best jobs, but they were working it. There was a sense of spirit. They were going to ball games at Oppenheimer Park," Campbell says of the large green space with the checkered past at Powell and Dunlevy Streets. "The streets were vibrant during the day with shoppers. At night they were hopping with nightclubs, like the Smiling Buddha. Late at night the streets were empty. The Chinese community was bustling. It was a poor neighbourhood, but a normal place."

Now-retired Vancouver police inspector Bob Cooper started his thirty-year career in 1974 in the department's so-called skid row district, and he remembers the community as an "edgy place" but not a dangerous one. Instead of radios, police carried big brass keys that opened call boxes attached to utility poles. Officers used the call boxes to check in at police headquarters once an hour. There were two pawn shops in the Downtown Eastside, Cooper recalls, but they were run by respectable businessmen; boosters had to sell stolen goods in beer parlours. "You could walk anywhere. A young woman pushing a baby carriage could walk right down Hastings, and no one would bother her."

The sex-trade workers in the Downtown Eastside then were referred to as the "low-stroll girls," Larry Campbell says. "Sex-trade workers were a visible presence but never seemed to be in the kind of shape you see them in now. There was sort of a panache about them. They had makeup on. They were down at the heel, but they weren't this jerking, convulsing poor group of people you see today."

Even in the mid-1970s, Campbell says, he wasn't interested in busting marijuana users, who usually carried pot around in small amounts for personal consumption. However, he did arrest addicts found with harder drugs. At the time, as a cop with only a few years on the job, Campbell thought it was right to charge them, because they were breaking Canada's narcotic laws. Three decades later, after seeing the results of people's addictions on cold gurneys in the coroner's office, Campbell would come to believe those policies were misguided. "I didn't see it in a moral way, as I do now. I saw it as enforcing the laws. I certainly didn't see it as a medical problem, like I do today."

Campbell remembers crawling onto ceiling tiles to spy into the washrooms in the rundown Brandiz Hotel, because it was still a challenge then to catch someone using drugs. Police targeted users and dealers by setting up sting operations in other notorious hotels like the Sunrise, which was located at the centre of the action: the corner of Columbia and Hastings. Officers knew who the dealers were, but they were hard to arrest. Heroin came in capsules, and dealers stored them in condoms or balloons, which they could swallow to avoid getting caught with dope. They knew that by the time the rubber sacks had passed through their systems, the cops would be long gone. The street crew members, who worked in plain clothes without protective equipment, would follow tips about the locations of dealers, busting down doors in sleazy hotel rooms to catch them with a stash. "One officer would go to the toilet, so they couldn't flush, and one guy to the window, so they couldn't throw," Campbell recalls. "And I can remember sitting in the Waldorf Hotel, watching the Palmer boys run their big heroin business." Twin brothers Douglas and Donald Palmer were convicted of operating a major heroin distribution ring headquartered in Vancouver's East End between 1969 and 1975. According to testimony at their high-profile trial, as reported in the *Vancouver Sun*, the brothers stored heroin caps in glass jars sealed with electrician's tape. The jars were buried in quiet spots, such as residential lanes, and maps leading to the hidden treasure were sold to buyers. One ounce of heroin, which made four hundred capsules, sold for $2,400 in 1971 and as much as $5,000 in 1974. The brothers maintained their innocence but were sentenced in 1976 to life in prison. Arresting the dealers and seizing their drugs made a difference in the 1970s; unlike today, it noticeably reduced supply on the street. "The sense I have looking back is that we had control," Campbell says. "We would seize a pound of heroin from Asia at the airport, and there would be panic on the street. They would be scratching at Oppenheimer Park. While we weren't gaining, we had control."

But for the poorest and most marginalized Downtown Eastside citizens, heroin and liquor were often not the drugs of choice. Many of the less fortunate relied on cheaper, more toxic substitutes. Bob Cooper can remember the tiny Cozy Corner store across the street from the Sunrise being one of Canada's top sellers of Lysol. Residents looking for a cheap high would also heat shoe polish, so that the alcohol would come out, and then strain it through a sock before drinking it. Cooper recalls kids buying glue-sniffing kits at a store at Powell and Jackson as well.

It was those young people that twenty-eight-year-old street nurse Bonnie Fournier was targeting in 1969 when she started a new Narcotic Addiction Foundation youth outreach service called InTouch. Since graduating with a psychiatric-nursing degree four years earlier, Fournier had been working with the mentally ill and the addicted. While employed at the Narcotic Addiction Foundation withdrawal unit near Vancouver General Hospital, Fournier had helped addicts from all walks of life coming off heroin; she also saw young hippies and Vietnam War protesters living in the trendy Kitsilano neighbourhood or camping underneath the Burrard Street Bridge go on terrible, mind-altering trips caused by psychedelics like LSD. Under her new program, she encountered teens on rooftops and in doorways sniffing or drinking easily available noxious substances.

Young people high on airplane glue, kerosene, rice wine, after-shave, or mouthwash often thought they could fly and would need shots of Valium to bring them down to earth.

One hot June evening in 1971, Fournier was called to the Ray-mur Housing Project, where a twelve-year-old girl was perched precariously on a window ledge, her bare feet dangling four sto-reys above the ground. The girl held a brown paper bag to her face and was breathing in nail polish remover fumes. The con-coction came ready-made in a twenty-cent kit purchased from a local Chinese grocery store: cotton balls soaked in nail polish remover had been placed inside a plastic bag, which was then tucked into a paper bag. The girl's frantic mother, who struggled with her own addiction to Talwin and Ritalin (prescription drugs sometimes referred to as "poor man's junk"), had phoned the Narcotic Addiction Foundation for help. Bonnie Fournier looped one leg through the·open window and leaned against the win-dow frame, anxious the girl might decide to jump. "It was a scary thing," Fournier recalls. "I asked her why she was sniffing, and she said it made her feel good." The girl talked about her fears, about being lonely and helping out at home when her mother was high. Eventually she became dopey, and Fournier was able to bring her inside and convince her to spend the night at a safe house. Fournier doesn't know what became of the girl, but she says that the supply of cheap, noxious substances was reduced somewhat in the early 1970s. Ingredients in nail polish remover were altered to take out the intoxicating elements, and airplane model glue and rice wine were moved to behind store counters.

Despite the neighbourhood's challenges, Fournier remem-bers the Downtown Eastside as a functioning community for those who lived there. She has schoolgirl memories of eating clam chowder with her grandfather at the Only Seafood Café and attending St. James Anglican Church on special occasions. Fournier was drawn to work with people in the Downtown

Eastside because she could relate to their lives. When she was two years old, her father had taken Fournier and her nanny (whom he had impregnated) on the run, abandoning his wife and four-year-old son in Powell River. Fournier remembers living an impoverished, nomadic life with her father, her stepmother, and two new half-sisters. Her biological mother tracked her down four years later and took her back, but Fournier never got over the uncertainty of her early childhood. "A lot of times I identify with people on the street because I've been through it," she says today. "A lot of times I'd say, 'You've got to learn from your experiences and move on.'" She started the InTouch program because there were few resources available for kids entrenched in their addictions.

Like Fournier, Jerry Adams felt compelled to work with teenagers in the Downtown Eastside. After graduating from the University of Victoria in 1977, Adams became a social worker at an alternative school for Aboriginal kids located in First United Church. The teens attending the Outreach alternative school couldn't fit into the regular education system, and many were tinkering with marijuana and psychedelic drugs. "I thought they needed to be heard. I was the only stable part of their life, from 9 AM to 3 PM," recalls Adams, who remains an Aboriginal leader in the Downtown Eastside today. Many of the teens couldn't face being in the big, mainly white high schools. There were no specific services for Aboriginal youth then in the Downtown Eastside, and Adams could relate to some of the demons haunting these kids. His own mother was an alcoholic whose first four children, including Adams, were fathered by four different men. Adams, like his siblings, was snatched away from his family in the Nisga'a Nation in northern B.C. and raised by white foster parents. Many of the alternative school students were government wards; others had parents who had come to the area for jobs in the fish canneries along the waterfront.

There were concerns in the late 1970s about young Aboriginal women being given alcohol, taken onto ships docked at the port, and passed around as sex objects. "Nobody really cared about our people; there was no services for them," Adams says. His friend John Turvey, who would be instrumental in the 1980s harm reduction movement in the Downtown Eastside, lamented that these girls were "throw-away kids." On a reserve, Adams says, grandparents and aunts would typically take in children when the parents needed help. "We've lost that, because we [often] don't have grandparents living in the urban setting," Adams says today.

When he arrived in the Downtown Eastside, Adams had the impression that a lot of the neighbourhood's old-timers were Aboriginal. Many had addictions to alcohol, in particular rice wine. He attributes the high rate of alcoholism among his people to the fact that, until the 1960s, Aboriginal people were not considered citizens of Canada and therefore could not vote or legally buy alcohol in liquor stores. When that changed, many Aboriginal people who lived off-reserve were anxious to find out what they had been missing. The alcohol also helped to suppress inner turmoil created by residential schools, abuse, and racism.

In general, as Libby Davies recalls, the services in the 1970s for people addicted to alcohol and drugs, such as the Salvation Army's Cordova Detox and the Pender Detox, were insufficient. DERA battled with many church-based facilities because, although well-meaning, their Christian philosophy of "saving the souls" of addicts wasn't always a perfect fit for vulnerable people, she says.

The distinction between legal and illegal drugs had begun to unravel for the larger society by the late 1960s. Millions of young people from Western countries were travelling by plane to places previously accessible only to the very wealthy: India, Lebanon, Colombia, Vietnam. They encountered the drugs of the Third World—hash from Afghanistan, Lebanese Blonde, Thai sticks,

Colombian marijuana, coca, and heroin—and they brought those drugs home, most notably marijuana and hashish. In 1967 roughly one thousand Canadians were convicted of possession of marijuana. Half of them went to jail, for terms of up to two years.

National governments set up the Shafer Commission in the U.S. and Canada's Le Dain Commission (known officially as the Commission of Inquiry into the Non-Medical Use of Drugs) to look into the emerging drug problem. Both commissions recommended legal amendments that would emphasize health as the agenda for action, rather than relying on criminal law enforcement. Clearly, the get-tough approach didn't work. By 1976, forty thousand Canadians were being convicted each year of marijuana possession, and fewer than five per cent of them were going to jail. There wasn't enough space in Canada's prisons to house even half of all marijuana offenders. Tough penalties for marijuana use were no longer seen as appropriate, and once the genie was out of the bottle—drugs were about public health, not morality—it became difficult to justify putting heroin or cocaine users, or indeed any illegal drug users, in jail. But there were no easy solutions on the horizon. Marijuana had become a booming import-export business, with boatloads arriving from Colombia, Mexico, and Thailand. For dealers involved with other drugs, these changes presented business opportunities. Heroin, cheaper and more potent than ever before, was gaining a foothold in North America by the late 1970s, and cocaine would soon follow on its heels. For marginal people, the changes produced new risks that would become all too evident.

Well aware of the challenges on the street, DERA argued that residents needed a community centre, a place to go and something to do that didn't involve booze or dope. The perfect place to put it was the boarded-up, rat-infested Carnegie Library, which had been closed for a decade. Bruce Eriksen was determined to fight city hall's plan to sell the land. Most mornings during the mid-1970s, Eriksen had breakfast with city councillor Harry Rankin, a member of the minority left-leaning civic party. Eriksen asked Rankin if he could get the mothballed building opened up to host the committee meeting that would decide the Carnegie's fate. The February 1976 meeting took place among cobwebs and bats, but it reminded councillors of the building's history, and they narrowly voted to give DERA the money to renovate.

DERA needed to wrestle funding from the province and the federal government, too. At the time, Ottawa had pledged $6 million to turn Granville Island, in Vancouver's popular False Creek area, into a shopping district. On green boards surrounding the Carnegie, Bruce Eriksen painted: "$6 million for Granville Island. $0 for the Carnegie." The federal funding materialized, and the Carnegie Centre opened in January 1980. It was an alcohol- and drug-free oasis, offering residents recreational and educational programs, a reading room, and a small gym. Within four months, an estimated one thousand people a day were using the centre. Some argue that the reopening of the Carnegie marked the official transformation of the community from Skid Road to the Downtown Eastside.

Another of DERA's main goals was to ensure that existing affordable-housing stock in the downtown area was protected. According to a March 1979 city hall document, A Report on Residential Hotels and Rooming Houses, the number of residential hotels and rooming houses in a portion of Vancouver that included the Downtown Eastside had dropped by thirty-six per cent, from 307 buildings in 1974 to 196 buildings in 1979. The report also found that the number of people living in SROs had fallen— seventy-nine per cent of the rooms were full in 1974, but only sixty-three per cent were full five years later. Many of the modest hotels in the Downtown Eastside had served as residences for off-season resource workers and families coming to Canada. But patterns of immigration were changing, and there was more stability now among loggers, miners, and longshoremen, along with better unemployment benefits, an improved minimum wage, guaranteed pensions, and newly available low-cost housing. The residents who remained in the Downtown Eastside were mostly single older men who depended on either welfare or an old age pension.

The average tenure of residents in the area was thirteen years, making the Downtown Eastside one of the most stable communities in Vancouver, second only to upper-middle-class Dunbar. But although there were enough rooms in the neighbourhood, the city hall report acknowledged that these tiny "sleeping rooms" had never been intended for people to live in for extended periods of time. "Most sleeping rooms have inadequate or no food storage facilities, no refrigeration, inadequate wiring for a hot plate and other electrical appliances, and no private bath," the report said. The city inspected twenty-three hotels and rooming houses and found 9,312 violations for issues like cleaning, maintenance, repair, and upgrading. One quarter of the rooms were adequate, with the rest in "poor physical condition." Some improvements had been made, such as the installation of sprinklers, but bylaw enforcement had resulted in the closure of ten facilities, with another fourteen in jeopardy of being shut down. The report called for the city to "aggressively work with the development community" to fix these problems, to avoid "abandoning the area to a speculative and uncertain future." It also called for the creation of special accommodation for the five to ten per cent of rooming house residents who were classified as hard-to-house. "The majority of these people are chronic alcoholics whose behaviour when they are drinking is destructive and/or disruptive. A number of others are either anti-social or mentally unstable whether drinking or sober," the report said. Similar recommendations for the Downtown Eastside would be heard many times in the years to come.

Bonnie Fournier frequently saw members of this vulnerable population when she became the nurse at the courthouse jail at 222 Main Street in the late 1970s. It was Fournier's job to ensure the two hundred or so prisoners in the holding cells were healthy enough for their court appearances. Most of the people arrested in the Downtown Eastside had addiction troubles, and they had been picked up for relatively minor crimes like theft, break-and-enter, mischief, and prostitution. The problems were not new, but the addicts Fournier saw just seemed sicker.

Fournier was not alone in noticing the escalating health problems associated with alcoholism and substance abuse among the neighbourhood's most needy citizens. Larry Campbell, who left the RCMP in 1981 to become a coroner, presided over a series of inquests looking into deaths of prisoners in jails, most of them linked to alcohol and/or substance abuse. After serving two years with the police street crew, Campbell had worked with B.C.'s then-elite Coordinated Law Enforcement Unit, become head of the drug squad in Langley, been promoted to corporal, and worked as an RCMP watch commander. He was wooed to the coroner's service by a former police colleague, Bob Galbraith, then B.C.'s chief coroner. Campbell was largely his own boss, responsible for investigating about seven hundred non-natural deaths (such as homicides, industrial accidents, and overdoses) annually in Vancouver. In one of his early cases, two prisoners in the police department's drunk tank were found dead within ten minutes of each other.

Forty-four-year-old Rob Laws, known as Spider on the street, was found lying in a pool of his own urine on Hastings, in front of the Army & Navy store, at 8:30 PM on July 29, 1982. Laws was shirtless, stretched out on his back with a T-shirt draped over his bare chest. Constable J.M. Wadley asked Laws to move along, but even with another man's help, Laws walked only twenty feet before falling down again. Wadley then ordered a police wagon to pick Laws up. Laws bummed a cigarette from a passerby, then choked out a raspy cough and spit a large amount of phlegm on the sidewalk.

A half hour earlier, fifty-four-year-old Matthew Krasko had been found by police sitting between two parked cars at 100 Keefer Street with another man who was also intoxicated. They were loaded into a paddy wagon and taken to the drunk tank. Both Laws and Krasko were labelled by police at the time as "skid row drunks," known to consume Chinese cooking wine, Lysol, rubbing alcohol, and aftershave lotion. Laws had been sent to the drunk tank five times by police over the past year. Krasko had been held six times and was once hospitalized "for drinking some toxics that were from a photo studio that he had broken into," according to a police report.

The drunk tank was a wild place that night, filled with people who had been bingeing after receiving their monthly welfare cheques. Laws and Krasko had to share a small cell with seven other men. Laws was checked several times and found to be sluggish, but he did wake up when shaken by police officers. Around midnight, Krasko was seen sitting up against the wall, sharing a cigarette with another inmate, but about an hour later he was found lying on his left side against the wall, with blood coming from his mouth. A police nurse performed CPR but couldn't get a pulse. Krasko was taken to hospital, where he was pronounced dead. At 1:15 AM, an officer found Laws lying motionless on the floor on his stomach. He was not breathing, had poor colour, and was cool to the touch. He also died that night.

At the inquest into Laws's death, coroner Larry Campbell ruled he died of a massive brain injury, most likely the result of falling down. His blood contained 0.28 per cent alcohol; a person is considered legally impaired at 0.08 per cent. The autopsy on Krasko did not find any evidence of trauma, but a pathologist told police he likely "died of too much alcohol." Krasko had 0.26 per cent alcohol in his blood.

The jury at the Laws inquest raised concerns about "the high rise in arrests due to alcohol abuse during the time when welfare cheques are given out." Jury members also said, "When we hear that the detoxification centre is full during this time, we feel that a staggered system of welfare payments should be made. We suggest that the Ministry of Human Resources study a staggered welfare pay day in an attempt to stop the gross abuse of alcohol associated with this day each month." Another recommendation from the jury was that the health ministry open more detox beds. When summing up the evidence for the jurors, Campbell had told them: "I am shocked at the expense and cost of life alcoholism is causing. When 35 to 40 per cent of police arrests are for 'intoxicated in a public place,' steps must be taken to not only lower the police involvement but assist the persons who suffer with the alcoholism on a long term basis... The alcoholic in the majority of cases is a social and not a law enforcement problem."

BRUCE ERIKSEN, himself a recovering alcoholic, found his own way to try to address the systemic problem of alcohol in the neighbourhood. He argued that the B.C. Liquor Store just east of Hastings and Main was fostering alcoholism, and he spearheaded the controversial move to close it. Not everyone supported the work DERA was doing during the 1970s, and there were concerns this closure would drive drunks to purchase dangerous substitutes like rice wine. But Eriksen always fought strongly for causes in which he believed, like arguing for funding so that the once-bare Oppenheimer Park could get some landscaping and trees—creating a much-needed green space for the area. Eriksen was also determined to portray the neighbourhood known as Skid Road as a residential community. Frustrated by the area continually being dismissed as home to a bunch of bums and drunks, he once famously retorted, "The people who live here, they call it the Downtown Eastside." It was another of Eriksen's victories: the more pleasant moniker would stick.

3 | Lethal Heroin, Killer Coke, and Expo 86

WITH LARRY CAMPBELL'S CHANGE IN career in the early 1980s came a philosophical shift in his thinking: he no longer viewed the victims of fatal overdoses in the morgue as lawbreakers but as people whose deaths could have been prevented. "The biggest change was the mindset that you were going from enforcing laws to keeping people alive," Campbell says today. "That is where my changes in attitude towards drug addiction took place. I was anxious to know, how do I keep these people alive? How do I prevent death?" Of mounting concern to the rookie coroner was the increasing potency of first heroin, then cocaine. He also found the overdose deaths upsetting because they were claiming victims from all walks of life: young and old, rich and poor, sick and healthy, occasional users and entrenched ones. By 1991, at an inquest into the death of a heroin addict, Campbell was telling the coroner's jury: "There is no doubt that this addiction is an illness as surely as cancer, heart disease or a tumour. The difficulty is in the treatment, and while certain successes have been registered, the problem appears to continue unabated." His conclusion was progressive at a time when many officials were still approaching addiction as a criminal problem.

The case Campbell was commenting on was that of Ken Hodgins, a man whose severe dependence on heroin had caused his life to fall apart. "Medically, no one has been able to explain how a 'good husband, father, worker' turns into a violent, driven heroin addict," Campbell told the jury. Hodgins, thirty-seven, was living in a Downtown Eastside hotel and was wanted for ten armed robberies when he was shot and killed by police on January 2, 1991, in east Vancouver after refusing the officers' repeated requests to drop his loaded gun. Hodgins had committed the robberies to support a habit that was costing him five to seven hundred dollars daily, and he had taken eight caps of heroin an hour before his encounter with police. In a report submitted to the jury, Hodgins's parole officer said, "Although the subject died of gunshot wounds, it would seem that in reality he died of heroin addiction."

Hodgins had a stable family life and a good-paying job as a tree faller on Vancouver Island when a series of tragedies led to him using a syringe to manage his grief. His habit had become extreme by 1986, a year in which he was charged with sixteen robberies and convicted of committing nine. A 1989 National Parole Board report concluded Hodgins was "not fundamentally anti-social or criminally oriented," and a Corrections Canada report added: "Kenneth Hodgins no doubt has a great deal of potential. He has employment skills that are marketable. He has a sincere desire to be a positive role model for his son. What he is lacking however appears to be the intestinal fortitude that it will require for him to leave heroin use behind him." Hodgins was dead less than four months after being released from prison. The head of the police bank robbery squad, Sergeant Ted McClellan, told the *Vancouver Sun* in 1990 that Hodgins exemplified the reason the city's bank robbery rate was the highest in the country.

"It's not done for personal gain," McClellan was quoted as saying. "It's done to support a habit."

In his address to the jury, Larry Campbell spelled out the dire consequences of not doing more to help those with debilitating drug habits: "Heroin addiction is such that life itself is controlled by the schedule set by the drug... If the demand is not listened to, the results are predictable: painful and debilitating withdrawal. The cycle continues with Ken requiring more and more money to support the habit. Soon, the proceeds from the armed robberies do not cover the cost of the drugs and the violence escalates due to the withdrawal and a frustration that this is never going to end. As the coroner for the city of Vancouver for the past ten years, I have dealt with literally hundreds of deaths involving heroin addiction. Fortunately most of them do not involve the police and shooting, but violence has almost always touched the lives of the addict at one time or another. You are just as surely dead from an overdose as from a bullet or knife."

The complexities of Hodgins's case were tragic but unfortunately not rare. The evolution of drugs through the 1980s had created chaos. Between 1984 and 1987 there were fewer than twenty heroin overdose deaths annually in the province of British Columbia, but in 1988 the number of overdose deaths jumped to thirty-nine and then began a meteoric rise. According to provincial toxicology reports, the purity of heroin seized on the street between 1984 and 1993 surged from an average of six per cent potency to more than sixty per cent. Unlike in eastern Canada, where high-strength drugs had always been a market option, users in B.C. had no idea about the purity of the drug they were injecting, and most of the carnage was taking place on the streets of the Downtown Eastside.

Michael Brandt, an MA student at Simon Fraser University's School of Criminology, examined the toxicology reports of all overdose deaths in B.C. during the 1980s and early 1990s. He found that about twenty per cent of heroin overdose deaths during the 1980s involved the consumption of alcohol to the point of impairment (an average blood alcohol reading of 0.10). By the early 1990s, that percentage had risen to about sixty. Were drinkers turning to heroin? Yes, very likely; the drug had become cheaper and more accessible, and its unexpected potency was producing fatal results. Cocaine, present in fewer than ten per cent of fatal overdoses in the 1980s, was seen in close to thirty per cent of fatalities by the 1990s.

Although the death rate was increasing, the street scene was still relatively calm in the early 1980s, Larry Campbell recalls. There were no violent turf wars among dealers, since the drug trade in Vancouver was controlled by three or four groups. Crystal meth and crack had not yet arrived in the city; most addicts were injecting heroin, a drug that made its users relatively mellow. The Downtown Eastside was still a functional, stable place for people to live. "The biggest eye-opener I had was how cohesive the community was," Campbell says of his early years as a coroner. "It was a place you could go where, if you were different, you wouldn't be judged. There was a sense that if you were down and out, someone would help you, would take you in for the night. For the retirees and widows, it was not a bad life. There wasn't the drug-fuelled craziness we see now."

Campbell remembers being called to a rooming house where a retired logger was slumped dead over his kitchen table, an open newspaper and a lottery ticket nearby. The man had just won the lottery, but whether the sudden windfall had caused his heart attack couldn't be known for sure. The man's relatives, who had long dismissed him as a drunk but would inherit his new-found money, wanted to cremate him in a cardboard box. The beat officers in the neighbourhood, outraged by this, devised a plan to ensure the man would be given a proper funeral, Campbell recalls. The officers told his relatives the man should be buried in an expensive casket at a proper wake with food and drinks; all of it could be paid for from the lottery winnings. Limousines were rented to take about thirty of the man's Downtown Eastside friends to the funeral. "I remember these guys showing up in suits out of the forties, with ties so wide you could land a jet on them. They were all just family down there. They had this incredible funeral," Campbell says today.

But he saw his share of disheartening events as well. In 1986, Campbell investigated the deaths of two men who had fallen three floors when a rusty fire escape collapsed at the Astoria Hotel, a rundown SRO in the Downtown Eastside. John Dyck, aged thirty-eight, and Matthew Wilson, twenty-nine, had plummeted into the alley below. An investigation found the external staircases were rusting off "hundreds of buildings" in the low-income area, recalls Campbell. He held an inquiry that ultimately called for tougher inspection methods. "It was unbelievable. I had been in and out of those buildings as a Mountie, but I had never looked at them for what they were: places with one bathroom for dozens of people. The majority of people in some rooming houses were retirees, loggers, fishermen, miners. The women were widows. This was just sort of where they ended up. Other SROs were for people on welfare, and those places were more frequented by drug users and sex-trade workers." The latter buildings, in the heart of the drug district, had the worst fire escapes.

Whether they were derelict or tolerable, the number of low-income hotels in the Downtown Eastside continued to decline in the 1980s. The person who fought hardest to reverse the closures was Jim Green, an outspoken football- and opera-loving guy with a master's degree in anthropology who became a fierce protector of the community's existing housing stock. Green took over the Downtown Eastside Residents' Association in 1980, when Bruce Eriksen was elected to city council and Libby Davies was elected to the city's Parks Board. In a DERA report

Green wrote in 1985, *Housing Conditions and Population in the Downtown Eastside,* he called on the city to start protecting low-income
rooms, especially with the World's Fair, Expo 86, coming to
Vancouver the following year. "Over the past four years approximately 2,000 units of housing have been lost in the Downtown
Eastside. With the approach of Expo the number of units lost will
increase drastically," Green wrote. The DERA report found residents were "fiercely loyal to their neighbourhood," which made
the Downtown Eastside one of the most stable communities in
the city. But the amount of housing was shrinking, and some of
the loss was due to the 1985 demolition of the sixty-room Georgia Rooms on Main Street, torn down to make way for a parking
garage. The typical evictees were older, single, retired resource
workers—including eighty-seven-year-old William Smith, who
had lived in the Downtown Eastside hotel for forty-six years.
"They told me I had to pull out because they were tearing it down.
I didn't want to move, but what could I do?" Smith told *Vancouver
Sun* reporter Bob Sarti at the time. DERA arranged for Smith to
move into a hard-to-find unit in a social housing complex.

William Smith was one of the more fortunate evictees,
because he adapted to his new home. But there are ghosts, like
that of Olaf Solheim, who continue to haunt the neighbourhood.
Solheim, a retired logger, had lived in the Patricia Hotel on East
Hastings for more than forty years, but he was evicted when the
hotel went upscale to house tourists during Expo 86. At eighty-
eight, he was relocated to the Columbia Hotel, but he wouldn't
unpack his meagre belongings, refused to eat, and often returned
to the Patricia in a confused state. Six weeks after his eviction, Solheim was dead. Vancouver's medical health officer said Solheim's
passing was caused, in part, by the shock of losing his home.

In his book *Fighting for Community,* Sandy Cameron wrote
about the tensions caused by rooming houses slapping on a coat
of paint and boosting rents for the five-month-long World's Fair:

"The Downtown Eastside is a tiny David compared to the Goliath of development, determined to build the corporate city, and the community is in crisis. Larry Campbell, the city coroner, has said that the stress people are under is far too much for many to bear. This is one of the reasons why there have been so many deaths in the past year."

For Jim Green, the battle to maintain existing housing in his community was personal. He lived in or near the Patricia Hotel for five years during the 1980s, and he went to the Patricia's beer parlour every night for a drink and a place to read the newspaper. Green organized demonstrations to boycott the hotel after Solheim died. For a long time, Green told the *Vancouver Sun's* Bob Sarti, he carried in his pocket Solheim's key to his former room at the Patricia.

While the population of residents in the Downtown Eastside declined during the 1970s, this trend had begun to reverse itself by the early 1980s. The city hall report *Downtown Lodging Houses and Tenant Profile,* by project director John Jessup, found the Downtown Eastside population had risen from a low of 2,182 in 1976 to 2,507 residents by 1981. During the same time, the steady loss of SROs and lodging houses continued, with the number of units being reduced by 1,987 between 1978 and 1982. In 1980 and 1981, these units were ninety per cent full. The average rental rate in 1982 for an SRO was around $175, lower than the maximum welfare shelter rate of $200. (That extra $25, which doesn't exist today, gave welfare recipients more money for food and other necessities.)

Vancouver's Expo 86 was officially declared a success, with government claiming the World's Fair had brought not only tourists but ongoing financial benefits to B.C. But not everyone in the Downtown Eastside agreed with that assessment. While Jim Green argued the biggest legacy from the fair was a loss of housing, Judy Graves would have said it was a shift in the community's drug culture. "[The government] told us they were bringing us a world-class city, but what they brought us was world-class drugs," laments Graves, who from 1979 to 1991 worked at Cordova House, a facility opened by the city in the 1970s to house the sixty-seven people police had identified as the most problematic in the neighbourhood. The violent people Graves worked with were mostly addicted, some of them with mental health problems as well. However, she remembers the community in the early 1980s as a safe place where she could walk to the corner store in the middle of the night to get snacks. Many service providers were unprepared for the changes more potent cocaine would bring to the neighbourhood; they hadn't even believed cocaine was addictive, because initially it was so weak. Stronger cocaine at the same low prices arrived with Expo, Graves says, and when people got hooked the prices were jacked up. After Expo, Graves saw dealers from other countries moving into some notorious Downtown Eastside hotels, and she recalls turf wars erupting over the lucrative drug business.

It hit the newspapers in July 1986 that so-called killer coke had caused six fatal overdoses in the past year; cocaine had evolved from being a drug only the rich dabbled in to one accessible to poverty-stricken addicts. Coroner Larry Campbell told reporters that more and more thrill-seekers were playing Russian roulette with injections of the so-called champagne drug. "People don't think it could happen to them," he said in 1986 of fatal overdoses. By the early 1990s, the availability of cocaine was combined with life-threatening purity levels of more than ninety per cent. In the past, cocaine sold at the street level had usually run between fifty and seventy-five per cent purity. Police were warning addicts to "step on" (street jargon for dilute) their scores to prevent more deaths. Young drug users were warned against a fashionable combination of heroin and cocaine called a "speedball," also proving to be lethal.

Donald MacPherson, today Vancouver's drug policy coordinator, had a front-row view of the neighbourhood's troubles through the late 1980s and early 1990s. MacPherson, who had been working on a master's degree in adult education, moved with his wife and children in 1986 from Ontario to B.C. He got a job at the Carnegie Community Centre, running its adult literacy program. His students were predominantly loggers and other middle-aged people wanting to finish their high school diplomas, along with some younger adults and those who spoke English as a second language.

At first MacPherson saw the core problems of the Downtown Eastside as alcohol or cheap substitutes like shoe polish and Lysol. He used as his unofficial measuring stick the roof of the Carnegie Centre. "It would be littered with Lysol cans from the Roosevelt Hotel next door," he recalls. But users were soon shooting up drugs in plain view on the streets. According to MacPherson, when the city cleaned up nearby Granville Street for Expo 86, it pushed the cocaine market into the Downtown Eastside. There were suddenly two or three twenty-four-hour grocery stores on every block with bare shelves and a booming under-the-counter cocaine business. In some restaurants, users did lines of coke on the tables. MacPherson's unofficial barometer was revealing different information by the early 1990s: "I'd go up to the top of the Carnegie Centre, and it was covered with syringes from the Roosevelt Hotel."

Along with increased drug use came the crime to fund it. The neighbourhood went from being home to two or three legitimate pawn shops to having forty-four second-hand stores within a few years. It was wild on the streets at the corner of Main and Hastings, and MacPherson recalls Carnegie Centre employees regularly helping people in distress. "Our door staff were reviving people every day in the washrooms who were blue," he says. There were so many memorial services for locals who had fatally overdosed that it seemed they were happening daily. Yet the drug-free Carnegie Centre maintained some normalcy during these turbulent times. "The Chinese ladies would come in for the ballroom dance classes from [the suburbs] on Sunday afternoons and weed through all the chaos out front," MacPherson recalls. The Carnegie was still offering a learning centre, a library, a kitchen program, a seniors' program, camping trips, coffee, and crafts, and it provided sports equipment at Oppenheimer Park. "Japanese women would come to play gate ball every Wednesday morning in their hats. Twenty metres the other way, you'd have your dealers with their drugs on picnic tables. It was a classic Downtown Eastside coexistence: no one bothered anyone," MacPherson says. "The problem was the picnic tables were beside the children's playground."

By late 1988, injection drug use had so increased in prevalence that John Turvey, the founder of DEYAS (Downtown Eastside Youth Activities Society), started single-handedly giving out three thousand clean syringes a month to try to reduce the spread of infectious diseases among addicts. Alongside him was Jerry Adams, who was hired by Turvey as a DEYAS outreach worker in 1986. He says Turvey, a former heroin addict who got clean in the 1970s, used donated money to buy clean needles because he was worried about the abscesses and scarring some users were developing. Turvey would walk the streets for hours, plucking clean rigs from his green army bag to give to surprised users. "I saw the first needles getting handed out," recalls Adams. "It was quite an amazing thing. Like anything else, it was scary for people, who would say, 'You're not supposed to be giving us these.'" Turvey received the Order of British Columbia in 1984 for his social work on the street, and he was recognized by the Atlanta Center for Disease Control in 1988 for his needle distribution work. DEYAS eventually secured $100,000 in government funding and got permission in 1989 to open Canada's first official needle exchange. Five hundred addicts were using it regularly by the end of its first month. DEYAS hired two extra staff, who drove around in a big green van, initially handing out about ten thousand new rigs a month and collecting old ones. "John did this work out of his heart. He had a volatile temper, but John was all heart. He was very concerned for these people. The work he did came from a passion," recalls Adams. DEYAS also handed out condoms to sex-trade workers and kept a "bad date" sheet about customers who had victimized the women. (Turvey would be mourned by many in the Downtown Eastside when he died in 2006 of mitochondrial myopathy, a fatal muscle and nerve disorder, at the age of sixty-one.)

Among those backing the needle exchange started by Turvey was Vancouver's chief medical health officer, Dr. John Blatherwick, who argued it was crucial that users be allowed to trade used rigs for clean ones. It was a foreign concept to the city council of the day. "When John Blatherwick started talking about needle exchange, we didn't know what he was talking about," recalls Philip Owen, who was then a Vancouver city councillor and would later become mayor. "Blatherwick saw the need. He was the one who quarterbacked it." Gordon Campbell, Vancouver's right-of-centre mayor at the time who would later become B.C.'s premier, was an unexpected champion of an official needle exchange. Campbell provided city funding for the controversial project and secured more money from the province. "Gordon is the reason why we got it through. When he really wanted something like that, he pushed hard," Owen recalls.

There was a public outcry from those who argued the needle exchange enabled drug users to keep injecting. Coroner Larry Campbell flatly rejected that position, saying the needle exchange was necessary to keep addicts healthy until governments could be persuaded to properly fund detox and recovery facilities. "All they were trying to do was keep people alive until someone woke up and put real money into this. If it had been any other disease, we would have been on it like a rash," Campbell says today. "There was certainly a recognition out there that addiction was an illness, but it was more often seen as a criminal event. And there was virtually no treatment. You needed a lot of money to get it and probably had to go outside Canada."

Manny Cu, who would go on to manage the DEYAS needle exchange vans, was originally one of the needle users. Cu moved from Toronto to Vancouver in 1988, trying to leave behind a youth scarred by racism, petty crimes, and minor drug use. Instead, he was wooed by the easy supply of drugs in the Downtown Eastside. He started to hang around with bikers and eventually full-patch members of the Hells Angels, wowed by their lifestyle: rides in limousines, the best seats in restaurants, lots of attention from strippers. Before long, Cu was the middle man for a big-time cocaine operation, selling to dealers who hawked their coke near Oppenheimer Park. He had an unforgettable run-in with B.C.'s Coordinated Law Enforcement Unit, which targeted gangs: "I had the CLEU boys stick a gun in my head, because at one point I was running a shooting gallery." But mostly Cu avoided the police by selling in Chinatown, where it was difficult for the mainly Caucasian CLEU members to blend in.

Cu received his supply in kilos, cutting it with glucose for junior dealers to peddle on the street. He had no idea how much he was snorting, because he had an endless supply at his fingertips. Once he started basing—cooking the cocaine to further refine it— he wasn't far from injecting. He and four friends would share one needle, using two dirty nickels to straighten the tip when it got bent. Cu drew water out of toilets and mud puddles to make his fix. "I didn't care if I was going to die or get HIV," he recalls.

In a short period of time, Cu ended up on the street, as the kind of entrenched addict he had "looked down on" when he first came to the neighbourhood. "It was a nightmare. I was sleeping on park benches. Stairwells in Chinatown. Abandoned houses. I couldn't pull it together to get a place to live. All the money went to drugs," Cu recalls. He developed the trademark scabs over skin where he frequently injected, making it almost impossible to find a vein. "You get so shaky from the cocaine that you can't even shoot yourself. I made a sex-trade worker named Tracy cry because she didn't want to shoot me anymore. Throughout all that is just misery. All your morals and values are gone. You get to the point that you'd use anything." Soon Cu was also injecting heroin. Life was so bad he wanted to end it countless times. "Christmas Eve in Oppenheimer Park, I remember sitting on the swings and wrapping the chain around my neck, but I didn't have the nerve. So what did I do? I went on the streets and did more drugs."

Cu tried detox several times, but he could never stay clean. A caring outreach worker urged him to go to a recovery home, and in May 1992, when his five-foot-ten frame carried just 115 pounds and he was severely dope sick, he agreed. Cu had been in the Downtown Eastside fewer than four years and had lost nearly everything. He says he went to hell and back in recovery, but he has remained clean. However, not everyone is that lucky.

By August 1992, the coroners service was lamenting that five young people a week—ranging from those homeless on the streets to healthy recreational users—were dying from drug overdoses. Campbell ordered a review of the tragedies, which were sweeping not just the Downtown Eastside but rural areas and urban centres across B.C. Existing social programs were making little difference. "The profile of the user had changed," Campbell says today. "In the seventies it was a guy who had done prison time, had been an addict for years. And then we started seeing people with no record, a different dynamic altogether. Then a shift started to take place towards younger people." As the effects of the drugs became more severe, the level of violence escalated. Firearms replaced knives as the common weapon on the street.

By the end of his first decade as coroner, Campbell was delivering tragic news to more and more families. "Part of the job was talking to the next of kin. Some of that was very difficult. Almost always, although the parents said they didn't know about the drugs, you knew instinctively that they had to know. Sometimes there would be an estrangement, where they hadn't seen their child for months. Sometimes mental illness and abuse came into it. The victims were young people, Native and non-Native, and all the potential was there." Campbell's morgue was becoming increasingly crowded, and the coroner knew something major needed to change.

4 | The Cain Report

IT WAS DAYTIME WHEN THE police paged the coroner: officers had found two dead bodies in an SRO building. When Larry Campbell arrived on the scene, police pointed him up the stairs, telling him it appeared to be another case of death by overdose. "Normally the police wouldn't say that. Until we work the room, they wouldn't say that. I remember thinking they should not jump to conclusions," Campbell recalls. But as soon as he entered the tiny room, he understood. Hypodermic needles were still embedded in the arms of both dead men, just below the rolled-up sleeves of their shirts. Campbell had never seen that before. "I just thought, 'What the hell did they shoot up that would take them down this fast?' Usually you shoot up and then go unconscious and your system shuts down. This must have just been 'boom!,' and they didn't have time to pull the needle out," Campbell says. The men, both in their forties, were not novice drug users. Their arms were covered in track marks from previous injections. But the heroin they took was later determined to be eighty per cent pure. It was late 1993, and notices would soon be posted around the

Downtown Eastside to warn addicts. Over the next two weeks, Campbell investigated five or six more cases of users dying in a similar way.

Fatal overdoses in B.C. had risen from 39 in 1988 to 331 by 1993. Thing were so out of control that B.C.'s chief coroner, Vince Cain, convened a task force made up of officials from the health, social service, and law enforcement fields as well as Aboriginal representatives, street workers, and recovering addicts. Cain travelled the province for eight months, seeking information about illicit narcotics in private meetings with drug users and during well-attended public sessions. The report he completed in September 1994 was a harsh indictment of the province's treatment of drug users. Cain was a former RCMP superintendent, and his verdict carried even more weight because it came from someone with a law-and-order background.

In his introduction to his *Report of the Task Force into Illicit Narcotic Overdose Deaths in British Columbia,* Cain said overdose deaths could not simply be explained as an "excessive intake of the drug." There needed to be "a greater understanding of who these people are, where they come from and where they are going." Cain was among the first officials to state boldly that drug addiction was a health problem and a social problem, not just an enforcement problem. No one is immune, he wrote. Doctors, lawyers, and others from affluent neighbourhoods had fallen victim, as well as those in low-income communities like the Downtown Eastside. The war on drugs, Cain's report said, "can only be regarded as an expensive failure." While there was no easy fix, he recommended some innovative harm reduction measures, "from facilitating safe use of illicit drugs to facilitating detox and addiction treatment for those motivated to discontinue their drug use."

Cain referred to the overdose deaths as an epidemic; by 1993, drug use had become the leading cause of death in British Columbia for men and women aged thirty to forty-four. Heroin was involved ninety per cent of the time. "The immediate apparent cause of this epidemic is the availability of unusually pure heroin resulting in inadvertent overdoses," Cain concluded. The purity of heroin had skyrocketed at a time when the price was plummeting because of a massive supply. Drug couriers from Africa and Asia were supplying Canada and using the country as a drug transit route to the U.S., where there had been a strengthening of drug enforcement in the 1980s. One ounce of pure heroin could be purchased for two thousand dollars in the 1990s; during the previous decade, that ounce would have been cut four or five times, with each cut sold for fifteen to twenty thousand dollars. Police believed the low prices were creating more traffickers and more users, Cain wrote.

The solution to the drug problem, Cain said, wasn't the war on drugs, with its "revolving door of arrest, detention, parole and relapse." He argued that drugs were readily available in jail, and the prison environment lent itself more to criminal mentality than to recovery. "The reputed 'war' in this field is perhaps better characterized as decades of skirmishes, with frankly 'no end in sight.' Perhaps some form of truce might best be called for," he wrote. "While a portion of the drug problem will remain a law enforcement problem, the time has surely arrived for society to re-examine, re-define, and clarify the balance between public safety and harm reduction." Cain's most controversial recommendations concerned the legalization and decriminalization of drugs. He suggested the decriminalization of simple possession of specific soft and hard drugs, so that addicts could be dealt with through the medical system, saying that "it would ameliorate many negative personal, family and social consequences arising from the punitive criminal model." He also suggested providing heroin to serious addicts through clinics, to "reduce the demand from the street trafficker." Additionally, Cain recommended looking into the merits of legalizing the possession of some soft drugs, like marijuana, a step that could "create that necessary 'window of opportunity' for the addicts who have lost hope and freedom of choice."

While Cain called for harsher sentences for drug importers and traffickers, he said that wasn't the answer for addicts. "The drug problem here cannot be altered through the criminal justice system, the police, the courts or the corrections system," he wrote. "We are going to have to adopt broader social strategies to deal with drug abuse." Money spent on policing and jails could be better spent on helping addicts, he said. "Removing threats and fears from users would allow them to 'come out of the closet' and, with some outreach mechanisms, would provide a variety of programs for treatment and ultimate harm reduction."

Society needed to compromise, Cain argued. There was no evidence abstinence-based programs reduced the ills related to drug use, and harm reduction strategies could at least "chip away" at the issues. "This approach ought not to be considered the answer to all of the problems related to drug abuse, but if it puts a dent in criminal activity, in robberies, assaults and murders; if it reduces the ambulance calls and Narcan injections; if it frees up court rooms and jail cells; if it cleans up our streets and public places from harassment and discomfort; and if it brings peace and quiet in families and increased employment and productivity, then the harm to all can be said to have been reduced—not completely, but perhaps to a socially tolerable level." The harm reduction Cain called for included expansion of and stable funding for needle exchanges, trials on the utility of methadone maintenance, a review of the feasibility of heroin maintenance, and the employment of recovering addicts in outreach roles.

Vince Cain's report painted a sympathetic portrait of the typical people addicted to drugs. He cited a disturbing study that had found as many as forty-six per cent of pregnant women in the Downtown Eastside were using drugs and alcohol, and he said the worrisome trend was usually the result of complex social issues such as "poverty, sexual abuse and violence, racial and gender marginalization, and HIV." Cain also concluded many people used drugs to forget a horrific past. "Nearly all addicts registered at needle exchanges have reported physical and sexual abuse in their homes as children," he wrote. "Many of the young women involved in sex trade work on the streets of our major cities have backgrounds of sexual and physical abuse by parents and family who took advantage of them, while under the influence of alcohol or drugs. The great majority of the First Nations people residing in Vancouver's Downtown Eastside report these conditions on their home reserves."

Cain recommended better funding for education, prevention, and treatment programs, as well as suggesting daycare and financial support be made available for mothers in treatment. He called for the expansion of detox and treatment centres across B.C. to reduce the one- to three-week-long waiting lists. In particular, he cited the need for more long-term recovery and residential care programs for youth and women, as well as facilities where mothers could keep their children with them. He recommended better counselling and treatment for troubled youth, improved drug prevention programs in schools, and "immediate across-the-board response for an adolescent in need of detox and follow-up treatment." Youth should not be sentenced to adult prisons, he said. "Of the addicts I spoke to, most started some form of substance abuse in their teen years, some in their pre-teen years. This was generally in response to a range of problems, complex and interrelated, including physical and sexual abuse, joblessness, homelessness, peer pressure, and boredom."

Cain also joined the chorus of people championing clean, decent housing, instead of dingy SROs—"not an eight by ten hovel with a cot and a hot plate," he wrote. "If the general public were to witness and experience the hovels some addicts exist in,

they would perhaps better understand why some of these people need alcohol and drugs to face the world day to day." The lack
of safe housing, for women in particular, meant some children
were being raised in rooming houses, many of them "shooting
galleries." Cain suggested, too, that recovering addicts needed
help finding good jobs. "It does not take a rocket scientist to figure out that if a person does not have meaningful work to go
to after treatment, then he/she is at risk to continue the cycle of
drug abuse." Cain reported that the typical drug-involved person
receiving social services was a "single female parent" who often
requested crisis grants to replace lost cash, was hounded by utility bill collectors, and "with growing frequency is involved in
robberies and other crimes."

One of the important findings in Cain's report was that
the incidence of overdose deaths increased dramatically on
the second-to-last Wednesday, Thursday, and Friday of each
month—the days just after welfare cheques were issued. He suggested "staggering social assistance payments throughout the
month" so that binges would not happen with the same intensity.
His recommendation echoed that made by the jury at the coroner's inquest into the death of Rob Laws twelve years earlier.

Cain's report also highlighted the plight of Aboriginal people, who by then made up thirty-seven to forty per cent of the
population of the Downtown Eastside, calling for a review of
outreach, support, and detox/treatment services for Aboriginals;
help for bands in addressing alcohol and drug issues in their
home communities; an expansion of multicultural training for
people who provided services to Aboriginals; and the full participation of Aboriginal people themselves in the planning of
substance abuse programs.

Lou Demerais, today executive director of the Vancouver
Native Health Society, recalls that the city's first urban clinic
specifically for Aboriginals opened in 1991, with funding from

the provincial government, precisely because of the concerns Cain would identify in his report. "The stats were abysmal on life expectancy rates and death rates," Demerais says of his people. "I'd talk to people on their way in and ask when they last saw a doctor, and they'd say they probably saw one once when they were a baby. And these were adults." The clinic, on Hastings Street east of the Carnegie Centre, incorporated modern Western medicine and traditional Aboriginal healing methods. The society also took over responsibility for an inner-city foster parent program that was largely serving an Aboriginal population. And in 1993, a doctor had proposed the clinic start a new program, which was named Sheway, to help keep pregnant mothers off drugs and alcohol. "The statistics were terrible. One in four babies born to Aboriginal women at the time were born with syndromes they'd have for the rest of their lives, poor kids," recalls Demerais.

Despite the need for these programs, there were constant funding battles to keep the society running. Demerais believes impoverished residents of the Downtown Eastside were easily overlooked in the early 1990s because they carried no clout with politicians. He can remember telling Aboriginal people they needed to start voting in elections so that politicians would listen. "But they had so many more other issues to struggle with—sickness, housing, eating," Demerais says. "Many of the most marginalized on the streets were residential school survivors." While working as a DEYAS outreach worker in the early 1990s, Jerry Adams lost a few young Aboriginal clients to suicide, and some teenage girls told him harrowing tales of abuse in their own homes. "A lot of them couldn't deal with the pain they felt at home, and the worse it was at home the more the addiction increased," Adams recalls.

As coroner, Larry Campbell was seeing a relatively high number of deaths, including suicides, involving Aboriginals. "I think that, generally speaking, the suicide rate among First Nations was higher because of the sense of despair and what people had gone through," Campbell says today. "The grandparents who were in these residential schools didn't have a prayer. A lot of it had to do with self-esteem and a long historical tale of being treated as less than human. Some people had no spirituality, no sense of community, no sense of civilization—we know that's wrong on all counts." The coroner suggested to some elders that the practice of naming new buildings after Aboriginal youth who had died by suicide be stopped—he feared it might encourage other fragile teens to kill themselves so that they could be memorialized. And Campbell once instructed a coroner's jury to take into account how Aboriginal Canadians were treated by the justice and the health care systems. "People would say to me that Natives couldn't get it any better: they don't pay taxes, the government treated them way too well. Which I didn't agree with," he recalls. In particular, he believed urban Aboriginals were extra-vulnerable because they were on their own, receiving no services from their home bands.

Larry Campbell didn't always see eye to eye with his boss, Vince Cain. Cain was a traditionalist, Campbell more of a renegade. But Campbell was amazed by the recommendations in Cain's report. "I was blown away by that report, by the depth of knowledge and by the conclusions," Campbell says today. "I walked into his office and said I couldn't believe he had written it. First and foremost, he said that drug addiction was a medical problem. It was not ambiguous. This wasn't a wishy-washy report. Coming from someone with his credentials, it didn't get any better than that. He bled red—this guy had been a chief superintendent with the RCMP. Certainly from police there was a sense of skepticism, but they couldn't argue with this guy because he was a former cop." Cain's report came at a crucial time, Campbell says, with people dying almost daily from overdoses.

In the letter to B.C. Attorney-General Colin Gabelmann that accompanied his report, Vince Cain said he hoped his findings would "creat[e] a greater understanding of the problem, as well as produc[e] tangible results that will have a positive effect on all of us." The public response to the report was mixed. Gabelmann, a member of the governing NDP, told reporters that he planned to raise the matter of decriminalization with federal Liberal justice minister Allan Rock. "This is an issue that has not had the kind of public discussion yet that it demands, and I'm going to ask my colleagues at the national level to participate with us in a broader discussion," Gabelmann said. "It's important now that Canadians debate this issue seriously and [this], I hope, will lead to a conclusion in the years to come." B.C's health minister Paul Ramsey told reporters that the government had formed a team to coordinate action on Cain's sixty-three recommendations and agreed with Cain that society should shift from the enforcement of abstinence towards a harm reduction approach. John Turvey, director of the Downtown Eastside Youth Activities Society, praised the report as "the best we could have hoped for." And the *Vancouver Sun*, the city's largest newspaper, while acknowledging that the issues of legalization and decriminalization were tricky ones, backed the report in an editorial published under the headline, "Cain report a good start on a tough problem." A senior Vancouver RCMP drug-squad officer, however, was critical of the suggestion that Canada should consider decriminalizing or legalizing street drugs. "We want a drug-free society," Superintendent Vince Casey told the *Sun*, adding he feared legalization could encourage more people to use drugs and lead to a possible influx of traffickers. Some senior doctors also spoke out against the recommendation to prescribe heroin to addicts, arguing that methadone maintenance was a better way of combatting heroin addiction.

In the end, the "tangible results" that Cain had hoped for just didn't happen. "There were no earth-shaking changes to anything that I saw," recalls Larry Campbell, who took over Cain's job as B.C.'s chief coroner in late 1996. As had been the case with the Le Dain Commission in the 1970s, which recommended using the health care system as the agenda for action against drugs, Campbell says there was no political will from any level of government to support Cain's recommendations. The only possible impact, Campbell says today, was that the report may have planted a harm reduction seed in the mind of Vancouver's new mayor Philip Owen, first elected to that position in 1993. Several years down the road, Owen would champion a harm reduction approach to the city's drug woes.

Vince Cain had held public hearings in the final stages of gathering information for his report, and the last one was held at the Carnegie Centre. Donald MacPherson, by then a manager at the Carnegie, told the inquiry what staff were seeing every day at the corner of Main and Hastings. MacPherson was ecstatic when he read Cain's final report. "In my mind, that was the moment when addiction became a health issue. The report was so powerful. One of his main messages was to take the money we spend on cops, courts, and judges and spend it on health. And this was coming from a former cop," MacPherson recalls. His excitement turned to disappointment when "fuck all happened" with the recommendations, the straight-shooting MacPherson says, because no level of government had the courage to make them a priority.

Although his report identified heroin as the main culprit, Cain determined that two-thirds of the 331 people who fatally overdosed in 1993 were using more than one drug at the same time. The most common combinations involved heroin, cocaine, and alcohol. According to Neil Boyd, a criminology professor and the author of High Society, a book about drug policy published in 1991, those studying heroin overdose deaths in other parts of the world were beginning to realize it wasn't accurate to blame heroin alone. In one widely cited 1996 study, published in the journal *Addiction,* Shane Darke and Deborah Zador wrote that the problem was "multiple drug toxicity," noting that, on average, cases of fatal overdose revealed morphine levels no higher than those of survivors of so-called overdose. It wasn't heroin that was killing people, the researchers said; it was a cocktail of legal and illegal drugs, in combination with the highly compromised physical health of many of the users.

In his book, Boyd had recommended that legal and illegal drugs be treated in the same way, since they were all part of the same public health problem; criminalization was only making matters worse. When the deaths had begun to mount in the Downtown Eastside, Boyd had become increasingly interested in figuring out why—it seemed likely to him that more than heroin was in play. The research into overdose deaths done by Michael Brandt, who was one of Boyd's graduate students, revealed that only eight per cent of those deaths could actually be attributed to heroin. While it was true that cheaper, more potent heroin was flooding the streets of Vancouver, users were becoming wise to its potency and were turning to other powerful stimulants, many of which were just making their way to the street. It was no accident that heroin began to slide in popularity at the same time a new drug, crack cocaine, became available, says Boyd, today the associate director of Simon Fraser University's criminology department. Drug distributors recognized the lucrative potential in crack, small rocks of cocaine that sold cheaply and produced a quick high. A heroin user could feel right on two to three injections each day, but the crack pipe demanded dozens of hits.

Police had a lot more difficulty controlling someone on crack, who was typically alert, angry, and hyper-vigilant, than someone on heroin, who might be angry but was also sleepy and stumbling. And law enforcement efforts had little impact on the illegal trade in either crack or cocaine, Neil Boyd says, in part because of changes to policing in the Downtown Eastside. By the 1990s, police were in their cars, driving around the area, rather than on foot patrol. The absence of patrol officers led to more open drug use and more public disorder. Additionally, crack users led a more frenzied life, and the new distribution networks were not easily controlled. Police were often reduced to playing a triage role, trying to clean up the mess the trade had created.

As the Downtown Eastside grew more and more unstable, it became a neighbourhood that officials and average Vancouverites alike started to avoid. The general sense, Larry Campbell recalls, was that if the chaos could be contained within a ten-block area it wasn't worth worrying about. A hue and cry didn't emerge until later in the 1990s, when drug users started sleeping on the steps of the fancy new downtown library and panhandling at intersections in the business district. It was only then, Campbell says, that people started paying attention to the concerns Vince Cain raised in his report. "I include myself in this," he says. "I was the coroner when this was going on. We didn't just wake up one morning and this had happened. It happened over a period of time, and there was concerted neglect." Other B.C. cities were doing even less to address their drug problems, he says, so their addicts were coming to the Downtown Eastside, too. "You'd come to town to score, you got a cheap place to live, and you stayed, because there were people like you, so you were not scorned. And you never went back to Nelson or Nanaimo. You stayed here. And sometimes you died here."

With governments failing to act on the pressing issues the Cain report identified, some Downtown Eastside residents decided to take matters into their own hands. At the time of Cain's June 1994 public hearing at the Carnegie Centre, Ann Livingston had just moved with her three young sons into the Four Sisters Housing Co-op, after separating from her husband in Victoria. While her oldest boy was at school, Livingston loaded her four- and six-year-old sons, along with a neighbour's toddler, into a wagon and headed to the Carnegie for the public meeting. She listened to the speakers as she continuously pulled the wagon across the back of the hall, the only action that would keep the three boys quiet. "The testimonies were a spectacle to behold," Livingston says today. "The drug users' testimony was completely raw. It was as if nobody had asked them anything for twenty years. Cain, he was the guy that got my hopes up."

But like others in the neighbourhood, Livingston went from optimism about Cain's recommendations to deep frustration that those in power were paying them little heed. Livingston had no personal experience with drug addiction, but activism for causes in which she believed was in her blood; she had been raised by parents who did volunteer work with marginalized people, and she began fighting for services for the disabled ever since her oldest son was born with cerebral palsy. Her son's disability had also altered Livingston's life goals, so she related to some of the challenges her new neighbours were facing. Shortly after moving to the Downtown Eastside, Livingston had seen someone overdosing in the alley from her bedroom window, and she ran downstairs to perform CPR. The experience convinced her that drug users should be organized into a lobby group. With others, Livingston created a group called IV Feed and got a small amount of funding for it from DEYAS, which thought the group intended to open a drop-in centre for addicts. But Livingston was convinced something more drastic was needed. She put up posters inviting drug users to discuss "setting up a junkies' union and co-operative drug buying and a safe injection site," as she recalls.

Livingston's group rented a storefront in a squalid building at 356 Powell Street, and in the fall of 1995 IV Feed began running an unsanctioned supervised injection site. Known as the Back Alley Drop-In, the drug-user-run facility operated for about a year and was used nightly by as many as two hundred addicts.

Livingston recalls that the biggest challenge at first was getting enough needles to provide each user with a clean rig. Finally, a street nurse with the B.C. Centre for Disease Control started giving the group boxes of syringes, which Livingston hid in her apartment because they were worth money on the street.

The Back Alley was a primitive place with poetry scrawled across the walls. But it provided users with a safer place to inject, offering a reprieve from the streets and clean water to make their fix. When someone fatally overdosed, volunteers dragged the body into the alley before phoning 911. (This was a common practice among marginalized residents in the Downtown Eastside; people were worried they'd get kicked out of their SROs or get in trouble with police if they were found with a dead body.)

While no medical staff was employed at the Back Alley, street nurses from the Centre for Disease Control would drop by. The police were frequent and curious visitors, although many officers were lenient at first because at least the place offered addicts an alternative to shooting up on the streets. Livingston would open the door when officers arrived and stall them while others inside hid the drugs. "I was always in a flowered dress," Livingston recalls. "That was my strategy. I looked like a Sunday school teacher—well, not really, because I had army boots on." She'd let the police in to have a look around when the coast was clear.

Coroner Larry Campbell accepted Livingston's invitation to speak at the Back Alley Drop-In at the height of the overdose epidemic. At that point in his life, Campbell didn't believe in supervised injection sites, but he was in awe of what these drug users had accomplished. "I was really amazed by the group of people who got this together. I said to them, 'You can't keep putting overdoses in the alley. The cops are going to come and kick your door down.' I wasn't too concerned about them shooting up in there, but the overdoses were going to be trouble." However, Campbell was also overwhelmed by the vulnerable state of the people inside the makeshift facility. "There were people injecting while I was speaking, and there were people going on the nod," he says. "I just looked at this humanity and I said, 'You know, people, you've got to raise some hell about this. That's the only way the government is going to hear you.'"

The Back Alley closed down in October 1996, when its funding was cut; DEYAS didn't want to back such a controversial site. Police were also concerned that the place was becoming a shooting gallery where violent drug dealers were threatening users. Ann Livingston admits the Back Alley was squalid and difficult, but she argues it rallied drug users to work together and may have reduced the number of overdose deaths in the area—which was the whole point of the Cain report.

Ironically, the only immediate change following the release of Vince Cain's report was a *reduction* in the detox services available to addicts in the Downtown Eastside, with the closure of Pender Detox in Vancouver—a move by the province that Vancouver mayor Philip Owen labelled "criminal." By 1997, three years after he had penned his report, Cain estimated that only one of his sixty-three recommendations had been implemented. "Frankly, I'm disappointed. I thought it was off to a flying start, but . . . it got shelved," Cain told the *Vancouver Sun* in July 1997. "That report is as good today as it was then, but nothing has changed. People are still dying. There are more addicts. There's more pain and suffering. The only way this can hit home is if the public really understands the issues." Cain told the media the one recommendation from his report that was implemented was B.C.'s College of Physicians and Surgeons taking over the existing methadone program from the federal government, to provide easier access to the synthetic replacement drug for heroin and morphine. In response to the criticism, NDP health minister Joy MacPhail said another Cain recommendation, for a heroin maintenance program, had not been implemented because heroin was an illegal substance;

she told the *Sun* that Attorney-General Ujjal Dosanjh had discussed the Cain report with the federal government and was still
waiting for a response from the justice minister in Ottawa.

A handful of people, including Vancouver deputy police chief
Ken Higgins, spoke out in 1997 in favour of legalizing or decriminalizing small amounts of some drugs, but, as with Cain, their
lobbying did little more than generate headlines. A 1998 report
by the provincial health officer claimed that some planning and
research initiatives had also taken place following the release of
the Cain document and that services such as needle exchanges,
street nurse programs, and methadone maintenance had been
increased, some of them in the Downtown Eastside. But even the
issuing of this government report, which also studied what to do
about B.C.'s burgeoning injection drug problem, was proof alone
that not enough had been done to enact Cain's recommendations.
And the report's author, Dr. John Millar, noted particularly that
Cain's suggestion to establish a substance abuse commission had
been ignored. Such a commission was key, Millar argued, because
it "could bring together services that, at present, are administered
in separate ministries such as the methadone program in the
Ministry of Health and alcohol and drug services in the Ministry
for Children and Families." In fact, it would be many more years
before the government merged services for drug addicts.

For those working in the Downtown Eastside, like Coroner
Larry Campbell, the sweeping changes called for in Cain's highly
regarded report seemed to have been largely forgotten. "Governments work to an agenda set by their supporters," Campbell
says. "I simply don't think the government saw Cain's recommendations as a high priority that would resonate with voters.
Obviously, they were wrong, as evidenced by the damage caused
to the community, to citizens, and to the public at large." The
Cain report was a lost opportunity to save lives, Campbell argues
today, when you consider what his boss had actually called for.

"The drug problem in British Columbia is very real and very serious. No one in this province is immune to the problem. It is costing the taxpayer an enormous amount of money," Vince Cain had written in his report. "It is a social problem, as well as a health problem. The answers are not easily found. Neither are the remedies cheap. The problems cover a wide range of issues, the solutions equally expansive and expensive, but unless these are dealt with head-on and now, future generations may well be unable to contend with the consequences of our generation's unwillingness to face up to reality." How prophetic his words would prove to be.

5 | Woodward's

IT WAS NOT ONLY ON the drug front that Downtown Eastside residents were proposing creative alternatives. Some were lobbying for systemic changes that would make the neighbourhood a healthier place to live. One of those was Jim Green of the Downtown Eastside Residents' Association, who was fighting to keep the heartbeat of the community: the venerable red-brick Woodward's building with the revolving, 652-bulb W sign perched on a mini Eiffel Tower on its roof. The department store on Hastings Street had fallen on hard times financially by the time Green became president of DERA in 1980.

Started by Vancouver's Woodward family in 1892, Woodward's expanded across western Canada as a chain. Hastings and Abbott was the flagship location, built in 1903 on what was then the city's busiest commercial strip, home to other department stores, newspaper offices, and theatres. The food floor, pharmacy, and wildly popular $1.49 Days provided staples for those on a limited budget; the store also carried fashions and other favourites popular with middle-class residents from wealthier parts of the city. At its height, Woodward's employed hundreds of people, many of them from the neighbourhood. But as the store approached its centennial birthday, it struggled to remain relevant. More and more shoppers were flocking to new suburban malls. In the early 1990s, after announcing massive losses, the store's owners made valiant efforts to restructure the company.

Woodward's was where Jim Green had regularly met friends for coffee, cashed his meagre paycheques (before the advent of ATMs), and taken his daughter for a low-budget treat. There were also the Christmas window displays, animated marvels of mechanical teddy bears and toys that always drew hundreds of spectators. "I would book my airline tickets there and buy my wife a dress for Christmas," he recalls. "Woodward's was the perfect epicentre of the Lower Mainland because it served everyone who was rich and also those in abject poverty." Green was among those who believed the enormous building on Hastings was crucial to the future of the neighbourhood, even if the store inside didn't survive. It would turn into a protracted David-and-Goliath battle, with Goliath—land owners and developers—taking an early and considerable lead. But Green, who'd made a career of being the scrappy underdog, was up for the fight.

Green was born to a religious mother and an alcoholic army sergeant father in the southern U.S., a place rife with class and racial prejudice. He left home at sixteen and drove a hearse to support himself while going to school. He moved to Colorado to pursue a master's degree in anthropology, thinking he'd find enlightenment on the west coast. Instead, he started fighting for the rights of migrant farm workers.

After launching a legal appeal of the draft that was trying to send him to Vietnam, Green moved to Vancouver, where he identified immediately with the community at Main and Hastings. Before becoming DERA's president, he worked as a college instructor, a cab driver, and a union shop steward during a stint

as a longshoreman. He also wrote a book on the Canadian Sea-
man's Union. DERA had gone through another funding battle
and could afford to pay Green only nineteen thousand dollars
a year. But with Green at the helm, DERA lobbied for financing, and it soon became one of the neighbourhood's most
successful developers of social housing. Green recalls a day in
the mid-1980s when he both attended the ground-breaking
ceremony for the DERA Housing Co-op (a fifty-six-unit social
housing facility that opened in 1985) and secured funding for
the Four Sisters Co-op (a 153-unit low-income facility that would
open in 1987). The financier for Four Sisters asked Green what
his next project would be as the two walked along Hastings near
Abbott. Green looked up at the neon W sign and said, "I want
Woodward's." His vision was to fill the ageing seven-storey building with a mix of housing and retail so that it could remain a
lifeline of the community.

It would be another decade before the Downtown Eastside Woodward's location went out of business, but it was no
secret the chain was in trouble: from 1986 onwards, it lost mil-
lions annually. Chairman and chief executive Charles "Chunky"
Woodward, grandson of the store's founder, blamed the losses on
increased competition, high interest rates, and a soft economy.
The store changed the type of merchandise it sold, including
a failed experiment in offering high-end clothing. The food
floor that had been so successful in the first half of the twentieth century just couldn't compete with mega grocery stores, and
it was sold in 1986. Staff were laid off in high numbers. For the
first time in its ninety-six-year history, the family-run company
hired an outsider to oversee its twenty-six Woodward's locations,
thirty lower-priced Woodwynn stores in B.C. and Alberta, and
four Abercrombie & Fitch outlets across Canada.

The doors to the trademark Hastings Street location closed in
January 1993. The news was devastating for Downtown Eastside

residents who depended on the store and for the other businesses along an already ailing commercial strip. "The old guys of the area use Woodward's as their corner store, for groceries. Where are they supposed to go if there is nothing to replace it?" Green said at the time. "And Gastown merchants depend on Woodward's to draw people in." His dream reactivated, Green began searching for financing to fill the building with four hundred residential units, half low-income and the rest market housing, as well as services and retail shops on the ground floor. There was a dire need in the neighbourhood for low-cost rental units, but Green feared some developer would follow trends in other areas of downtown Vancouver by filling the iconic building entirely with high-priced condos.

Green was ideally placed to broker such a deal. Before leaving DERA in 1992, he had turned it from a one-man show into a fifty-employee organization that orchestrated more than six hundred new units of social housing for the area. He then started working with the provincial New Democratic Party, which had toppled the ruling Social Credit Party to gain power in Victoria, to promote deals between private developers and non-profit groups to finance housing projects. Green knew how the political system worked, having run for mayor of Vancouver in 1990. But even he couldn't close a deal on the Woodward's building. Some powers in the financing and development game wanted to tear the building down, and many politicians were loath to enter the fractious debate. However, Green remained committed to the cause during the tumultuous years that followed.

While the Woodward's building sat empty, Hastings Street morphed into a ghost town, recalls Larry Campbell, who was regional coroner in the early and mid-1990s. Among the bleakest stretches was the 100-block of West Hastings, on the south side of the street across from the boarded-up Woodward's. All but one of the fourteen buildings there had been constructed between 1899 and 1909; nine had been designated heritage buildings by the city. In the glory days of the 100-block, customers walked along wooden sidewalks to visit dentists and doctors and pharmacists, upscale hotels, tailors, cafés and restaurants, newspaper offices, and the Vancouver Stock Exchange. By the late 1990s, the buildings were rotting and mostly vacant, aside from pawn shops, rats, and the odd homeless person looking for shelter. No one washed the bird poop off the sidewalks, or fixed broken windows, or cleaned the urine stains from the doorways.

In 1981, George Chow and two business partners had opened the Bonanza Market, a South Asian grocery store, in the 200-block of East Hastings near the Blue Eagle Café. It had been a fantasy for Chow, who was by then an engineer at B.C. Hydro, to open a business in the neighbourhood where he'd spent his teen years. At first, business was good. The daily receipts from the store were deposited at the Royal Bank at Main and Hastings, across from the Carnegie Centre, and although there were some "bad elements" in the area they were never violent, says Chow. But the street and the retail scene worsened, and Chow ended his association with the store in 1991. Nearby Chinatown was also in demise; it had been "in full bloom" in the 1980s, Chow says, with steady traffic on Pender Street between Main and Gore. Like many other retired Chinese people in Vancouver, Chow's elderly parents lived in an apartment in Chinatown and went to the Carnegie Centre for dances, to use the library, and to chat over coffee. But people arriving from Hong Kong and China in the 1990s moved instead to Richmond or other parts of Metro Vancouver, where malls and stores catering to Chinese Canadians had started to open.

Tom Laviolette, who prepared a report in 2000 on the changes in retail on Hastings Street over thirty years, concluded that although drug addicts filled the vacuum left by departing retail, it's unlikely they had chased the store owners out. In the

1970s, says Laviolette's report, written on behalf of the Carnegie Community Action Project, "Hastings was not rich, but it was bustling." In addition to anchor stores like Woodward's and Army & Navy, the street had many other shops, restaurants, and bars catering to moderate-income customers. When Vancouver's main downtown shopping district began shifting west following Expo 86, and consumers converged in ever greater numbers on comfortable indoor malls, the stores along Hastings were forced to close, including stalwarts like the Peggy Shop, Pierre Paris shoes, Ripley's men's wear, Philip Clothier, and Wosk's. Three major banks (TD, Nova Scotia, and CIBC) also left Hastings, along with several restaurants and other entertainment facilities.

Al Hersh had opened Ripley's in 1947 near Pigeon Park, a popular neighbourhood gathering place, and closed it nearly fifty years later after witnessing the decline of the community. "This area has been going downhill for five years, since Woodward's closed. They were the cement that kept us together. But look at the boarded-up windows, the places that have closed. We had a bank at every corner, but they've all pulled out, one by one. There's drug-dealing on every corner," Hersh told the *Vancouver Sun* in 1994, when he was seventy-eight years old. "When I started, having a place down here was a license to print money. People came down here to watch other people, to shop. They spent money. We got to know them. I met people from across the street and from across the ocean. I took the name and address of every new customer and sent them birthday and anniversary cards. We used to send out 5,000–6,000 cards a year... Now there's no reason to come down here like there used to be. Sweet Sixteen is gone. Pierre Paris is gone. Wosk's is gone. Woodward's going out of business knocked us all out."

Things worsened when three other retail giants on Hastings closed: Fedco, Woolworths, and Fields. Without those stores, most people simply stopped coming to the Downtown East-side to shop. The only new businesses opening up were fast food joints, convenience stores, and pawn shops. The vacancy rate along Hastings soared to thirty-six per cent. A few long-time merchants did remain, however, including the seventy-year-old Only Seafood Café, which initially packed its fish on ice in the front window because it didn't have refrigeration; the Ovaltine Café, with its eighteen-metre-long vintage counter and stools; and a Downtown Eastside icon, the Army & Navy department store.

"The aftermath of Woodward's closing and leaving the block empty was devastating," says Jacqui Cohen, Army & Navy's president and CEO. The first Army & Navy store was opened on Hastings in 1919 by Samuel Cohen, and the discount department store chain now has six locations in B.C. and Alberta. The company's heyday was in the early 1980s, before the arrival of Walmart in Canada. By the time Cohen took over her grandfather's company in 1988, it was a big decision to keep soldiering on, especially on Hastings Street. "A lot of people didn't think Army & Navy would survive, but I have a passion for this area and I hunkered in," she says. As a teenager, Cohen took the bus from her family's West Side house to the store, where she worked as a salesgirl. "It was just like having a second home, and I never thought of this area as anything more than normal." Cohen opted to keep the Hastings Street location operating for a couple of reasons. First, she carried merchandise the area's low-income residents bought, like sardines and cat food—both cheap dinners for someone without teeth and with pennies a day to spend on meals. Second, Cohen says that for her the Hastings Street store is akin to the family homestead Scarlett O'Hara fought to save in *Gone with the Wind*. "People said, 'Sell the thing. What do you need that for?' But it's still my Tara." Cohen loves the architecture of the Downtown Eastside, and she respects the residents who live courteously in the 'hood, despite being frustrated by the graffiti on the buildings and the general chaos outside her store's front doors.

The Woodward's building was sold in December 1995 to Kassem Aghtai of West Vancouver–based Fama Holdings. Aghtai planned to put 350 upscale market condos inside, which prompted about thirty outraged Downtown Eastside groups to join together to rally for social housing. "Let's be honest about it—there is going to be a lot of collateral damage to the low-income people from this project," Jim Green told the media at the time. "This project will cut a swath through the heart of the community, drive up property values and make it harder to build social housing." The groups caught the ear of NDP premier Mike Harcourt, who in 1996 offered $25 million so that Aghtai could include two hundred low-rent units in the building. A year later, however, Aghtai announced the deal had collapsed because of certain agreements he couldn't reach with the province; his plan was again to build all market housing inside Woodward's with some retail space.

Bud Osborn, a neighbourhood activist, published poet, and former addict, had been speaking at churches and community meetings across Metro Vancouver to try to convince voters to support the idea of social housing in the Woodward's building. "What I tell them is what the Bible says, 'That Jesus is with the poor, and if you drive the poor out of a neighbourhood, you are driving Jesus out, too,'" Osborn explained to the *Vancouver Sun* following one of his church meetings. Osborn, who was on the DERA board and the Vancouver/Richmond Health Board, argued that what happened to the Woodward's building—the "cornerstone" of the neighbourhood—would foreshadow the future of the area. Church members and leaders from outside the Downtown Eastside began lobbying city hall to protect social housing in the vulnerable neighbourhood, he recalls.

Shortly after Aghtai's decision, about a dozen members of Osborn's new Political Response Group met in a cramped room, where the walls were decorated with homemade posters that read "Displacing the poor is a crime against humanity," "Pain and suffering the results of homelessness," and "Where do we live when there is no place to go?" Members brainstormed about how to oppose the Woodward's decision. Later that day, the protesters used red and black paint to declare that the empty Woodward's building belonged to the people, writing "Public Property" and "Give It Back" on the boards. Vancouver police spoke to Osborn about the demonstration, but he was not charged. Some passersby, who were captured on camera by a documentary crew, were critical of the action, accusing drug addicts of wanting a free ride. Members of Osborn's group fired back that while there were drug addicts in the Downtown Eastside, there were other poor people who desperately needed affordable housing: pensioners, the handicapped, single mothers.

Bud Osborn wrote a poem about the importance of the issue and mailed it to Aghtai, who invited the activist to his office for tea. At the end of their meeting, however, Aghtai explained he was not going to hand Woodward's over for low-income housing. "I thought, the next time I come here, it's not going to be on these terms," Osborn recalls today. At a subsequent Political Response Group meeting, Osborn illustrated on a flip chart the layout of Aghtai's office. On April 15, 1997, armed with yellow pamphlets that read "Woodward's belongs to us!," Osborn and half a dozen protestors barged into the developer's West Vancouver premises. They stayed in the office for an hour or so, handing out their pamphlets and emphasizing that the company's decision was disrespectful to the community.

The protests continued in the months that followed. About one hundred people marched through the Downtown Eastside, chanting "We want Woodward's!" and waving placards with slogans like "Woodward's belongs to the people of the DES" and "We need welfare-level housing, not condos." Balloons, more painting on the security boards (some done by children), and chalk drawings on the sidewalk also appeared. As the rain fell on one demonstration, Osborn told the crowd that a housing crisis in any other neighbourhood would have brought a more immediate response.

Instead, Woodward's continued to sit empty. The owners of some of the closed businesses on Hastings hired private security firms to guard their vacant buildings. Many of the empty spaces were inside heritage buildings that couldn't be torn down, and the city required the owners to keep the squatters out; city hall made that ruling after a dozen young people living in a vacant apartment building accidentally set it ablaze in October 1997. In the mid- to late 1990s, city hall enforced bylaws that prevented more unsavoury second-hand shops from opening in the Downtown Eastside, suspended a few business licences and forced a handful of bars to close earlier. More police officers were assigned to walk the beat, leading to the seizure of stolen property and charges against several shop owners. The effort reduced criminal activities by at least ten per cent between 1996 and 1998, according to a report by city hall's general manager of community services, Nathan Edelson. Thefts from vehicles were down by sixteen per cent, and drug trafficking arrests were up by thirteen per cent. Sidewalks were repaired and power-washed, garbage was taken out of lanes, and graffiti was removed from buildings. Still, Edelson wrote, conditions in the community had made it "unlivable" for the residents and "virtually impossible for many legitimate businesses to survive." Edelson's 1998 report called for community-based initiatives that would help attract new businesses to the area. But the imbalance in the Downtown Eastside would continue: while more stores sat empty, homeless residents clamoured for a roof over their heads.

The ultimate showdown over this dilemma was still five years in the future. When it happened, it would pit activists against the establishment in a long, heated protest held right inside the neighbourhood's venerable Woodward's building.

6 | Homeless and Mentally Ill

BRIAN SHAW WAS IN AND out of mental health institutions for much of his life. When the schizophrenic man was stable, he volunteered in the community and was known by many to be kind and friendly. However, the forty-year-old man had fallen on difficult times by the early 1990s, often panhandling to supplement his six-hundred-dollar monthly handicapped pension and becoming agitated when people didn't give him enough spare change. In addition, Shaw had not been keeping up his medications. He was a regular at the Kettle Friendship Society in east Vancouver, but on August 19, 1991, he arrived too late for the centre's free dinner. When the frustrated man threatened a drop-in centre employee and refused to leave, the police were called, but Shaw disappeared before they arrived. The next morning he returned for a cup of coffee and apologized for his actions. An hour later, Shaw jabbed a kitchen steak knife at a person on Commercial Drive who wouldn't give him a cigarette. When a police officer arrived, Shaw would not drop his knife.

During a tense exchange, he lunged at the officer, who then fired one shot. It was fatal.

Shaw had lost weight and was looking desperate and unkempt before his death. "He had been slipping for sure," Mark Smith, then the Kettle's executive director, told the *Vancouver Sun*. "We have good recreational programs for people with a mental-health disability. But what we don't have is money for them to live on... For him, it was the lack of money—he was broke and frustrated. He was hungry a lot." Marilyn Sarti of the Mental Patients' Association also spoke out at the time of Shaw's death: "This is what happens to people who don't have short-term acute care available—they just stay on the street and deteriorate... There's no one who looks into it for these people. At night they have to go home alone and live with their demons."

Among the recommendations of the coroner's inquest into Shaw's death, which was led by Larry Campbell, was a suggestion that police be better trained to deal with the mentally ill and that governments provide more services, especially since institutions were increasingly discharging patients straight into the community. "As deinstitutionalization of the mentally ill continues, we find that funds *must* be directed to the community sector to provide services to support those who are mentally ill, e.g., counsellors, care teams, home care workers, food banks, meals on wheels, adult day care, drop-in centres," the five-person jury said on March 24, 1992. Another of the jury's recommendations was that the hours for Car 87, the police car in which a mental health worker rides along with a Vancouver police officer, be increased to twenty-four hours a day, seven days a week.

Campbell still feels what he describes as a "sense of futility" about Brian Shaw's death. Because society had let Shaw down, Campbell says, the police were forced to act as mental health experts, which they weren't trained to do. "In the purest sense, Brian Shaw was killed because he was crazy. Somebody in their right mind realizes you can't pull a knife and do this and expect to walk away. That's the tragedy, because in so many cases, with proper care and treatment, mental health patients are fine."

The shortcomings in the system that were experienced by Shaw would only get more severe. Like many other Western governments, Canada's federal Liberals were focused on cutting spiralling deficits and in 1993 decided, among other things, that Ottawa could no longer afford to build social housing. At the same time, British Columbia's only long-term psychiatric hospital, Riverview, located close to Vancouver in the city of Coquitlam, was continuing to discharge record numbers of patients. By 1993, Riverview's population had fallen to just 800, from a high of 5,500 patients in 1955. The situation had the makings of a perfect storm.

Deinstitutionalization had been taking place across Canada since the late 1960s, in the belief that psychiatric patients would be better off living in a community with support services than locked up in a hospital. In B.C., the plan had been to create new beds and health services for the mentally ill around the province. The concept was well intentioned, but it depended on sufficient services being in place to help patients once they were released. The NDP, while B.C.'s opposition party, had argued in the provincial legislature that plans by the Social Credit government to phase out Riverview would create a "crisis," because there was already a severe shortage of mental health beds in the province. Some doctors also worried that certain patients shouldn't be free from rigid supervision, as they could potentially put themselves and others at risk. Socred health minister Peter Dueck defended the government's program, saying communities would easily be able to care for mental health patients through a "comprehensive infrastructure" of services. In March 1989, however, a city health department report found that the majority of Vancouver's thirty-six boarding homes for the mentally ill were "substandard."

Vancouver health officer Dr. John Blatherwick told the *Vancouver Sun* that before the provincial government released more Riverview Hospital patients into the community, it had to improve the boarding home program. "[Otherwise] they might as well stay in Riverview," Blatherwick argued. "We want them to live quality lives and not be warehoused." An agency that provided outreach services to the mentally ill told the *Sun* that same year that it couldn't cope with the workload of taking on any new clients. John Russell, executive director of the Greater Vancouver Mental Health Service, said the agency's 100 therapists were already struggling to provide adequate services for their 3,800 clients. In October 1991, the Socreds were criticized for not yet spending any of the $26 million the government had pledged a year earlier for community services to replace Riverview beds. As a result, Riverview administrator John Yarske announced, "we have basically put a hold or a freeze on any further bed closures or reductions here at Riverview until such time as adequate alternative programs are developed in the community." When the NDP under Mike Harcourt won the provincial election in October 1991, unseating the Socreds, the party vowed that the plan to discharge more patients from Riverview would continue only when there were enough community services in place.

Deinstitutionalization was taking place across Canada, but its effects were particularly acute in B.C., where the days of care provided for patients of psychiatric hospitals dropped by almost sixty-five per cent between 1985 and 1999, in contrast to a national decline of about forty per cent. B.C.'s faster pace was a reflection of a relatively more significant political commitment to deinstitutionalization by the provincial governments of the day, both the Social Credit and the NDP, though that commitment was not always backed by the necessary funding. On the housing front, what little social housing did exist was typically not equipped to assist people who had been institutionalized or who suffered from mental illness and/or substance abuse disorders. Many ex-patients were evicted from the housing they found after being released or were unable to find housing in the first place.

Darrell Burnham, executive director of Coast Mental Health, identifies 1993 as the year the difficulties began in earnest, with the cost-cutting federal government's decision to pull its support for social housing. For B.C., that meant the loss of a program that had built 1,800 new units of social housing each year across the province, he said. Quebec and B.C. were the only two provinces that continued to construct some low-cost units on their own; but without federal dollars, B.C. could afford to build only about six hundred units a year, Burnham added. Demand escalated, with discharged psychiatric patients from other provinces now joining those from B.C. in looking for places to live. In 1995, the provincial NDP and Vancouver's ruling centre-right municipal Non-Partisan Association (NPA) party formed an unlikely alliance to create new units of social housing in the ailing Downtown Eastside. In some cases, the city provided the land and the province the capital costs; in other cases, the city required developers to include some low-rent units in new downtown projects.

The number of SRO rooms in Vancouver's downtown core fell steadily from the 1970s to the 1990s, from a high of 13,412 in 1970 to 7,044 in 1998. The decline was slightly offset by the province and the city building low-cost housing for single people; the number of those units actually increased, from 256 in 1970 to 3,996 in 1998. Nonetheless, the result was a net loss of about 60 units a year for low-income single people in downtown Vancouver. Over the same period of time, low-income rooming houses in other parts of the city (Kitsilano, Fairview, and the West End) had been closing, replaced by middle-class condominiums. According to a report by Vancouver senior housing planner Jill Davidson published in 2007, the most significant reasons for the persistent decline in SROs during the 1990s included conversion to budget hotels, buildings being destroyed by fire, the city enforcing health and safety bylaws, and a switch to government-owned, subsidized units. SRO vacancy rates went from twenty-one per cent in 1973 to about thirteen per cent in 1998.

There was another complicating factor: although all the new non-market housing built by the government was affordable for welfare recipients, many existing SROs were increasing their rents to above the $325 provincial shelter allowance—putting their rooms out of reach for the most needy. The number of units in downtown Vancouver renting at or below the welfare allowance dropped from 9,100 in 1992 to 7,800 in 1998. During that time frame, real estate values in Metro Vancouver steadily climbed, and rental increases across the city made things difficult for the working poor as well.

The situation was a disaster in the Downtown Eastside, to which many mentally ill people were drawn because of cheap rent, soup kitchens, and community tolerance of their disabilities. Unfortunately, the neighbourhood also offered access to increasingly cheaper and more potent drugs. Many people went from struggling with a mental illness to becoming drug addicted, very sick, and often homeless. "When we deinstitutionalized, we promised these people that we would put them into the community and give them the support they needed. But we lied," Larry Campbell says today. "I think it's one of the worst things we ever did. We said we'd put them in the community with care and help. Instead, we gave them medication and a bus ticket, and they came to Vancouver. Then they started self-medicating with alcohol and, later, illegal drugs."

Mark Smith agrees with Campbell. "None of this shit needed to happen to these people. People need a home, a friend, and something to do. And we failed them on all three counts," he says. Smith has worked with the mentally ill for thirty years. When he was hired by the Kettle in 1978, he says, he felt connected to clients like Brian Shaw who were mostly "outside the norm." As a child, Smith himself had often felt like an outsider, because his father's academic career required the family to move frequently from city to city in western Canada and the U.S. In the beginning, Smith found his mentally ill clients were mostly abusing alcohol and pot. Cocaine was far too expensive at the time, unlike today's crack. Very few of the people he worked with were homeless. But that had changed by late 1991, when Smith was recruited by the Downtown Eastside's Triage Emergency Services & Care Society to take over a twenty-four-hour-a-day shelter that gave "society's cast-offs" a bed for the night and a short reprieve from the drug-fuelled streets. "No other organization would deal with them, often including emergency rooms. So we really were the safety net. If they weren't landing here, they weren't landing anywhere," Smith says.

The Triage Shelter was located in the former Bank of Montreal building at Main and Prior. There were nineteen cots for men in the main area, where bank customers had once lined up for their financial transactions, and a handful of cots for women on the other side of the counter, where the tellers would have stood. A small former waiting area had two cots for transgendered people. The vault was home not to gold bars and bags of cash but to valuables of a different sort: used clothing donations, and the limited personal possessions of the shelter's clients. Smith worked in the bank manager's office. But "the real work," he says, took place in the basement, where the staff, toiling alongside rats and cockroaches, juggled intake forms and medication requirements for the clients. "There was a lot of acceptance there," Smith says. "In its own time and place, it was bloody progressive, the work we were doing." The building's windows were always closed, because homeless men in the alley routinely peed against them. Despite a job that took him to some gruesome death scenes, Larry Campbell can remember being spooked the first time he visited Triage's administrative offices in the decrepit former bank building. "It was scary. I was freaked out. There were things that bumped in the night down there," recalls Campbell, who would later become a member of Triage's board of directors.

The Triage building was eventually condemned by public health officials, but when Triage tried to move the shelter, there was a huge uproar from other local residents and business owners about the agency bringing "those people" into their backyards. It did finally relocate on July 1, 1993, to 707 Powell Street, with room for twenty-eight shelter beds. That year, Triage also opened Windchimes Apartments at Heatley and Powell to provide permanent, long-term housing for chronically homeless men and women. The agency offered services to help homeless people manage their welfare money and their medications and started a meal program at the shelter.

Larry Campbell says it was the small success stories at Triage that affected him most. One young woman who left the streets when she got a place to stay through Triage went on to get her Grade 12 equivalent and go to Simon Fraser University. "I was moved to tears, and I thought, this is what can take place if you put the services in place," Campbell recalls today. "The staff at Triage gave unconditional love: 'We are here to help you.' You would go in there, and they would know everyone. I took clothing down there once, and this sort of scruffy guy said, 'Can I try these on?' He left Mark's office with the clothes. He matched jacket and shirt and tie and shaved in the washroom. He came out and said, 'I'm going to get a job.' I asked Mark later if he could, and Mark said, 'No, but for a while he is going to think he can.' You can't pay to get that kind of feeling, because it's personal."

Despite the amazing work they did, however, Triage and shelters such as the Lookout (forty-two beds) and Dunsmuir House for Men (thirty beds) could not handle the flood of people arriving in the Downtown Eastside. The trend was unmistakable:

between 1991 and 1993, Triage was forced to send people to other shelters maybe fifty to sixty times a month because it was full; that number would grow to four to six hundred times a month in the coming years, and often the other shelters would be full, too. By 1995, people reported sleeping instead in parks, at the beach, under viaducts, in alleyways and doorways, and in abandoned buildings and cars. By 1996, doctors complained that psychiatric patients with nowhere else to go were overloading the emergency departments of Vancouver's two largest hospitals. After the Riverview Hospital board told the government in February of that year that "the inability of the over-all mental health system to provide essential support to clients has reached a crisis point," NDP health minister Joy MacPhail ordered a temporary halt to bed closures at Riverview until adequate community care facilities could be put in place. A year later, the government announced $125 million for better housing and assistance for the mentally ill. "Our review showed that we weren't doing things wrong so much as we weren't doing enough of what's right," said MacPhail at the time. "The goal of this [new] plan is for every person disabled by a serious mental illness to be connected with the mental health care system." The B.C. branch of the Canadian Mental Health Association supported the plan, saying there was a waiting list of about 3,600 people who needed safe, decent housing. One former Riverview patient and long-time foe of the government's mental health plan, however, was not convinced anything would change; Roderick Louis told the *Vancouver Sun* that the province's rush to downsize the hospital had created a "disgusting ghettoization" of the severely mentally ill in areas such as Vancouver's Downtown Eastside.

That there were more mentally ill people in need of help in the community was unquestionable, but not all experts believed the downsizing of Riverview played the most significant role. The blame has more to do with the lack of housing, argues Darrell Burnham of Coast Mental Health. Burnham says deinstitutionalization was begun for good reasons and administrated well through the 1970s and the 1980s. Support services were offered to former Riverview patients as they were gradually released in the early 1990s, too, he says, but not all accepted them. "Riverview had two doors," Burnham explains about the release strategy. The front door was a planned exit, involving social workers helping the ex-patients adjust to the community. The euphemistic back door was for patients who demanded to be released and didn't want help. "Many of them went to the SROs. Those hotels ended up being a short-term hostel for Riverview's back door," Burnham says.

Nonetheless, with little support and nothing to do, Vancouver's homeless people were sitting targets for "friendly" dealers when the supply of cocaine rose and the drug's price fell. The result was catastrophic: cocaine was an "up" that made behaviour even more extreme, and because it had to be injected more than a dozen times a day to maintain a high, desperate users resorted to crimes and prostitution to fund their habits. Things became even worse in 1995 when crack hit the streets. "Crack was a seismic shift in addiction and behaviour, and it had a major impact on people's ability to care for themselves or give a shit about themselves," Mark Smith says. He witnessed some mentally ill people addicted to crack become isolated from their friends, with dealers taking over their welfare-supported rooms as payment for drug debts.

By 1998, B.C.'s medical health officer Dr. John Millar was strongly recommending improved coordination between mental health and addiction services in B.C. "Many services in the past have been based on an abstinence model. While this is changing, there are still many barriers to effective care because of a carryover of the old approach. For example, injection drug users who are being treated with methadone or being maintained on other drugs may be denied housing or access to mental health services because they are not drug-free," he wrote.

The 1998 report by Vancouver's general manager of community services Nathan Edelson called for both more housing and more addiction services in the Downtown Eastside. By his count, the neighbourhood had, at the time, fewer than six thousand rooms in 145 SROS and rooming houses; about ten per cent of those were either unsafe or "virtually unlivable," while others were "under threat" to be converted into tourist accommodations or condominiums. "These problems have been compounded by the withdrawal of senior levels of government from their traditional roles in providing an array of treatment services for the mentally ill and those with addictions, as well as subsidized housing for low-income people," Edelson wrote. "To be successful, all of this work should build on the community's many strengths, especially the caring and sense of community which most of its residents have."

A 1999 Vancouver/Richmond Health Board report found outbreaks of serious diseases among SRO residents with compromised immune systems, individuals who had limited access to toilets or sinks because up to ninety residents were sharing one washroom. But the report did acknowledge several good examples of social housing that offered support services for residents: the sixty-seven-unit Jim Green Residence, opened in 1996, and the seventy-unit Portland Hotel, opened in 1991. The latter had originally been the rundown Rainbow Hotel, but DERA, with financial help from the province, had leased the rooms from the building's owner, who still ran the first-floor beer parlour. DERA had fixed up the four residential floors and named the initiative after Portland, Oregon, a city DERA president Jim Green admired for its innovative approaches to housing the homeless. The Portland Hotel would become the first SRO to be operated by a non-profit agency, and before Green left DERA, he'd needed to hire someone to run it.

He found the answer in a determined twenty-six-year-old registered nurse, Liz Evans. Evans had become disillusioned while working on the Vancouver General Hospital psychiatric ward—she thought the system was trapping patients in a cycle of poverty and homelessness, and she wanted to offer them alternatives. Evans was offered twelve thousand dollars a year to help the most challenging of the Portland's seventy residents, most of whom had both mental health and addiction issues. Her part-time job description also involved unclogging the four toilets, cleaning up vomit, and doing any other menial labour required to keep the place resembling a home. "There were tidal waves of every conceivable problem," Evans recalls today, flashing an improbable smile. She remembers one of her earliest tenants, Tom, cradling a dead pigeon in the lobby of the hotel and then later jumping naked out of his window because he thought boxer Mike Tyson was in his room. Tom broke his arm but survived.

Evans had not had the life experience to prepare her for the challenges faced by the hotel's residents. "How could I, a twenty-six-year-old middle-class girl, relate to a thirty-eight-year-old Native woman who had been raped and had a drug addiction?" she remembers thinking. But once she discovered that her initial goal of curing or "fixing" people was unrealistic, her philosophy evolved into one of giving them space and dignity, because this population had been given very little respect so far: people were sick or dying, blamed and brutalized, with limited access to housing or medical care. Evans's first few years at the Portland coincided with the height of the overdose epidemic in the Downtown Eastside, and although no one ever died from an overdose inside the hotel, she regularly gave mouth-to-mouth resuscitation or administered Narcan to shock tenants out of overdosing. The Portland, which also received funding from the Vancouver/Richmond Health Board, brought in counsellors, nurses, a doctor, and mental health workers to assist the tenants. Evans tried to create a culture in which the tenants would feel safe to tell her when someone had overdosed, so that people would stop abandoning bodies in hallways. It was a difficult time. Evans recalls vomiting on the way to work some mornings, wondering who from the Downtown Eastside would die that day.

The Portland Hotel was among the first sros to allow tenants to use drugs in their rooms; the alternative was to sentence entrenched addicts to the alleyways. And those running the Portland also believed no one should be evicted. If a fight broke out, Evans might have a tenant arrested for assault but would keep his room for him so that he had a place to return to. "We believed everyone deserves housing. The very act of housing this population and not evicting them was shocking at that time," she recalls now. The Portland's cutting-edge policies brought some stability to tenants' lives, but Evans learned to measure success in baby steps. "Safe housing didn't mean they weren't addicts anymore or would go to college. But it might mean they would take their TB meds from me because I had changed their sheets or cleaned up after them when they shit themselves at the bottom of the stairs," she says.

Larry Campbell can remember being called to the scene of a natural death at the Portland one Halloween night during the hotel's first few years in operation. He was amazed by the "decrepit" place and the unusual tenants, joking today that he couldn't tell who was dressed up in costumes and who was in regular clothes. Evans, he said, was cooking a big vat of hot dogs, an island in the storm of chaos. When the body pick-up guys arrived that night, they were "bewildered" by the place, Campbell recalls with a laugh. Campbell stopped to have a hot dog, and he became a huge supporter of this woman who he says is "committed day in and day out" to helping people often overlooked by society.

The staff also tried to have fun with their tenants at the Portland, recognizing the people there craved happy pastimes like anyone else: camping, cribbage tournaments, talent shows, poetry lessons, communal cooking, outings in the neighbourhood. The residents were given disposable cameras to document what they saw in their community. For the most part, they did not take the stereotypical photos of homeless people sleeping on benches or drunks passed out in alleys but captured instead smiling images of friends and family in the Downtown Eastside.

The Portland was so successful that Liz Evans and Mark Townsend, partners in life as well as work, created the non-profit Portland Hotel Society (PHS), a multi-employee, multi-service agency. In 1995, Townsend phoned renowned Vancouver architect Arthur Erickson and described to him how difficult it was for the seventy Portland residents to share four toilets and four showers in an old building with tiny rooms and insufficient electrical outlets. Erickson, accustomed to creating much more upscale projects, accepted the challenge to design a brand new Portland. The modern $7-million building, financed by the province and the city, opened in June 2000, just down the street from the original hotel. The eighty-six rooms in the new Portland were tiny at only three hundred square feet, but each had a private bathroom and a kitchen-like space with a bar fridge and sink, all inside a modern building with extravagances like pipes that didn't leak and a sufficient number of electrical outlets. The second floor of the new Portland Hotel became a buzz of activity, where residents could have their hair done in the beauty parlour, get massages, and participate in celebrations in the large activity room or attend barbecues on the outdoor deck. In the examination rooms, tenants lined up to see the full-time nurse or veteran family doctor Dr. Gabor Maté.

From the beginning, the PHS made the decision not to force people out once they were stabilized. "If we take them and later say they have to move on, then it defeats the purpose of giving them something they've never had—a fixed address," Liz Evans says. Portland Hotel Society workers have been criticized as enabling drug users by doing too much for them, but Evans argues staff are teaching the residents to ultimately fend for themselves, not trying to "fix" people, an unrealistic goal that just burns out workers. Evans has had some unpleasant encounters with tenants, but the good has outweighed the bad. "I've been around seventeen years, and I've never felt so loved by a community," she says. When Evans and Townsend had a son in 2000, residents celebrated the occasion, giving her greeting cards, a Tonka trunk they had found in a dumpster, and their penny collections.

Whenever its government-funded budget allowed, PHS tried to give tenants something to be excited about. A handful of residents went on cruises, stayed in fancy hotels, or were flown to a dream destination. It never went completely smoothly, says Mark Townsend with a laugh. An angry hotel manager phoned once about the water damage to his building when a Portland tenant had "an episode" in the bathroom. Downtown Eastside residents didn't have the typical cruise ship wardrobe. And often the tenants had to be walked to the check-in counter at the airport and booked onto the flight, so that they didn't sell the tickets for drug money. In 1998, the *Vancouver Sun* named Evans and Townsend two of B.C.'s most influential people.

Throughout 1996 and 1997, all 280-plus beds in Vancouver's seven shelters were constantly full. Drop-in centres that allowed people to stay overnight, like the Salvation Army's Crosswalk, were also turning people away because of the unprecedented demand. In response, a group of charities worked with city hall and the province to open extra beds during the winter. "It's not

an elegant situation," Judy Graves, by then a senior city hall housing worker, told a reporter in 1998. "It's sleep-on-the-floor. But
it's a heated building, with the security of people who know how
to deal with such a situation." Graves estimated at the time that
about six hundred people lived on Vancouver's streets, many
of them not from Vancouver itself. Despite the wider problem,
few outlying suburbs opened more shelters or built more social
housing.

That same year, the province announced a new six-year mental health plan to increase from 300 to 1,300 the number of
mentally ill people living in existing social housing, and to boost
rent subsidies for those living in private-market rental housing.

In 1991, exhausted from her shift work at Cordova House
and raising two children, Judy Graves had begun working for
city hall, helping seniors, disabled people, and single parents find
housing. It wasn't until 1995, she says, that homelessness became
an emergency. By then, it was common to see multiple people
huddled in doorways under sullied sleeping bags or shopping
carts packed with personal possessions parked beside cardboard
lean-tos. Graves predicted publicly that the city's problems could
explode in the 2000s. She started to walk the alleys between
2 AM and 6 AM, asking the people sleeping there what had led to
them to being homeless. "People were telling me about service
cutbacks, that it was harder to stay on welfare, that there were
changes in employment insurance, that it was really hard to find
a room in a rooming house because almost all of them had been
torn down," Graves says. Among them were former psychiatric
patients who had drifted to cheap Downtown Eastside hotels
because there were few other options. Outside their new front
doors, the local drug dealer seemed like the nicest person, hawk-
ing something that would chase away all their anxieties. "You've
got a psychiatrist with an unpleasant drug or a dealer treating
you like a valued customer, offering a drug that makes you feel so

good. Which one would you choose?" Graves asks. "People want to say that homelessness is caused by mental illness and addiction, but what has changed is there's no housing available."

As many of the people Graves met knew well, it had become more difficult since the early 1990s to qualify for unemployment insurance; the federal government had changed the program's name in 1996 to "employment insurance," in fact. There had been cutbacks in provincial welfare services, too, and those lacking skills to navigate the system—people without family or friends to help, or who couldn't read, or who had mental or social challenges—couldn't get the help they needed. The waiting period to get government assistance was now longer, so people who'd lost their jobs went on to lose their housing as well; they had no money to keep up rent or mortgage payments. Graves also met people sleeping under awnings who had jobs but couldn't find an affordable place to live. Some were older women who had experienced major upheaval (divorce or the death of a relative) and couldn't get back on track. It was Graves's goal to find places for all of these people to live. "Any time a person can put a lock between themselves and the rest of the world, it improves their mental health," she says.

Larry Campbell echoes Graves's words. "My argument is you can't start healing without a house and a lock, but you also need support," he says today. "If they had deinstitutionalized people and the promise of in-community care had been kept, that would have been okay. But the government wasn't ready for it; they didn't plan effectively for it. They opened the gates without these people having anywhere to go or enough resources in place." On the streets, the mentally ill are the first targets for dealers, pimps, and other bullies, Campbell says. "They are at the bottom of the food chain, and everyone picks on them." Society should not have let that recipe brew in the Downtown Eastside. "It doesn't matter why you're there—you're there. As human beings we should do something about it, and we didn't." Campbell does praise the B.C. NDP for continuing to build some social housing after the feds pulled out in 1993, but what the province could do on its own just wasn't sufficient to meet demand.

In 2001, a report from Vancouver's city hall noted a lack of progress on Victoria's part towards the promised additional spaces and rent subsidies for people with mental illness. The document said that the B.C. Mental Health Monitoring Coalition had also severely criticized the overall lack of funding and support for the mentally ill. "The move towards deinstitutionalization of the mentally ill without adequate housing, medical and support structures has left many homeless and hopeless. Mental health services are desperately inadequate," the city hall report said. Other reports were equally critical. A 2002 Vancouver/Richmond Health Board report found there were currently only about eight hundred institutional beds across B.C. for the mentally ill, a shocking decrease from the five thousand beds of the early 1990s. "Many" of those people, the document said, had become residents of the Downtown Eastside, for lack of any other place to go.

Drastic as they were already, the mental health and homelessness issues in the Downtown Eastside would soon be compounded by an emerging health crisis. The shocking fatal disease that became universally known as AIDS would spread through this vulnerable population with frightening speed.

7 | Vancouver's HIV/AIDS Epidemic:
The Worst in the Western World

"MORE HELP IN OUR OWN area!" demanded Bill's wind-whipped banner as he marched with about sixty other Downtown Eastside residents on Sunday, December 1, 1996, World AIDS Day. Bill, aged thirty-seven, was among the at least 750 Downtown Eastside drug users who were HIV-positive at that time. He had become infected in 1991, after sharing needles while injecting cocaine, and was protesting for more provincial money for inner-city counselling, housing, and health care. "I know some people who aren't getting any health services at all and don't want anybody to know they're positive... they're getting ill and dying without any help at all," Bill told reporter Lori Culbert as the march progressed from Oppenheimer Park to the provincial health minister's constituency office on Hastings Street. "The worst thing down here, in my mind, is the housing. Having to share a washroom with thirty other people, living in an eight-by-ten hole. And there's a lot of people down here who can't even read, so they can't access the few services that are available."

Bill and others at the rally were outraged that most of the AIDS services in Vancouver were located in the middle-class West End, while a growing number of drug users and sex-trade workers in the Downtown Eastside were contracting the deadly virus. That was true, agreed Lorne Mayencourt, who was executive director of Friends for Life, a support, counselling, and resource organization for people with life-threatening illnesses. The vast majority of clients at the Diamond Centre for Living, a wellness centre he had founded in the West End, for example, were HIV-positive gay white men from the same neighbourhood. Mayencourt, who would go on to become a Liberal MLA, told the *Vancouver Sun* a similar facility was desperately needed for Hastings Street, one targeted particularly towards the residents there. Roland, a forty-year-old Downtown Eastside resident with full-blown AIDS who was marching in the rally, argued his life expectancy was far lower than those in more affluent neighbourhoods. "People in our community are getting ignored," Roland said. "I would say in the next few years we'll have people starting to drop dead right on our streets."

In fact, people had been dying from AIDS for years. As Vancouver coroner in the early 1980s, Larry Campbell had investigated deaths caused by an illness that seemed mysterious. Most of the victims were white gay men. Their skin was red and blotchy, their once-healthy physiques now frail and gaunt. Some funeral parlours refused to take the bodies, worried that the strange illness could be contagious. "Nobody knew, if you touched the body, what was likely to happen," Campbell recalls today. "It was just something that came out of nowhere, and all of a sudden it was here. This was the first time I came into contact with prejudices involving disease and certain segments of our society. But it was not the last time. The gay community didn't know what was going on. You start marginalized, and now you are even more marginalized—there was an us-and-them mentality. It was a frightening time." Once the fast-moving and painful disease was given a name—AIDS—and some explanation of how it was transmitted, the gay community began practising safe sex and generally protecting themselves. But by the 1990s, the disease was spreading at an alarming pace among a new demographic: drug users and sex-trade workers.

In 1994, the B.C. Centre for Disease Control reported a growing outbreak of HIV infection among injection drug users. It was the first year that group surpassed gay men for recording the most new infections. Among drug users alone, 338 new infections were recorded in B.C. in 1995, 387 in 1996, and 253 in 1997. (Among gay men, who had registered more than 700 new infections in B.C. in 1987, the infection rate was below 200 for each of the years 1994 to 1997.) Several hundred people suffered AIDS-related deaths in B.C. in the mid-1990s. The death rates steadily declined in the latter part of the 1990s, mostly because gay men were taking precautions, but the HIV-infection rate was certainly not falling among drug users in the Downtown Eastside.

Lou Demerais saw the faces behind those statistics every day at the Vancouver Native Health Clinic on East Hastings. Recalls Demerais, "We had a sense that things were about to explode when the AIDS pandemic got a foothold in this community down here. We had an RN and a licensed practical nurse on our HIV/AIDS team. We thought they might get one hundred patients, but it wasn't long before they were looking after the needs of six hundred people. Most of them couldn't go to doctors uptown; they'd be turned away." There was a sense that physicians in other parts of the city were hesitant to accept very sick patients with complex issues from the Downtown Eastside. And a small minority of doctors in Vancouver and other North American cities were refusing treatment to all drug users; they feared improper use of the antiretroviral drug cocktail treatment could lead to a multi-drug-resistant strain of HIV that could be passed to others.

Demerais says Downtown Eastside residents who injected cocaine had such frenzied lives that they knew very little about HIV or how it was spread. Most did not realize they were infected until they got very, very sick. Often they would have full-blown AIDS by the time they came to the Native Health Clinic for help. Most of them were Hepatitis C–positive as well. "An average Aboriginal person with HIV would die within a year and a half of diagnosis. We just had to sit back and watch these people waste away," Demerais says, noting that richer people, usually healthier to begin with, had much longer life expectancies. "It was a feeling of utter hopelessness. We used to sit around and console ourselves. Many of us thought we could empathize with people from African countries, because there wasn't a damn thing we could do about it. There was a time when the bulk of [the AIDS] staff were spending their time planning and going to funerals."

It was also a challenging time for nurses, police officers, and outreach workers, who needed to learn how to keep themselves safe from the fatal virus. Larry Campbell, like many others, scared himself by accidentally pricking his finger with a dirty syringe, after being called to examine a dead body lying beside the hydro station on Main Street. He hadn't been expecting any needles on the man, who looked healthy, had no track marks, and was in clean clothes. "I don't know what I was thinking, but I put my hand into his fanny pack, and it was just full of needles. And I stuck myself. I normally wouldn't do that; usually I'd cut the pockets open, usually do pat-downs. I wanted to beat on the dead body. That was my gut instinct. And afterwards I was so ashamed of myself." Campbell, in the end, was not infected. It turned out the victim, an electrician who was also an amateur photographer, had been using for only about a year, after meeting a new girlfriend who was hooked on drugs. The man had lost everything—his business, his truck, all his money—to support their habits, and then died alone of a drug overdose. "His parents were in complete shock. His whole life had just fallen apart," Campbell remembers.

Campbell also recalls a different type of death related to the virus in the early 1990s: suicides. The suicide manual *Final Exit* was found in the bedroom of a Matsqui man with AIDS who killed himself in October 1991, and the book was used by three other B.C. residents who killed themselves that month. When another B.C. coroner suggested publicly that the manual be banned, Campbell responded with outrage. He didn't believe in censorship, he says, and for a determined person the book offered some painless ways to end a life. "I believe you have the right to die, but you have to have the ability to understand the decision you are making," Campbell says. The AIDS-related suicides were not cases of vulnerable children or the mildly sick but of people with a painful, debilitating fatal illness. "You had a terminal illness that was going to get really, really awful. I think there were lots of incidences of people helping people to die during that period of time," he says.

Campbell can remember going to see David Lewis, then director of the Vancouver Persons with AIDS Society, after Lewis admitted in July 1991 to helping eight AIDS victims commit suicide. The resulting controversy generated an emotional public debate and requests for the coroners service to hold an inquest. With reporters camped outside the society's office, Campbell sat having a cup of coffee with Lewis. "I said, 'I know you've done this, but there is no need for an inquest because you sure don't need this hassle,'" Campbell recalls. At the press conference they called following their meeting, Campbell said Lewis would not supply him with the names of the eight people he had allegedly assisted. Without names or dates or places of death—or bodies, which Lewis said had been cremated—Campbell told the press, there was nothing the coroners service could do. Police did not pursue charges for the same reasons.

In May 1996, Dr. Elizabeth Whynot, a Vancouver medical health officer who would later become president of B.C. Women's Hospital, wrote a report that called for better coordination of health care funding for injection drug users, to reduce new infections of HIV/AIDS. Whynot argued for more non-discriminatory social housing, more needle exchanges and outreach nurses, and improved mental health and counselling resources. She recommended the creation of safe injection sites as well, along with expanded services for drug users in the Downtown Eastside who already had HIV. There were only seven family physicians in the area, her report stated. Just one clinic, Vancouver Native Health, was open evening and weekend hours. There were no short-stay places for homeless people infected with HIV, and the only long-term care facility in B.C. for AIDS patients couldn't cope with drug users, Whynot wrote. She noted the city had just two alcohol and drug detox centres, only one of them located in the Downtown Eastside; the community had no outpatient detox clinics or rehabilitation centres, though there were outreach workers employed through various agencies. "Accessibility and relevance of programming for intravenous drug users are *huge* issues... The current set of alcohol and drug services is largely inadequate to the needs of injection users. There is no comprehensive plan regarding development of resources in the area of highest injection drug use concentration, i.e., the Downtown Eastside."

Whynot's report noted that only one doctor in the Downtown Eastside was licensed to prescribe methadone, the synthetic heroin replacement. There should have been more, but Whynot also argued methadone was not a silver bullet: it didn't mitigate cocaine symptoms and wasn't effective for all heroin

addicts. She recommended instead something far more controversial: doctors prescribing heroin to their patients. "Increasing
evidence from other countries [shows] that such prescriptions
can be managed safely and have great potential to reduce many
of the consequences of the illicit drug trade," her report said. The
HIV/AIDS prevalence rate among injection drug users in Vancouver was then estimated at a staggering twenty-five per cent,
massively higher than in cities like Liverpool where physicians
were permitted to prescribe heroin, she wrote.

At the time Dr. Whynot's report was released, she estimated
there were as many as fifteen thousand injection drug users in
B.C., roughly a third of them in the Downtown Eastside. Of the
thousand or so Downtown Eastside drug users known to be HIV-
positive, sixty-five per cent were men, a disproportionately high
number were Aboriginal, and there were increases in the numbers of both pregnant women and mentally ill people becoming
infected. Needle sharing was thought to be the main reason HIV
was spreading among drug users, Whynot wrote, and there
were systemic reasons for the risky practice: the frequent injections required to maintain a cocaine high, unstable housing and
homelessness, a history among many users of sexual abuse, and
depression and despair. About six thousand people were registered to use the Downtown Eastside Youth Activities Society
needle exchange, which had swapped 1.8 million clean rigs for
dirty ones in 1995. The irony was that having North America's
largest needle exchange didn't appear to be slowing down the
HIV infection rates. The bottom line, Whynot wrote, was that
there was an overall increase of HIV-positive drug users: the
number of clients at the downtown health clinic had doubled
in just eighteen months, and she predicted that would continue
without more active prevention programs.

Whynot's report had both supporters and detractors. The
National Task Force on HIV/AIDS, funded by Health Canada, had

also suggested the spread of HIV could be reduced by allowing doctors to prescribe narcotics to drug users and by decriminalizing possession of small amounts for personal use. Those measures were supported by some members of the Vancouver Police Department (VPD), including deputy chief Ken Higgins, who had spent much of his thirty-year career in the Downtown Eastside, and Constable Gil Puder, who voiced his opinions at a Vancouver drug conference in 1998 even after his chief had forbidden him to do so. However, some equally high-profile police officers and doctors in Vancouver thought those ideas were absurd and instead lobbied for more funding for abstinence-based solutions like detox and therapy.

Vancouver was also at the heart of international medical breakthroughs related to HIV/AIDS. Dr. Julio Montaner had moved to the city in 1981 from his native Argentina to work in pulmonary research. Shortly after his arrival, Montaner started to encounter patients, mainly gay men, with dire pneumonia caused by a mystifying disease. After treating some of these patients with only limited success, Montaner became involved in drug trials. In 1994—basing the work on his father's own experience with research into tuberculosis—he started providing a combination of three drugs, instead of a single one, to infected people. One year into Montaner's study, the virus was no longer detectable in about half of the participants. American researchers had near-identical results in a similar study, and within a few years an antiretroviral drug cocktail was responsible for a ninety per cent reduction in AIDS deaths in the developed world.

It should have been a time for celebration, but it wasn't for Montaner and his colleagues in Vancouver, who in 1992 had opened the Centre for Excellence in HIV/AIDS. They had noticed the centre's clientele changing from mainly gay men to injection drug users; while the former responded well to the new drug cocktail, there was much less hope for the latter, because of their chaotic lives. Many infected people in the Downtown Eastside were battling the demons of poverty, sexual abuse, and despair. "The treatment was getting better, and we were having dramatic improvements in the outcome of HIV-related markets in the well-adjusted gay population, but we were having absolutely minimal or no impact in other sectors of the epidemic," Montaner recalls.

When the Centre for Excellence's Dr. Steffanie Strathdee began the VIDUS (Vancouver Injection Drug Users Study) of 1,006 users in 1997, she found twenty-three per cent were HIV-positive and eighty-eight per cent had Hepatitis C. As a group, these users were more likely to share dirty needles, be involved in commercial sex work, not eat properly or live in sufficient housing, be undereducated and poor, and have such low self-esteem that they didn't want to get tested to see if they were HIV-positive. It was "alarming," Strathdee wrote, that the HIV prevalence rate was so high when a vast majority of the study participants reported frequently using the DEYAS needle exchange. The explanation, her report said, may have been that one needle exchange was not enough to keep the infection rate down; adequate addictions treatment, detoxification, and counselling were also needed. Critics of the needle exchange argued instead that the program encouraged drug use by handing out free rigs and so facilitated higher infection rates.

In the spring of 1997, the B.C. Ministry of Health pledged $3 million to combat the spread of HIV/AIDS in the Downtown Eastside. Dr. Penny Parry, commissioned by the province to determine how best to use the money, was asked to get input from the community in preparing her conclusions. Parry's powerful report, *Something to Eat, a Place to Sleep, and Someone Who Gives a Damn*, declared there was an HIV/AIDS epidemic in the Downtown Eastside, especially among drug users. Parry said the problem in Vancouver distinguished itself from that in other cities because of the intense concentration of people who were either homeless or living in SROs, the drug of choice shifting from heroin to cocaine, and the lack of integration of services to those most at risk. There was no way to curb the epidemic, she wrote, without addressing its victims' day-to-day experiences. "Such basics as safe, stable housing, good physical and mental health, a sense of self worth because you have meaningful things to do with your time, friends, personal safety, and respect from those around you, are absent for most of the people at risk," Parry wrote. "As one individual put it: it is hard to think about HIV/AIDS when you're wondering where you're going to sleep tonight and where you'll get your next meal." Parry also pointed out that drug addiction was seen in Canada as a criminal matter, not a health issue, which further marginalized vulnerable people and made assisting them more difficult.

The problem of HIV/AIDS was also becoming significant among drug users in Vancouver suburbs, places like Surrey and New Westminster, Parry wrote. She suggested new services for drug users be located outside the Downtown Eastside, so that people could leave the congested area if they wanted. She also called for the creation of outreach resources in the 100- and 200-blocks of West Hastings, where many users spent their days. Parry raised concerns, however, that even those who tried to take the complicated AIDS drugs would struggle. Many, for example, had no access to cooking facilities and a limited income for food, when the pills were supposed to be taken with meals. "Not having a fridge or even a hot plate adds greatly to the already complex regimes that these medications require," she wrote.

Parry's report, released one year after Whynot's, estimated there were 1,500 HIV-positive people living in or near the Downtown Eastside. In 1996 alone, 713 people in B.C. had tested positive, more than half of them injection drug users. Seventeen per cent were Aboriginal, though Aboriginal people comprised only four per cent of B.C.'s population. Parry found that there were few culturally sensitive detox programs to help Aboriginal people get off drugs and that some people unknowingly took the virus back to their reserves after they'd been infected. Other high-risk groups for HIV/AIDS included women (eighty per cent of female drug users were active in the sex trade); those with mental illness, who were twice as likely to share needles; and youth, a growing population in the Downtown Eastside. Parry's recommendations called for the province's $3 million to be spent on alcohol and drug treatment and other outreach services, a housing support program, transportation for people to and from services outside the Downtown Eastside, improved access for drug users to community centres and other public facilities, and more public education programs about HIV/AIDS.

In 1997, some of the $3 million earmarked by the province was used to start the Native Health Society's Positive Outlook Program to provide Downtown Eastside residents with a drop-in centre staffed with doctors, nurses, and counsellors. Nurse Doreen Littlejohn left the Greater Vancouver Mental Health Services Society to start running the program. The ground-floor facility, located beside the Vancouver Native Health medical clinic on East Hastings, was created to be culturally sensitive, and it did not dictate what the clients might need; instead, the staff first built relationships with people, then found out what they required. Unfortunately, many people had end-stage AIDS before even seeking help from the clinic, Littlejohn says. A study conducted in 1998 by the Centre for Excellence, St. Paul's Hospital, and the University of British Columbia found that only forty per cent of infected drug users were receiving antiretroviral drugs, despite the fact that the drugs were free in Canada. Four outreach workers, two intake workers, two drug and alcohol counsellors, Littlejohn, and a second nurse shared the workload at the clinic, which included cooking the soup for the meal program and cleaning the toilets. Staff encouraged those who could to sign up for the life-prolonging antiretroviral drugs. Recognizing that people who were unstable, homeless, or living in SROs couldn't keep their pills at home or take the proper doses, the new drop-in centre, operating on a shoestring budget, used egg cartons to organize the complex combination of drugs each client had to take. If the patients forgot to come in to get their meds, outreach workers would search for them throughout the Downtown East-side. "We'd outreach them three times a day to make sure they took their handfuls of pills," recalls Littlejohn. "We found them in parks, we found them in doorways. We put medication in their mouths and gave them food. And we were very successful at it." The centre got about one hundred of its patients onto anti-retroviral drugs. Two independent studies later found that a good percentage of Downtown Eastside residents took their treatment regularly and therefore saw their viral loads diminish. While that was a positive turnaround, the death rates in the neighbourhood were still high relative to other communities. Each year Positive Outlook lost about ten per cent of its clients, with an average of thirty to forty people dying annually of AIDS-related causes.

Some people also refused the treatment. Littlejohn had one client who was funny and outgoing, she says, and reminded her of comedian Robin Williams. The man, whose name was Robert, was HIV-positive, but he would not sign up for the cocktail. When Littlejohn asked him why, he offered a harrowing explanation. Robert had been snatched from his family at age five and sent to residential school, where he endured torturous punishments for wetting his bed at night. After he ran away from school at twelve, he ended up working with migrant farm labourers in B.C. fields. The workers introduced the young boy to alcohol, which Robert told Littlejohn was the best thing that had ever happened to him; the booze made him feel good for the first time he could remember, and it blocked out terrifying memories. The alcohol led to drug use, and before long Robert was Hepatitis C–positive and had HIV. He wasn't interested in taking the antiretrovirals, though, he told Littlejohn, because he didn't want to cut back on the illicit drugs he was using to block childhood memories. Robert developed end-stage AIDS and died in a hospice in his thirties.

Positive Outlook built up trust in a community that was hesitant to be trusting. Regulars at the clinic were given jobs—peeling potatoes or staffing the front desk for a small stipend—and started telling friends to come by. Soon, two hundred people a day were using a space that was designed to hold no more than fifty. The Native Health Centre offered other incentives for patients to come in, too, such as a food bank, a meal program, and free telephones. Still, despite all the hard work, infection rates and death rates remained far higher among Aboriginal people than any other group. "There was a sense of despair at the time," Lou Demerais recalls. "There was no guarantee that we might see a person who came into the small space on a Monday again the following Friday—because they were dead."

Activist Bud Osborn was so saddened and outraged by the loss of his friends in the Downtown Eastside that in 1997 his fledgling organization, the Political Response Group, staged eighty demonstrations to lobby for things like better detox centres and housing for addicts—whose "life expectancy was closer to Hades than the rest of Vancouver," as he put it. Osborn's group, working with the Portland Hotel Society, held its most high-profile demonstration in July of that year. About two hundred people marched from Main and Hastings carrying a large red banner that read "The Killing Fields—Federal Action Now." In Oppenheimer Park, they erected more than a thousand crosses to commemorate those who had died of drug overdoses and AIDS in B.C. over the past four years. The speakers at the event were powerful. Dr. Elizabeth Whynot said drug usage in the

Downtown Eastside was a disaster "we can't seem to do anything about" and predicted that deaths would almost certainly increase. The father of a young man who had died of an overdose demanded government regulation of heroin and cocaine so that users would know the potency of the drugs they were taking. A university professor, saying that most addicts' lives were unbearable without their fix, warned the death toll would continue unless doctors were permitted to prescribe the drugs and users were given a safe place to inject them.

Osborn wrote his poem "a thousand crosses in oppenheimer park" for the event, and he read it with passion that day. A young woman in a floppy white hat wiped tears from her eyes. An older man snoozed on a bench. A young girl ran squealing in the grass. A Native man sang a traditional song, beating his drum. Osborn could have been one of the haunted faces in the crowd; he had spent two decades hooked on drugs, sleeping in flophouses, and, occasionally, making suicide attempts. He had managed to get clean just a few years earlier, and that day he stood at the microphone and read for the crowd:

These thousand crosses are symbols
of the social apartheid in our culture
the segregation of those who deserve to live
and those who are abandoned to die
these thousand crosses silently announce
a social curse on the lives of the poorest of the poor
in the downtown eastside
these thousand crosses announce an assault
    on our community
these thousand crosses announce a deprivation of possibility
for those of us who mourn here
the mothers and fathers and sisters and brothers
the uncles and aunts and grandmothers and grandfathers

the sons and daughters
the friends and acquaintances
of those members of our community
of a thousand dreams
of a thousand hopes
of a thousand yearnings for real community
lost to us
but memorialized today
brought finally into a unity
here in this community park
this park which is the geographical heart
of the downtown eastside
these thousand crosses are a protest
against the abandonment of powerless and
    voiceless human beings

The demonstration garnered some publicity, and Libby Davies, today an NDP MP, believes it galvanized community members into action—even if government response was slower. "It was dramatic. Imagine walking into Oppenheimer Park and there are one thousand crosses," Davies says. "My constituents were dying, and nobody gave a shit about these people." A few Downtown Eastside activists didn't support the demonstration because they thought it portrayed the neighbourhood—also home to families, labourers, shop owners, and others—in an unfair light. But Mark Townsend of the Portland Hotel Society said the event was intended to show the community's problems would be solved not by throwing people in jail but by increasing health care funding. "There was no public sympathy whatsoever until people saw addiction as a medical issue," Townsend says today.

Bud Osborn also wanted the rest of Canada to know the

Downtown Eastside was ensnared in a "global health catastrophe." He looked up the definition of "public health emergency" at the Vancouver Public Library, then made a motion at the next Vancouver/Richmond Health Board meeting that the declaration be applied to the situation in the Downtown Eastside. Osborn had been appointed the Downtown Eastside's representative on the health board by the provincial government earlier that year. Although his high-profile advocacy work for the disadvantaged frustrated more traditional board members, they did approve Osborn's motion, and the Downtown Eastside was deemed to be a medical emergency in September 1997. The drastic step was taken because of both Osborn's actions and Dr. Penny Parry's damning report.

In October 1997, there was another startling announcement: the HIV/AIDS rates in the Downtown Eastside were declared the most rampant in the developed world by the B.C. Centre for Excellence in HIV/AIDS. "It was part of our frustration at the time, to try to bring attention to the fact that this was not a trivial thing that we were talking about. We were talking about rates of HIV in the Downtown Eastside comparable to the worst epidemics in the world," recalls Dr. Julio Montaner. "The rate of HIV was up to thirty per cent in some communities in the Downtown Eastside. The rate of Hepatitis C was up to ninety per cent. We got more vocal and put pressure on various levels of government to do something. We were not very successful, though—and still are not today."

Later that month, the health board added $1.65 million of its own money to the $3 million pledged by the province and directed staff to devise an action plan on how to enact many of Parry's recommendations. Following the meeting, Osborn told the press he was frustrated by the slow, bureaucratic response to the HIV/AIDS crisis and warned of dire consequences to come if action was not taken more quickly. "One month has passed and nothing has happened in this public health emergency, the first in Vancouver's history. And that's a disgrace." But while activists like Osborn criticized the health system for waiting so long to act, their work and that of others had finally pushed officials to start looking for some answers.

Crowds assemble outside the courthouse at Hastings and Cambie Streets for a visit by the Duke and Duchess of Cornwall and York in September 1901.

City of Vancouver Archives, SGN 382

A man poses in front of the Pierre Paris retail store, located underneath the Strathcona Hotel on Hastings Street, in the early 1900s.

Vancouver Public Library, Special Collections, VPL 84917

The Carnegie Public Library in 1904, one year after it opened, beside
Vancouver city hall (*shown at left*). Today the building operates as the
Carnegie Community Centre.   *Philip Timms photo, Vancouver Public Library,* VPL 3433

Jim Green (*left*), then an organizer with the Downtown Eastside Residents' Association, walks through the neighbourhood with community activist Don Larson in November 1981.

Deni Eagland/Vancouver Sun

Bruce Eriksen takes a break while restoring his mural at the
Four Corners Community Savings bank in November 1996.
He died of liver cancer four months later.

Bill Keay/Vancouver Sun

Bud Osborn leads demonstrators in April 1997 to protest
Fama Holdings' decision not to build social housing in the old
Woodward's store. *Mark van Manen/Vancouver Sun*

Executive director Lou Demerais, with nurses Kathy Churchill
(*left*) and Carol Kellman, stands outside the Vancouver Native
Health drop-in centre in October 1997. *Glenn Baglo/Vancouver Sun*

A drug user returns old needles and collects new rigs from
Ron Graham of the DEYAS Needle Exchange van in a back alley in
August 1997. *Jeff Vinnick/Vancouver Sun*

Karen Darbyson, whose troubling childhood led to a heroin habit,
poses in front of the Balmoral Hotel, where she lived in November
1997. *Mark van Manen/Vancouver Sun*

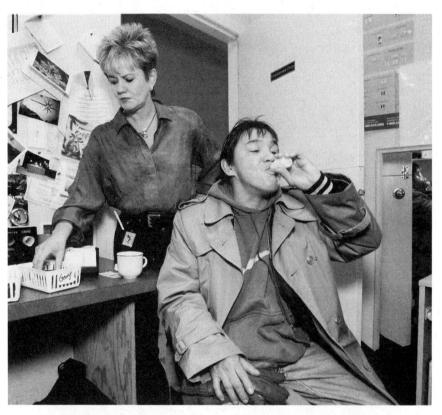

George Guiboche drinks an HIV cocktail with nurse Doreen Littlejohn
at Vancouver Native Health's Positive Outlook Clinic in February 1999.

Kim Stallknecht/Vancouver Sun

Women walk along Hastings Street in 2000 during the annual Valentine's Day march to remember women who died in or disappeared from the Downtown Eastside.

Ian Smith/Vancouver Sun

Liz Evans and Mark Townsend (*with his hand on her shoulder*) show
their nine-week-old baby, Kes, to tenants of the new Portland Hotel in
June 2000. *Mark van Manen/Vancouver Sun*

Vicki Fraser mourns among the two thousand crosses erected in Oppenheimer Park in July 2000 to commemorate those who had lost their lives to drug addiction. *Ward Perrin/Vancouver Sun*

8 | Harm Reduction:
A Grassroots Struggle

IT WAS BY THE GIANT CHESS board in Oppenheimer Park, where the large chess pieces had been replaced by dealers plying their dope and addicts sleeping it off, that Bud Osborn held the first public meeting of the group that would become VANDU (Vancouver Area Network of Drug Users) in the fall of 1997. He had put up handmade posters throughout the Downtown Eastside inviting people to come to the park to discuss the strife in their community. As the neighbourhood's representative on the Vancouver/Richmond Health Board, Osborn wanted to know how people thought they could make their neighbourhood healthier. He didn't know what to expect, and he was thrilled when about twenty people showed up.

"It was a remarkable meeting," Osborn recalls today. "Families came, and seniors were already there because they lived in the housing project across from the park. There were users and dealers, and a lot of rice wine drinkers who were in the worst shape of anyone. There was this whole conglomeration of people." Osborn's friend Ann Livingston used a flip chart to record the wish list of those at the discussion group: better housing, safer streets, a supervised injection site. The families and seniors wanted less drug dealing in the park. The eclectic group had one unified request: a place for addicts to go where they could have a cup of coffee, socialize, and receive medical treatment and counselling without their lifestyle being judged. (At the time, people were banned from most resources in the Downtown Eastside, like the Carnegie Centre, until they had sobered up.) Osborn took their comments, which also included changing government drug policies and ending discrimination against users, to the next health board meeting, marking one of the first times the voices of this marginalized group were heard by officials at a government table.

"We decided we were going to have another meeting, too," Osborn recalls, shaking his head with amazement. While a posse of addicts and non-users forming a lobby group was a novel idea, it was also a crucial one. Their message was that drug users were a part of society, and it was perilous for the rest of the province to ignore the issues ravaging the Downtown Eastside.

Bud Osborn's journey to becoming one of Vancouver's harm reduction leaders was a difficult one, from a horrendous childhood in the working-class city of Toledo, Ohio, to years of self-medicating his turmoil with heroin. Osborn's father, Walt, had returned from World War II with physical and psychological injuries. He found work as a newspaper reporter but struggled so badly with violence and alcoholism that he hanged himself in jail in March 1950. Bud was just three years old at the time. Walt Osborn's employer wrote a scolding editorial, saying the family's troubles were "the consequence of flaunting contempt for the moral laws on which our society ultimately rests." Osborn's mother suffered from her own mental health and alcohol problems. She met men in bars and often brought them home; one of them raped her while Bud, then a preschooler, cowered in the corner. His mother would marry four more times, and the young boy was bounced from house to house, from stepfather to stepfather. The only anchor in Bud's early childhood was his paternal grandmother who, just a few years after her son Walt's death, was fatally shot by her daughter, who then killed herself.

Bud Osborn played sports in high school and tinkered with university courses, but he always felt like he was running from his past and tried several times to commit suicide. He began working for outreach agencies across the U.S.: detox centres, group homes, and places for the mentally ill. He had started smoking pot, and then a co-worker gave him some heroin. "I thought if I had enough of this I'd have something to live for, because I'd be able to sleep through the night," he says today. "I wouldn't feel like I hated myself, like I was a worthless piece of shit." If heroin was one way of coping, his poetry was the other, and a small U.S. magazine was the first to publish his dark words.

In 1969, when he was twenty-one years old, Osborn was drafted to serve in Vietnam, a war he did not support. He fled to Toronto and spent years adrift on drugs before coming in the 1980s to Vancouver, where he moved into an abandoned warehouse on Railway Street with some friends, most of them artists. He became involved with an anarchist group and was arrested because of its association with the Squamish Five, five young militants who in the early 1980s used firebombs and dynamite (once at a B.C. Hydro station) in a notorious campaign against capitalism. Osborn was eventually acquitted of all but a few minor marijuana-related counts.

In Vancouver, Osborn's love for writing poetry accelerated, as did his affection for heroin. He was in and out of the few treatment centres available. He was often homeless and shoplifted to fund his habit. It seemed unrealistic to think he would ever get straight until a caring friend let him sleep on her couch, made him meals, and allowed him to use her phone to call the detox centre continually until he got in. Osborn started living a more stable life in 1993, though he still had his difficult days. He did not leave the community he had come to call home but instead became involved in DERA, DEYAS, and the Carnegie Centre and began speaking at events and to groups about protecting the rights of the poor.

The need for such grassroots action was intense. Despite the problems in the Downtown Eastside, other areas of the city were still commanding much more attention. In October 1997, there was a Hepatitis A scare at a restaurant in the Waterfront Centre, which was located in an upscale section of the downtown core. Health and government officials acted swiftly, setting up an immunization clinic and issuing public bulletins to warn people who might have eaten contaminated tortilla wraps or rice pots. "Six blocks away, people were dropping dead year after year, and no one did anything," Donald MacPherson recalls. The problem was that there was no specific level of government in charge of cleaning up the Downtown Eastside. "No one was driving the bus," MacPherson says today.

What little response there was from government was inadequate and not coordinated. Larry Campbell says that Ottawa was indifferent to B.C.'s problems because of the buck passing in the late 1990s over whether Canada, like Switzerland, should legally distribute heroin to reduce the risk to addicts. Liberal health minister Allan Rock dismissed the issue as a Criminal Code matter, while justice minister Anne McLellan said it was a medical matter. Noting neither politician was from B.C., Campbell told the *Vancouver Sun* in September 1997, "They don't have the guts to address it, that's what the whole problem is. They don't see it as being in their back-yard. They don't see it as being their problem. Well, when it's costing you billions of dollars a year, it's your problem. I don't want to be parochial, but I can tell you something: if there were 300 people fatally overdosing each year, on top of an AIDS epidemic, somewhere other than Vancouver, we would be seeing action. My response to them is if you can't handle it, then give it to us and let us treat it as a British Columbia local problem, but make up your mind. While you're doing this people are dying."

In November 1997, the federal health minister announced $1 million to fight the HIV/AIDS epidemic in the Downtown Eastside, for use in areas such as expanding prevention programs, increasing substance abuse services, and creating more resources for Aboriginal people. Many community activists rejected the amount as too little, too late, arguing much more was needed to improve housing and substance abuse programs, not just in Vancouver but right across the country. "It was a drop in the bucket. Completely insufficient to make a difference," Donald MacPherson recalls. In December 1997, seven people— a mix of entrenched addicts and middle-class recreational users—died of drug overdoses in a twenty-four-hour period in Vancouver, prompting the police to issue an unusual warning about lethal drugs on the streets. Larry Campbell, who had been promoted to chief coroner of B.C. and was now supervising about forty full- and part-time coroners across B.C., recalls, "What surprised me was how much broader the spectrum was now. We had everything from rich stockbrokers who were casual users to hard-core, homeless addicts. It would be wrong to say there was a typical victim."

Reaction to the action plan adopted by the Vancouver/Richmond Health Board in response to the public health emergency in the Downtown Eastside was slow at first, as prevention programs such as expanding the needle exchange were introduced and a drug overdose marketing campaign was launched. The idea was to keep people alive and contain the spread of communicable diseases until more sweeping solutions could be found. The most high-profile action the health board took, with part of the $3 million the province had freed up the preceding spring, was to give Bud Osborn money for his fledgling group to provide "outreach support and education" to health care professionals in the Downtown Eastside. By early 1998, the group had grown to about one hundred members, most of them current or former drug users, and it was holding regular meetings at the so-called hot dog church on Hastings (the Foursquare Street Church, where hot dogs were served). VANDU was working to gain addicts some level of official acceptance and an improved ability to fight for what they needed. The message Bud Osborn wanted to instill in group members was this: "No matter what I've done, I've got worth and value."

When VANDU first began meeting, program coordinator Ann Livingston used her paltry welfare cheques to make low-budget sandwiches for those in attendance. After the group received the health board grant, members could be given a snack and bus fare. Eventually, VANDU rented a modest office space, which was decorated with the names of two thousand overdose victims, along with replica coffins propped up in corners. A 2001 report prepared for Health Canada by two professors from UBC and the University of Victoria, with the assistance of three VANDU members, said the group was groundbreaking and could serve as a template for other user groups around the world. "VANDU has performed a critical public education function by bringing policy makers, researchers, and other external stakeholders face to face with the realities of the Downtown Eastside," said the report, which was called *Responding to an Emergency: Education, Advocacy and Community Care by a Peer-driven Organization of Drug Users*. The authors found VANDU could bridge gaps often faced by health care providers, such as effectively reaching out to drug users, communicating with them, and gaining their trust.

But there was persistent debate within the community about whether fighting the public health emergency should involve

harm reduction measures or more initiatives focused on abstinence. A report prepared in February 1998 by Dr. Stan de
Vlaming, a longtime Downtown Eastside doctor, along with several like-minded physicians, rejected the idea of decriminalizing
narcotics possession as a way of lowering the spread of HIV and
Hepatitis C among injection drug users, arguing that it would
only encourage more young people to use heroin and cocaine.
Aside from some liberal members of the Vancouver Police
Department, like Inspectors Kash Heed and Ken Doern, police
also argued harm reduction measures would enable addicts and
addiction. Many politicians, with the exception of NDP MP Libby
Davies, NDP MLA Jenny Kwan, and a handful of others, argued
decriminalization was morally wrong.

As a former drug cop, Larry Campbell could relate to the concerns of the naysayers. The concept—even the vernacular—of
harm reduction was foreign, and Campbell initially accepted
"the common thought of the day": that many harm reduction
measures were "honey pots" that would attract addicts to the
area, increasing crime without solving the underlying problems.
Even after Campbell started speaking to John Turvey about his
groundbreaking DEYAS needle exchange and to other "unsung
heroes" like Bud Osborn and Ann Livingston, he was "still
pretty torn in my own mind," he recalls. "I remember saying to
Bud Osborn, 'There is no fucking way.' Bud said, 'You don't get
it, Larry. You just don't get it yet.'" Campbell's view changed
gradually, he says, as Osborn and others set him straight about
injection sites being health facilities and abstinence not being
possible for some addicts. "I had to be taught. I had no problem with the idea that this was a medical problem, but I hadn't
come to grips yet with looking at it as a wide-open problem
that required many different solutions," Campbell says today. "It
finally occurred to me that drug addiction was no different from
being an alcoholic—but drinking was socially acceptable, and

you couldn't get the same help for an addict." Campbell came to realize, too, that harm reduction wasn't presented as a replacement for treatment, which was the argument of many critics. Instead, it offered a crucial bridge between heavily entrenched addiction and beating that habit one day. "If you work through this in a logical fashion, then you realize it's a health care issue," Campbell says. "Nothing more. It's not the same as condoning the use of drugs."

Campbell's conversion was also due to what he witnessed every day as chief coroner. A huge number of cases involved injection drug users, and the situations were harrowing. In one instance, Campbell was called to the external stairwell of an office building on the waterfront, just a few blocks off the main drug strip. A young, well-dressed man was collapsed in a corner. The man's parents were devastated by their son's death and by the lack of help they'd been able to find for him while he was still alive. "There was a huge sense of despair," Campbell says, "about what might have been if we'd treated things differently." Anyone was now susceptible to the epidemic. "Things accelerated, and I've never found a logical explanation of why. It was a switch from heroin to cocaine to crack to meth. But why? There are probably as many different reasons as there are people. There is abuse; there are the rebellious youth who run away from home; there is poverty." During the summer of 1997, the number of youth living on the streets in Vancouver had been estimated at between three and five hundred. "We weren't dealing with it, and the community continued to suffer. I feel guilty, too, because I didn't do anything. I was down there every day. I don't know what it was, if I didn't see it grow until it was too late. It's frustrating, because as a coroner your role is to prevent death. On the other hand, with the exception of treatment and enforcement, how do you go about it?"

The report released by provincial health officer Dr. John Millar in June 1998 recommended a province-wide, multi-agency strategy to address the epidemic of deaths and disease among injection drug users. Injection drug overdoses had become the leading cause of death for adults age thirty to forty-nine in B.C., Millar wrote, with more than three hundred deaths a year—most of them in the Downtown Eastside. It was not a problem that was Vancouver's alone to fix, he said. "The outbreak is a symptom of broader problems—child abuse and neglect, drug use, untreated addiction, poverty, and marginalization—that need attention throughout British Columbia." Millar described drug dependence as a relapsing medical condition as chronic as high blood pressure, diabetes, and asthma. "Addiction is neither a lifestyle choice nor a moral lapse. Research shows clearly that addiction is a disease of the brain," he wrote. Millar called for the system to invest more money in treatment, both to stem the spread of communicable diseases and to reduce the crime associated with drug dealing. He also recommended establishing a substance abuse commission that could oversee goals such as improved child care and drug-awareness education, to lower the chances youngsters would try drugs; better mental health and social services, including housing, street outreach, and needle exchanges; more methadone, detox, residential care, and counselling for injection drug users; pilot testing of heroin prescribed by doctors; and a trial use of "drug courts" instead of jail for people possessing small amounts of drugs.

Millar's report estimated there were fifteen thousand regular injection drug users in B.C., one quarter of them HIV-positive and eighty-eight per cent with Hepatitis C. In fact, B.C. accounted for more than half of all Hepatitis C cases reported in Canada, the report said; the province's rate of infection was more than four times the national average owing to both a higher number of drug users and more reliable data collection. "The continuation of this epidemic represents a failure of societal values and attitudes," Millar wrote. "Our improved understanding of addiction suggests that it is time for this to change and for society to recognize that injection drug users—like people with other chronic diseases—are suffering human beings deserving of our compassionate care and respect." The Canadian Centre on Substance Abuse, the report said, estimated illicit drugs cost the B.C. economy $209 million annually for law enforcement, health care, and social services. Millions could be saved by providing extensive treatment and harm reduction measures, Millar suggested. "The problem of drug abuse will never be entirely eliminated, but certainly the harm and costs resulting from drug abuse can be greatly reduced."

Also in June 1998, the B.C. Ministry for Children and Families, which had jurisdiction over addiction services in the province at the time, released a review of drug and alcohol services in Vancouver. The report included a scathing self-critique of the job the ministry was doing. A new sobering centre, a safe haven to which police could take people intoxicated with alcohol or drugs, was in the planning stages for Vancouver, but all other resources were insufficient. "The lack of adequate resources cannot be overstated," the government report said. "The simple fact is: there is not enough of anything, there are waiting lists for everything and we are chronically under-serving many. There is not only a need for more of the same, but new and innovative approaches need to be developed to attend to emerging trends and issues."

Around the same time these two critical reports were released, Donald MacPherson left the Carnegie Centre to work on drug policy initiatives for the city of Vancouver. MacPherson had no personal background of drug addiction, but after years of working in the trenches he'd come to believe true change would happen only when a courageous political leader took the helm. He didn't know who that person would be, but he went to city hall to start his search.

MacPherson used his sister's frequent-flyer points to travel to Europe in 1999 to check out the harm reduction policies already in effect there. He attended an international harm reduction conference in Geneva, where the Swiss health minister explained how the country had cleaned up the notorious needle park in Zurich. MacPherson also went to Frankfurt, where he visited safe injection sites. European research showed that when users got into the drug scene they typically stayed there for six years; by then, they were extremely sick and entrenched in their addictions. In response, the Europeans had introduced low-threshold access to various forms of help, such as clean syringes. At the time, most Vancouver treatment centres required people to be thirty days clean, a goal the majority of addicts could not achieve. In Switzerland, MacPherson learned, making treatment more readily accessible had also made it easier to connect with difficult-to-reach groups, such as women, youth, and immigrants. MacPherson saw users in Europe who were much healthier than those on Hastings Street. "I had a real epiphany," recalls MacPherson. When he got home, he wrote a report entitled *Comprehensive Systems of Care for Drug Users in Switzerland and Frankfurt, Germany,* which advocated a harm reduction approach for the Downtown Eastside. He gave the controversial document to Vancouver mayor Philip Owen. "He really liked it, and he immediately got it," MacPherson says.

MacPherson invited Werner Schneider, the head of Amsterdam's drug program, to Vancouver, and together they visited the city's nine-year-old needle exchange program. Although Vancouver workers were connecting with thousands of addicts, Schneider observed, they were doing nothing tangible with the contact—not distributing information about treatment programs or even handing out sandwiches. "He basically saw us practising sloppy harm reduction," MacPherson recalls. Schneider also noted there didn't appear to be one person in B.C. who was responsible in an overall way for taking on the issue of drug addiction, a role he was filling in Amsterdam.

Donald MacPherson had no sense he would find the political leadership he was seeking from the NDP government in Victoria or the Liberals in Ottawa. As it turned out, he would find his harm reduction flag-bearer in an unlikely candidate: Philip Owen, who had succeeded Gordon Campbell as Vancouver's mayor in 1993. Owen had spent a quarter century with a centre-right municipal party, and he lived in a conservative Vancouver neighbourhood. He had no experience with drug policies, but growing up in Vancouver had shown him the current strategy wasn't working. Although Owen was raised in the tony South Granville area, his grandfather had owned a business on Railway Street in the Downtown Eastside. Every Saturday morning, young Owen and his brother would go to work with Grandpa and then walk to Oppenheimer Park to play. They'd kick a ball around the gravel field and play with any kids who showed up. In the early 1940s, the neighbourhood was a little seamy but safe enough for two school-aged boys to wander about alone; fifty-five years later, crack cocaine was wreaking havoc on a generation of newly homeless people.

Vancouver's chief medical health officer, Dr. John Blatherwick, started talking to Owen in the mid-1990s about the problems requiring medical solutions, not criminal enforcement. Owen raised this concept at a big-city mayors' conference but found his words fell on "mostly deaf ears." He also met with Prime Minister Jean Chrétien and Allan Rock, the health minister, and although both men appeared sympathetic to his message, Owen knew sympathy alone wasn't going to save any lives. He wrote blunt letters to the newspaper accusing senior levels of government of failing to act despite the "social decay" being caused by drug addiction. Owen took to walking the alleys of the Downtown Eastside at night, asking addicts what they were injecting, how often, and what the government could do to help. Whether they were huddled in doorways to keep out of the rain or sifting through dumpsters for something to sell, Owen found the people he met open, honest, and not the least bit frightening.

Owen was re-elected as mayor of Vancouver in 1996, and the following year he created the Coalition for Crime Prevention and Drug Treatment, bringing together a diverse group—including police, school board, health authority, business, and social service representatives—to tackle injection drug–related health and crime problems. The incidence of most Criminal Code offences across Canada had fallen sharply in 1996, but that was little comfort to residents of the Downtown Eastside, who witnessed property crime and public disorder related to substance use every day. Larry Campbell, as chief coroner of B.C., was a member of the coalition, and he remembers there being a "fairly substantial divide" at the first meetings as this wide spectrum of people debated possible solutions. Eventually, though, there was more order. "When all the deaths started coming, we knew clearly that interdiction wouldn't work," Campbell recalls. The group held five public forums in the late 1990s at which more than 350 people debated something called the four pillars approach to drug policies: prevention, treatment, enforcement, and harm reduction.

The four pillars concept had begun in Switzerland and Germany during the late 1980s and early 1990s, and nowhere was it more dramatic in its evolution than in Zurich, Neil Boyd says. Initially, policy makers there had determined it was best to confine injection drug users to a large park area bounded by bridges; the original notion was one of tolerance of use within a zone of geographic containment. Zurich's Platzspitz attracted global attention as an open drug scene with overdose deaths and violence—apparent proof that tolerance of drug use was doomed to failure. In fact, says Boyd, who visited Zurich to observe the scene, it was proof that simple tolerance wasn't enough. Zurich police closed Needle Park in 1992, only to have the open drug scene move to Letten, a nearby former train station, where the violence and the overdoses continued. From the chaos arose a coordinated approach—a coalition of police, social workers, physicians, and politicians with enforcement, therapy, prevention, and harm reduction all part of the strategy. The four pillars plan included commitments to housing those with substance abuse and mental health problems; providing off-street consumption rooms for addicts; offering improved health care, including heroin prescription in the most intractable of cases; and efforts by police to channel users to services whenever the open drug scene flared out of control. Though the dire situation in the Downtown Eastside required the Vancouver Coalition for Crime Prevention and Drug Treatment to "think outside the box" for solutions, Larry Campbell admits he was skeptical at first that a radical four pillars proposal—especially some of the harm reduction elements—could be realized. "I just didn't know how we were going to change the mindset of people to go for this," he says. Some of the coalition's initial plans did fizzle out, but the exploratory effort set the stage for Philip Owen's eventual political legacy.

Owen attended a harm reduction seminar in California in early 1998, and he invited a spectrum of European, American, and Canadian harm reduction experts to Vancouver in June of that year for a conference called the International Forum on Drug Treatment and Crime Prevention. Owen experienced a "watershed" moment on the first morning of the conference, he says today, while sitting at the head table between Vancouver's police chief Bruce Chambers and B.C.'s Attorney-General Ujjal

Dosanjh. A man with a few scraggly friends in tow approached a microphone set up for participants and said there was something missing from the city's first drug policy forum: the perspective of people who used drugs. As Owen recalls, "The man said, 'My name is Theo Rosenfeld. I've been clean for a few years. My friend George here is a user still. Bill is in relapse; Henry's in bad shape.'" Owen apologized for the oversight and said Rosenfeld and his friends would be welcome to participate. Harm reduction advocates in the crowd cheered. The reaction from those in suits was initially less jovial, Owen says, until they discovered the drug users had some salient comments. From then on, most drug policy events organized by the city included users, most often from VANDU.

It was clear by November 1998 that the crisis in the Downtown Eastside was worsening. (In total, 417 B.C. residents would fatally overdose that year, representing the worst year on record.) The Portland Hotel Society threw together a last-minute conference that month to try to galvanize public support for innovative solutions that were working in other countries. In the span of just a few weeks, the tenacious folks at the PHS had secured Health Canada funding and convinced international harm reduction speakers to attend, including the head of the Frankfurt drug squad; a Swiss drug policy coordinator; a Portland, Oregon, drug court judge; and experts from Liverpool. On the agenda were ideas that some Canadians had dismissed as "immoral and controversial," including heroin maintenance, safe injection sites, and drug courts. Organizers wanted the community's drug users to feel comfortable attending the event, so a large tent was pitched in Oppenheimer Park. Meals and musical entertainment were provided for the diverse group of participants, and although it poured rain, roughly eight hundred people came. The PHS's Mark Townsend was encouraged to see police officers, the chief coroner, nurses, addicts, residents, and bureaucrats sitting side by side at the conference taking notes, though he was disappointed that more politicians didn't openly endorse some of the ideas they had heard after the event.

In 1999, two years after declaring a public health emergency in the Downtown Eastside, the Vancouver/Richmond Health Board decided to investigate the current state of affairs. Heading up the investigation was Heather Hay, a nurse with two master's degrees who had been a senior manager in emergency services at Vancouver General Hospital before joining the health board's staff. The health board's evaluators determined that although the $3 million provided by the province in 1997 to stem the HIV/AIDS epidemic had reached infected people, the overall health in the community was still bad because of overlapping challenges: inadequate facilities for people with mental illness, an increase in a troubled Aboriginal population migrating to the city, the closure of treatment centres, the arrival of crack cocaine, insufficient housing, limited needle exchanges, poor access to health care, and few public washrooms. Hay's team concluded there was, in fact, a prolonged public health emergency in the tiny neighbourhood. "What we discovered was that we were dealing with multiple epidemics," recalls Hay, who today is the health board's director of addictions, HIV/AIDS, and Aboriginal health services.

Besides the worrying rates of overdose deaths and HIV infections, the Downtown Eastside was experiencing a syphilis outbreak among sex-trade workers, tuberculosis among rooming house residents, a ninety per cent Hepatitis C infection rate from needle sharing, and the spread of both Hepatitis A and Hepatitis B, given the compromised immune systems of many of the neighbourhood's residents. After fact-finding inside and outside Canada, Hay's consultation group—which included representatives from the B.C. Centre for Excellence in HIV/AIDS, the Centre for Disease Control, and the University of British Columbia—reached a unanimous but controversial conclusion: no more government money should be directed towards HIV or communicable diseases in the neighbourhood until the underlying problem—injection drug use—had been attacked. It became apparent, Hay says, that officials needed to find a way to keep the users alive while a far better system of care and treatment was designed to support them.

The shift in attitude marked the beginning of mainstream health care professionals embracing the concept of harm reduction in a comprehensive way. In June 1999, the health board adopted Hay's integrated health approach plan, which recommended immediate action on health care, treatment, harm reduction measures, and housing. An immunization program for Hepatitis A and B, influenza, and pneumonia was launched. The health board partnered with B.C. Housing, the provincial social housing agency, to buy four notorious and decrepit hotels—the old Portland, which was already operating as a non-profit SRO, plus the Washington, the Sunrise, and the Regal Place—and spruce them up. B.C. Housing had no rooms specifically identified for addicts anywhere in the province, so Hay brokered a deal: she wanted roughly a dozen rooms set aside in the newly purchased buildings for drug users, in exchange for the health board running support-recovery programs in the hotels. The health board would also train B.C. Housing managers on how to interact with people struggling with substance use so that escalating eviction rates could be reduced. Work began on other facets of the integrated plan, including getting Downtown Eastside residents better access to primary health care. A new city bylaw forced the closing of twenty-four-hour stores in the neighbourhood, which often sold illicit drugs, between 2 AM and 6 AM, reducing the number of people on the streets at night. Vancouver police put an extra 162 officers in the neighbourhood at night, and an extra 192 at dawn, to try to quell some of the public disorder.

Change was happening slowly. But despite VANDU being funded by the health board to provide advice on what Downtown Eastside residents needed, the group was still waiting for the final go-ahead for its first proposal—a drug users' resource centre. Bud Osborn had worked on the resource centre proposal, assuring potential funding bodies no drugs would be done inside the centre, which was a concern raised by police and local merchants. The plan was for the centre to be staffed by public health nurses, as well as housing and job advocates. While Osborn was in Ottawa for a poetry reading, MP Libby Davies asked federal health minister Allan Rock to meet with him, and by late 1999, Health Canada had offered $1.6 million to buy and renovate a location (575 Powell Street) for the centre. By then, further funding had been secured from the health board to operate the centre, which would be run by users but overseen by a board of nonusers. The centre also had the active support of some doctors who worked in the area, some health board officials, and Mayor Philip Owen. "We had everything ready, even the front door key," Osborn recalls.

A February 2000 city hall meeting about the proposal stretched into the wee hours of the morning, as supporters and critics took to the podium. Chief Coroner Larry Campbell told council that addicts hung around the streets because they had nowhere else to go. "I would do anything to save the lives I see so needlessly wasted," he told the crowd. "If we do nothing, more will die." But a long list of opponents said the area already had too many services for street people, that the noise from the centre could disturb elderly residents, and that the facility would be located too close to an elementary school. A group of Gastown, Strathcona, and Chinatown community and business leaders had formed a coalition called the Community Alliance to demand the city stop providing services for drug users unless they were accompanied by treatment facilities. Ultimately, there was so much opposition to the proposed resource centre, from inside city hall and without, that it was killed at the eleventh hour.

Five months later, Philip Owen made a shocking announcement: a ninety-day moratorium on any new services, housing, or resources in the Downtown Eastside. It made advocates furious, especially those who had thought Owen was on their side. Larry Campbell, though a staunch supporter and good friend of Owen's, told the media the mayor's move would trap drug users in an escalating cycle of overdose deaths. "Time means that people are dying," Campbell said. VANDU members responded by storming city hall, carrying a makeshift coffin and planting ninety crosses on the front lawn to represent the people who would die while the city was dithering.

Owen explains today he believed the moratorium was the only option available to him. While activists, some liberal-minded officials, and the mayor himself were pushing hard for alternatives to the war on drugs, there were others, including politicians and staff at city hall, who "were not quite up to speed" on the concept of harm reduction. Owen says he needed to calm everyone down and regroup as a united team before figuring out what step to take next. He also hoped during that ninety days to convince the federal and provincial governments to develop a comprehensive plan for the region and to ante up more money.

The volatile topic of harm reduction had divided Owen's municipal party, health care officials, and the public into pro- and con- camps. Larry Campbell was one of many calling publicly for some unity. "Somehow we have to get rid of the polarization in this area," Campbell pleaded. "At the moment, the right wing says everybody with a habit should go away and die and the left wing says everybody should be able to get anything they want. That's hurting people who need care." The debate was far from over. Harm reduction would become one of the most contentious issues in the ongoing struggle to turn things around in the Downtown Eastside, and the heated discussions about the hopes and fears it inspired would intensify far beyond the neighbourhood's borders.

9 | *Da Vinci's Inquest*

IN 1998, IN THE FIRST EPISODE of the premier season of CBC's *Da Vinci's Inquest,* a police officer and a pathologist wait for coroner Dominic Da Vinci in his office. They have disturbing information about the unsolved case of an Aboriginal woman found dead in the Downtown Eastside. "She had a blood alcohol reading of 0.9," reports the pathologist, Sunny Ramen—three times the lethal limit. Seven similar cases had been investigated as possible intentional alcohol-poisoning murders, police officer Mick Leary tells Da Vinci, before they were ruled accidental.

The gritty new TV show was filmed in Vancouver's Downtown Eastside, and its episodes were based on stories drawn from newspaper headlines. The title character, Dominic Da Vinci, was a former drug cop turned Vancouver coroner who was divorced from a pathologist, drank too much, and flashed a quick temper. When the show's producer, Chris Haddock, had first pitched the idea to B.C.'s real chief coroner, Larry Campbell had laughed at the personality traits he shared with the lead character. "I said to Chris, 'Okay, that's good. I'm still married to a pathologist, so no one will know who Da Vinci really is,'" recalls Campbell. (Today, Campbell is also divorced from a pathologist.)

Campbell began freelancing as a consultant and occasional scriptwriter for the successful show, which would go on to run for seven seasons. He says the show's stark plots accurately portrayed the struggles in the Downtown Eastside and provided some dignity and respect for the downtrodden. "We were addressing all kinds of issues, and people in Vancouver got a whole new look at the Downtown Eastside and what was going on there. Lots of the *Da Vinci* stories were hopeful. Certainly I think people watched it because it was real, because its stories were taken right from the headlines, because they could relate to it. The show raised the profile of the neighbourhood, but it didn't sugar-coat anything. It addressed the issues going on down there."

The first three episodes of season one were loosely based on a mystery that had unfolded throughout the 1980s in the Downtown Eastside. As coroner, Campbell had responded to an unusual number of deaths of down-on-their-luck women who had outrageously toxic levels of alcohol in their systems. Campbell found it odd that one man, barber Gilbert Paul Jordan, was at three of the death scenes the coroners service had attended. "Jordan was with the victims, or he would have phoned to say there was another dead body somewhere. I have a picture of him in bed with a dead body, because he jumped into the bed to show a detective where he had found the body," Campbell says. "Jordan kept saying, 'I don't know why this keeps happening to me.' He was creepy. He was a real piece of work." All of the deaths had been classified as accidental; it was hard to contemplate that someone was intentionally killing these women with alcohol. But when Vancouver police and the coroners service reviewed ten old files in 1987, they found signs pointing to one suspect. Patricia Thomas, aged forty, had died in 1984 with an alcohol reading of 0.51 in Jordan's barbershop in east Vancouver. Twenty-five-year-old Mary Doris Johns, who died in 1982 with a staggering blood alcohol reading of 0.76, had been found lying face-down on a foam mattress in Jordan's barbershop. One woman who had escaped accused Jordan of pouring alcohol down her throat, but police at the time had insufficient evidence to have charges laid. Following the 1987 review, however, police arrested Jordan as evidence mounted, and he went on trial for manslaughter in connection with the alcohol-poisoning death of twenty-seven-year-old Vanessa Lee Buckner. The victim had been found naked in a Downtown Eastside hotel bed, with a blood alcohol level of 0.91, and a prosecutor told the court Jordan was linked to the similar deaths of six other women. Jordan was found guilty of manslaughter and given a nine-year sentence. After his release from prison, he faced several more charges related to supplying alcohol to women. He died in 2006.

Da Vinci producer Chris Haddock had deep roots in Vancouver. He shopped at Woodward's as a child, busked on city streets to get a fledgling music career going, and played with his band in the Balmoral and other Downtown Eastside bars when the area had a hopping night scene. "I knew the Downtown Eastside as a comfortable neighbourhood for many years," he says. He eventually worked as a producer in California but moved back to Vancouver to raise his family. The CBC phoned in the mid-1990s, wanting to know if he had an idea for a new series. He did. He wanted to create a show that was "real" and spoke to Canadians about "daily life"—something he witnessed every day from the windows of his low-rent office in the historic Dominion Building across from Victory Square, at the corner of Hastings and Cambie Streets. Haddock had met Larry Campbell in 1995, when he was looking for advice on forensics for a different show. The two became friends, which is when Haddock floated the idea of a series about a crusading coroner. Campbell, he recalls with a laugh, wasn't enthusiastic. "When I first started, Larry was very skeptical. He was blunt and brusque and snorted, 'Hollywood!'" Haddock says with a chuckle. Campbell was, Haddock assumes, protective of how the show would reflect the coroners service. But as the process continued, Campbell changed his mind. Downtown Eastside residents got to know the *Da Vinci* actors and the behind-the-scenes people because so much of the filming was done in the neighbourhood. Some locals were hired as extras. Before filming in an alley, the show's contract required the crew to wash it down so it was clean and then litter it with fake garbage. Judy Graves jokes that the alleys haven't smelled as nice since *Da Vinci* stopped filming.

The award-winning show focused on—at times even predicted—the most controversial topics being debated by politicians, police, and the public. The failed war on drugs, abysmal public policies for the mentally ill, and safe injection sites were among the themes the episodes explored. The show also tackled the prickly topic of tensions between the residents of fancy new condos being built on the outskirts of the Downtown Eastside and the marginalized people who had always been there. Ninety-one *Da Vinci* episodes were created, and Larry Campbell co-wrote eleven of them, winning both a Gemini and a B.C. Leo Award for scriptwriting.

Some of Campbell's real-life experiences while coroner were rejected as too improbable for the fictional show, however—like the time he was held up at gunpoint in 1997 while shopping for a new jacket at a sports store on Vancouver's West Side. Three guys with a sawed-off shotgun screamed for everyone to hit the floor, and they taped people's ankles and wrists, including Campbell's. "They dragged us by our feet underneath the clothing racks and told us to keep our heads down," Campbell remembers. "I told the young guy beside me not to look at them." As the robbers started taking merchandise out the back door, Campbell realized they'd left the shotgun lying on a jacket about ten feet away. The former cop had known enough to put his hands back-to-back, with his palms facing outwards, while the robbers were taping him, so that he could work his hands free of the bindings. He grabbed the pocket knife he always carried, cut open the tape around his ankles, and started to reach for the shotgun. Then, Campbell remembers, "I hear a voice say, 'What the hell do you think you're doin'?' I say, 'Nothing,' and lie back down again." Campbell was terrified the robbers planned to shoot everyone in the store because they hadn't been blindfolded. "I was scared shitless, because these guys were not professionals. I could tell they were addicts," he says. But the robbers fled without harming anyone. Campbell later testified at the trial of the young men, who were charged with a slew of other hold-ups as well. The experience gave him nightmares for a while. It also gave him a first-hand glimpse of the desperation drug users feel when they need money for their next fix.

Drug addiction was also fuelling crime in the Downtown Eastside, despite efforts by police and city hall to shut down unsavoury bars and businesses. The city hall policy report by Nathan Edelson released in July 1998 concluded there was a worrying trend of intoxicated people becoming violent, since the area had both the highest concentration of bars and the most prominent drug trade in the city. In 1997, Vancouver police stationed in the Downtown Eastside had responded to 1,400 crimes against people—more than 18 per cent of the city's total, in an area that was home to just 3.3 per cent of its population. However, the majority (55 per cent) of crimes in the neighbourhood had been committed by people who did not live there. Regardless, the public had begun to perceive the Downtown Eastside as unsafe. "The generally high levels of drug- and alcohol-related crime have created a profound sense of fear for most of those who currently live or work in the area," said Edelson. The report lamented the lack of a common vision for the area, with its diverse mix of ethnic and socioeconomic groups. "The issues facing the Downtown East-side are unprecedented for Vancouver and are undermining the community's health and economic viability. International media coverage has also begun to tarnish our reputation as one of the world's most livable cities."

In fact, the Vancouver Board of Trade and some other Vancouver officials scolded Chris Haddock for presenting "the back side of the postcard" on *Da Vinci's Inquest*. However, Haddock says viewers liked the gritty but truthful portrayal of people's lives and the way that marginalized characters in the series were presented as normal folks. "Not everyone was painted with the brush of scumminess," Haddock points out, and those who were weren't always the characters you might suspect. One of the show's main themes was the sticky issue of red light districts and safer working conditions for sex-trade workers. The true story of prostitutes vanishing from the Downtown Eastside was worked into the series over several years, long before the arrest in 2002 of serial killer Robert "Willie" Pickton. Haddock wove hypothetical possibilities into his plots, such as the theory that the women were being snatched by a sailor in port, to remind viewers, he says, "that [the Downtown Eastside] is a hunting ground that attracts predators." The series also took pot shots at the Vancouver police, who were under criticism for not putting enough resources into the initial investigation in the 1990s. One Vancouver officer who diligently worked on the case, with limited support, was Detective Constable Lori Shehner, who was later hired by Haddock to be a consultant on *Da Vinci*. With her input, the show began hinting that the disappearances of the women were more than a coincidence.

In one of those provocative episodes, first aired in the fall of 1999 when police thought just twenty-eight women were missing, fictional chief coroner Jim Flynn admonishes his renegade employee, Da Vinci, for speaking in favour of red light districts at a convention. Flynn suggests mandatory HIV testing would save more lives by reducing the spread of AIDS.

"Twenty-eight women didn't die of AIDS, Jim. They were murdered or disappeared," Da Vinci angrily replies.

"You've got another serial killer theory going?" Flynn asks.

"Well, if you don't like that, my other theory is it's twenty-eight different individuals all killing one hooker apiece. Or fourteen killing two apiece, or four killing seven each—I'd take more comfort thinking it was just one madman than a dozen or two," Da Vinci responds.

Later, standing around the dismembered body of a murdered sex-trade worker, Da Vinci and veteran constable Leo Shannon complain to Flynn that there would be a greater response to the violence if the victims were in any other profession. Flynn repeats the concern raised by real-life police in the 1990s: there were no bodies for the missing women and no proof they were dead.

"Hey, Leo, you got an opinion on a red light district?" Da Vinci asks the police officer after Flynn leaves.

"You mean like Amsterdam or something? I dunno. Makes sense to me," the veteran cop replies.

10 | The Missing Women

ANNA DRAAYERS KNEW SOMETHING was wrong when her foster daughter, Sereena Abotsway, didn't show up for her own thirtieth birthday party on August 20, 2001. Abotsway regularly called her foster parents, who lived in the Vancouver suburb of Surrey, from the free phones at various agencies in the Downtown Eastside. Abotsway, diagnosed with a mental illness, was selling sex on the low-track to support her drug habit. "She would phone us every day, and sometimes when she was older and she couldn't remember she would phone two, three times a day," Draayers remembers. But the calls had stopped suddenly in late July 2001. Draayers reported her foster daughter missing on August 22, two days after her birthday. Later that year, Abotsway's name would be added to a police poster of women who had vanished from the Downtown Eastside, a poster that by 2005 would be covered with the faces of sixty-five women who disappeared between 1978 and 2001.

Abotsway had lived with the Draayerses since arriving at their home as a "furious" four-year-old, Draayers recalled in an interview in 2007. The young girl had been taken from her biological family and was skeptical of new people after enduring abuse as a toddler, but she developed into a bubbly little child who sang loudly and out of tune at church. "Those things now I think about, and wish I could hear it one more time," Draayers said. "I love her dearly." Abotsway's at-times erratic behaviour meant she needed to be home-schooled and struggled to make friends. However, she was raised with her half-siblings, Jay and Michelle, and was close to some of the other fifty foster children who rotated through the Draayers home over the years.

When Abotsway was eighteen, Bert and Anna Draayers made a heartbreaking decision: the teen's behaviour was so out of control that they were forced to ask the ministry to send her away to protect their other foster children. Although Abotsway had grown up physically, Anna Draayers said she remained "a child inside." Near the end, Abotsway owned nothing more than the clothes on her back. Anything Draayers gave her, she would either lose or share with others. By then Sereena Abotsway had become a well-known character in the Downtown Eastside, and in February 2000 she took part in the annual Valentine's Day march for women who had gone missing from the neighbourhood. She carried a poster she had made, which had a photograph of a funeral and the words "grief" and "tears." Two years later, hers would be one of the names marchers were chanting.

At a memorial tribute held in 2002, Jay Draayers fondly remembered his older half-sister as someone who would both bully and fiercely protect him, and who had volunteered to help others at Downtown Eastside organizations. "We hope that Sereena has found the peace and love which she always hungered for," he said. "Sereena did not choose to live life the way she did; circumstances chose it for her . . . Sereena quite often, when talking to us on the phone, would ask us to make sure that the younger [foster] children would never end up living the life that she was living."

According to historian John Atkin, prostitution in the Downtown Eastside area goes back one hundred years. At that time, there were separate brothels set up on the piers for white, black, and Asian sawmill workers who came by ship to Vancouver for their days off. But there were always citizens who were morally opposed, and when the brothels were closed by city hall in 1906, business decentralized and the women started working on the less-safe streets. The social gospel movement of the first decade of the twentieth century was remarkably successful, Neil Boyd points out, accomplishing the criminalization of smoking opium, greater restrictions on alcohol distribution, and the closing of buildings designated as brothels. The trades in opium, alcohol, and sex continued, of course, but with less public regulation. The majority of Vancouver's prostitutes, in particular those in the survival sex trade, were later pushed into the Downtown Eastside by public policy decisions banning them from other areas of the city. Larry Campbell notes that Mike Harcourt, Vancouver's mayor for much of the 1980s before becoming B.C. premier in 1991, had floated the idea of a red-light district outside of the neighbourhood, by a row of warehouses on Quebec Street. But the plan was axed because of community opposition.

The women missing from the Downtown Eastside were a varied group, but the majority had suffered some tragic life event that led them to the streets. The names on that 2005 police poster began with Lillian O'Dare, missing since 1978, followed by eight women who vanished in the 1980s, sixteen gone without a trace between 1990 and 1996, fourteen who went missing in the year 1997, nine who dropped out of sight in 1998, another nine who disappeared in 1999 and 2000, and eight missing in 2001. Port Coquitlam pig farmer Robert "Willie" Pickton was finally charged with the deaths of and/or was linked by DNA to thirty of the women. Pickton was convicted in 2007 of second-degree murder in the deaths of six of them: Sereena Abotsway, Marnie Frey, Andrea Joesbury, Georgina Papin, Mona Wilson, and Brenda Wolfe. Their partial remains had been found on Pickton's seventeen-acre property in a growing suburb east of Vancouver. Pickton was given the maximum sentence of life in prison with no chance of parole for twenty-five years. "I hope that her death doesn't go in vain, and it will change the way we look at those most vulnerable in our society," Andrea Joesbury's mother, Karin, said, outside the courthouse. "It's hard to lose a child or loved one, but [it's more] the way in which she was taken." Pickton was also charged with killing twenty more sex-trade workers from the Downtown Eastside, but it is unlikely he will ever face a second trial.

Both the Crown and the defence appealed the verdict from the first trial (the Crown saying Pickton should have been convicted of first-degree murder; the defence saying he should have been acquitted). In June 2009, the B.C. Court of Appeal denied Pickton's bid for a second trial. It also ruled that Pickton's trial judge was wrong when he divided the charges into two trials but said there would be "no useful purpose" to having a new trial on all twenty-six counts when his life sentence stands. The ruling upset relatives of the twenty women, who wanted their day in court. "I'm so hurt that the system doesn't seem to have a heart for the remaining families," said Lilliane Beaudoin, sister of victim Dianne Rock. It also left all twenty-six families in limbo, because the defence plans to appeal to the Supreme Court of Canada.

The DNA of at least four other women on the police's missing women list, as well as the DNA of four more unidentified women, was also found on Pickton's suburban farm. Names on the poster have fluctuated in recent years as police have discovered the whereabouts of some women, but no trace has yet been found of thirty-four of them.

Some friends and relatives of the vanished women had complained over the years that police were not responding quickly enough to missing person reports. Most of the women supported their drug habits with prostitution and, therefore, had unstable lifestyles. Without any bodies, police argued, it was nearly impossible to know whether the women had truly disappeared or just moved somewhere else. However, family members of the women (some of them still missing today) pointed out many of the victims did have schedules, even though they didn't involve nine-to-five jobs or yoga classes. Those schedules stopped abruptly, which should have sounded alarm bells.

Evidence presented at Pickton's trial in 2007 suggests Sereena Abotsway's semi-regular contact with people ceased at the same time the phone calls to her foster mother stopped. Abotsway had regular prescriptions dispensed, but PharmaNet records show that they ended on July 19, 2001, when she picked up her last asthma inhaler. Medical Services Plan records show that Abotsway's fairly regular health care use did not continue after July 18, 2001, when she attended St. Paul's Hospital. The last time she collected her welfare money was July 18, 2001. Vancouver police had had interaction with Abotsway in the Downtown Eastside over the years, with July 19, 2001, as the last occasion. The final day she was seen at the emergency housing facility where she had been living for seven days, after staying on the streets for a month, was July 18, 2001.

Among the most vocal critics of the Vancouver police has been the family of Marnie Frey, who was raised in the small city of Campbell River on Vancouver Island by her fisherman father, Rick, and stepmother, Lynn. Marnie was described as a carefree spirit who loved animals so dearly she'd try to nurse sick ones back to health. She was just eighteen when she had a baby girl, Brittney, whom she ultimately asked her parents to adopt and raise, believing that would be best for the child. While still a young woman, Marnie was drawn to the bright lights of the big city. She regularly phoned home, though, until, when Brittney was in kindergarten, the calls stopped. According to records, the last time Marnie went to a drug treatment program; paid the rent on her SRO room; picked up a welfare cheque; visited a pharmacist, doctor, or dentist; or interacted with police was in 1997. Her parents last heard from Marnie in August of that year, and they reported her missing after Christmas, when she hadn't tried to contact Brittney. The Freys maintain Vancouver police did little to respond to their concerns until Marnie's DNA was discovered on Pickton's farm in 2002. "We felt ignored and brushed aside. And we felt Marnie was being brushed aside because people just saw her as a drug addict and a prostitute, not a mother and a daughter," Rick Frey said in an interview.

In 2001, a *Vancouver Sun* investigation revealed that the initial police probe into the cases of the missing women, which had started in 1998 with one detective and been expanded in 1999, was assigned to inexperienced officers without the time or resources to do a thorough job. Although police had said publicly that up to nine officers were working on the case, the truth was that many of those officers were either assigned part-time or working two jobs at once, reported the *Sun*'s team of journalists Lindsay Kines, Kim Bolan, and Lori Culbert. Philip Owen, who as mayor was also head of the police board, was quoted as saying the nature of the women's disappearances made them difficult to solve; he was also not convinced the women were truly missing because there were no details about where any crime might have occurred. Police had offered a $100,000 reward in 1999 for information on a series of residential garage robberies in Vancouver's upscale West Side. But a reward in the missing women case, Owen said, might end up being used as a "location service" for runaways. After some public pressure a reward was approved; the city put up $30,000 and the province $70,000. John Walsh from television's *America's Most Wanted* was brought to town to publicize the police poster, which in 1999 bore the names of thirty-one missing women.

Larry Campbell remembers being frustrated himself at the lack of evidence surrounding the disappearances for law enforcement to pursue. "We never had any bodies. We never had a crime scene," he says today. As coroner, he met with police investigators, but it was hard to glean answers. Some women had been reported missing in Vancouver, while relatives of others phoned their hometown RCMP detachments instead. In some cases, women weren't reported missing until weeks, months, or even years after they had last been seen. Campbell says different police agencies rarely shared information with each other back then. "People would like to believe this was a failing on the part of the police, because these victims were of lower socioeconomic value, but I think it was more a breakdown in communication. And I don't think it was a matter of not listening to the victims' families, as much as not having the capability of starting an investigation from a set point or a set day that the person went missing. One of the reasons this happened is because these women were easy prey. The answer is to protect the sex trade and keep the workers in it alive and healthy."

The Vancouver Police Department team on the missing women was scaled back in the fall of 2000. There had been infighting among some members, but a few officers—Detective Constable Lori Shehner and team leader Sergeant Geramy Field among them—were praised for making some progress. Detectives had located four women reported missing by following up leads: two were located alive, and two had died—one of a heart condition, the other of a drug overdose. In early 2001, a new

RCMP-VPD joint task force was formed to kick-start the stalled investigation. The task force announced in late 2001 it was adding eighteen new names to its official missing women poster, raising the tally to forty-five.

Some of the "new" missing women files were actually several years old. However, Vancouver police chief Terry Blythe defended his department's handling of the case. He also suggested the VPD should have received help from outside police agencies sooner, since not all the files originated in Vancouver. "Right from the beginning, I think we've acted very responsibly and we've done as much as we could with the resources we had and with the information we had," Blythe told the *Sun* in 2001. "The other thing that really annoys me is why we're taking the brunt of this...I mean this is not solely our investigation, and I don't think we need to be blamed for it."

A minority of officers within the department thought it a distinct possibility that the disappearances could be the work of a serial killer. One of those was Detective Inspector Kim Rossmo, who created the department's geographic profiling unit after developing a unique computer system that identifies where a serial offender is most likely to live, based on the location of his crimes. In the summer of 1998, Rossmo had been approached for advice after a beat cop said he was hearing concerns from social service agencies about an increasing number of women in the Downtown Eastside going missing. Rossmo reasoned that serial killers are rare, and those who hide bodies are rarer still, so it was most likely there was one organized predator in the neighbourhood. He suggested that Vancouver police issue a press release indicating they were trying to determine if a serial killer might be preying on women in the Downtown Eastside. His advice was rejected outright by the inspector in charge of the major crimes unit, who refused to believe the serial killer theory. A more sympathetic senior manager asked Rossmo in 1999 to write a report on the case. Rossmo reviewed twenty years of data on people missing from the Downtown Eastside and discovered that between 1978 and 1994 almost everyone had eventually been found. But that had changed significantly by 1998. Rossmo concluded that there was most likely a single murderer (or partner murderers) targeting the missing women. He didn't have enough information to create a suspect profile, his report said, but he did note that serial murders often involve "cluster body dump sites"—something police would discover in 2002 when they raided Pickton's farm.

Today, it is known that Vancouver police received a tip about Pickton in 1998 but lacked either the resources or the evidence to follow it up. In his 2008 book, *Criminal Investigative Failures*, Kim Rossmo says the tip came from a person who had seen women's purses and identification in Pickton's home—exactly what the RCMP would find while carrying out a search warrant there in 2002. Had Vancouver police and the RCMP pooled their resources earlier, Rossmo writes, they could have targeted a suspect sooner—and potentially saved some lives.

Rossmo, now a research professor in the criminal justice department at Texas State University, unsuccessfully sued the Vancouver police after his five-year contract to run the geographic profiling unit was not renewed in 2000. Rossmo complained he was pushed out by vindictive senior officers, but Vancouver brass had publicly questioned the benefits their own department was receiving from Rossmo's work since his expertise was increasingly being used by outside police agencies investigating serial crimes.

Neil Boyd supervised Kim Rossmo in directed readings on homicide at Simon Fraser University while Rossmo became the first police officer in Canada to earn a PhD in criminology. Their collaboration led to a detailed investigation into David Milgaard's wrongful conviction, and their report was submitted by counsel for Milgaard to the Supreme Court of Canada in 1992. "Kim has been able to take questions of probability to a new level," Boyd notes. "He has developed a sophisticated method of analyzing serial crimes spatially and temporally." Larry Campbell is not convinced that Rossmo's reports or his geographic profiling tool could have helped in the hard-to-solve missing women case, but by the late 1990s he had also concluded that a serial killer was the only likely explanation. Although it never became a coroner's case, Campbell regrets not having been able to do more to help solve the mystery. "What I wish I had done better was get more involved with the women's disappearances. I have a real sense of guilt about that, because it didn't let up."

Under the direction of the joint RCMP–Vancouver Police Missing Women Task Force, the list of missing women ended up at sixty-four names. RCMP Inspector Don Adam testified at Pickton's trial that his task force had identified a number of systemic problems facing the Vancouver police: the lack of a missing persons DNA data bank in B.C., no method for comparing the DNA of missing women to the 130 unidentified remains at the coroners service, and the DNA of suspects in similar but older cases never being analyzed. In addition, Adam testified, the task force's efforts to review the 1,300 tips collected by Vancouver police was initially slow because the city department's computer system was in "disarray." More members had been added to the task force by the summer of 2001, and a new "pro-active team" liaised with agencies that worked with sex-trade workers in the Downtown Eastside—an approach that arguably should have been adopted years earlier. When officers travelled to Seattle and Spokane to compare notes with other police departments investigating the murders of prostitutes, the information they received was jarring. A serial killer is always ahead of an investigation, they learned; while police are doing background work on the last killing, the murderer is out there committing a new one.

Although the official police poster of missing women never grew to include women who disappeared after Pickton's arrest in February 2002, sex-trade workers continued to vanish and to endure unspeakable violence in the Downtown Eastside. Very little had changed for these vulnerable women, who were still falling victim to dealers, pimps, johns, and other abusive men. Many people argued there were still not enough medical, social, or financial structures in place to keep sex-trade workers safe, and women's lives continued to be in danger. That was something a number of groups in the Downtown Eastside pledged to change.

11 | Four Pillars

RAY AND NICHOLA HALL LIVE IN a leafy neighbourhood on Vancouver's chi-chi West Side, where the average home is worth more than $1 million. Ray is a filmmaker and emeritus professor of theatre at the University of British Columbia, and Nichola works in community development at the same university. Their friends Rob Ruttan, a Crown attorney, and Susie Ruttan live nearby. The manicured front lawns and immaculate schools look a world away from the Downtown Eastside, but behind the front doors of some of those well-maintained homes are problems similar to those faced by homeless addicts at Main and Hastings. In 2000, the Halls and the Ruttans started a support group called From Grief to Action, for parents of drug addicts.

When her sons were younger, Nichola Hall had spent little time thinking about the struggling residents of Vancouver's Downtown Eastside. "I'm ashamed to say that my attitude before my own children was very judgemental," she says matter-of-factly today. "You think you're immune, and your family isn't going to have this kind of experience, but it's not true." Reality hit when the Halls' first son, and then their second, began experimenting with heroin. The boys had both battled mental health issues (one has attention deficit hyperactivity disorder (ADHD), the other suffers from depression) and were outsiders at school with few friends. But though she and her husband were open parents who spoke to their children about traditionally taboo subjects like sex and pot, Hall says, "We had no idea, no suspicion. We had no idea how cheap the drugs were. When we were growing up, it was only pop stars who could afford heroin." The truth, however, was that dealers were selling heroin for ten dollars a flap right outside one son's prestigious high school. The other boy, who went to an alternative school, could easily buy it by hopping off the bus in downtown Vancouver.

As young men, both sons ended up on the streets of the Downtown Eastside. Ray Hall would drive around at night, trying to spot them. If he was lucky, he'd find one and take him to McDonald's for dinner so that he'd know his son had some food and a little pocket money. "My only objective was to keep them alive," Ray Hall recalls. There was pathetically little help available; the Halls were told by the Vancouver/Richmond Health Board in the mid-1990s that there was an eight-week waiting list for counselling, let alone treatment. They sent their sons to private treatment centres, but the demons could not be chased away. "Addiction is so terribly complex," Nichola Hall says. What didn't exist, she adds, were sufficient long-term rehab facilities. She concedes they would be costly, but no more expensive than the money spent on continually rotating very sick people through emergency rooms and prisons.

The Halls and the Ruttans began meeting at a local church with a few other families with addicted relatives in 1999. "We supported each other in our feelings of shame, perceived guilt, helplessness, and grief. We also shared our anger and disbelief about the lack of treatment alternatives that were available to help either us or our children," Nichola Hall recalls. They invited experts to talk about drug addiction, and Chief Coroner Larry Campbell could see the potential for the group to have an effect when he spoke at one of their meetings. "They were normal people who wanted to work on a solution," Campbell remembers. "It was a powerful thing to sit around in a circle and hear them share their experiences and little successes, like that sons or daughters were still alive and still in care."

When Bud Osborn was invited to speak to the group, he left amazed at the stories he'd heard. He had read about a group of parents in Australia who were advocates for drug policy reform, and at their next meeting he tried to convince the members of the Vancouver group to begin speaking publicly. Nichola Hall remembers being surprised, and a bit scared, after that conversation with Osborn. "Bud said to us, 'People will listen to you. You will have clout,'" she recalls. But the idea made sense. The public would be able to relate to the group's members because they had bank accounts, houses, cars, and jobs, like the majority of Canadians. If they complained that there wasn't enough treatment for their drug-addicted children and that some harm reduction measures could be life savers, people would be less likely to dismiss them as radical.

It was difficult for the group's members to expose their personal stories at first. "The stigma and the shame are so great, and I don't think most people have any idea how big the problem is outside the Downtown Eastside," Nichola Hall says. But rather than being ostracized by neighbours or acquaintances, the Halls encountered overwhelming support and sympathy. Nichola Hall says she found discussing her family's story almost therapeutic, because it meant she was doing something about a terrible situation. "Instead of being helpless, we would turn that around and do something positive to help other people," she says. At the first public forum From Grief to Action held, in May 2000, they expected maybe fifty people. They scrambled to find chairs when four times that number showed up. "We realized we were the tip of an iceberg and that there were many silent people out there who were incredibly grateful that someone was prepared to speak out," Nichola Hall says.

From that point on, From Grief to Action's goals were concrete. As Hall explains, "We felt that change in the average voter's understanding of issues around drug addiction was critical. We hoped to increase people's understanding that addiction can affect anyone's family, and the problem is not limited to the Downtown Eastside. People who become addicted have made stupid mistakes—and who hasn't?—but the element of choice is lost very early on; if we want 'junkies' to turn their lives around, even if it is only so that they will no longer bother us on the streets and by stealing, then we need to provide treatment and rehabilitation and support, not punishment and prison. I think that the voice of experience—of families saying addiction can happen in any family, in any socioeconomic strata, no matter how loving or dysfunctional the family may be—has helped to raise awareness of drug addiction as a disease, rather than a moral lapse. And if we can remove the stigma and marginalization of addicts, this will play a large part in helping them to recover and become healthy, contributing members of society."

Like that of the Halls, Gillian Maxwell's activism in the area of harm reduction was not something she could have anticipated. Maxwell had moved in 1996 to Strathcona, a residential community bordering the Downtown Eastside. Her stepdaughters attended the local school, where the student population had plummeted. Maxwell, a former real estate agent, was at first nervous of her new neighbourhood, where renovated historical homes like hers stood next to houses ravaged by poverty and neglect. However, her emotions grew to shock and outrage over the number of people she saw living on the streets. She joined the

Strathcona Residents' Association but quickly learned her ideas of how to help her homeless neighbours differed from those of most other association members. While they were advocating hiring more police, Maxwell started to research harm reduction. Through a community health committee, she met Vancouver/ Richmond Health Board member Bud Osborn and invited members of Osborn's group, VANDU, to help out at the residents' association's annual community cleanup day. The drug users ate pancakes at the kick-off breakfast before pitching in to beautify the neighbourhood. "Having face-to-face connections with people solves a lot of things," Maxwell says.

In 2000, Maxwell was invited to join the Vancouver Police Board, which split travel costs with the health board to send her to Miami for a harm reduction conference. There she heard first-hand about "acts of courage" like running needle exchanges, a particular challenge in parts of the U.S. "The big thing for me was just getting the whole human rights part of it," Maxwell explains, "and being able to articulate how oppressed these people were and that we were victimizing them rather than them being leeches on society." Vancouver mayor Philip Owen chaired the police board, and during a meeting in his office Maxwell discovered they were "soul mates"—two non–drug users who wanted to change policies for injection drug users. With his ninety-day moratorium on new drug services in the Downtown Eastside set to expire, Owen told her about his interest in devising a four pillars drug policy plan.

In Vancouver, a groundswell of grassroots support for harm reduction had come as drug-overdose deaths jumped by thirty per cent in the first six months of 2000. "We're way out of proportion to the rest of Canada," Chief Coroner Larry Campbell said as he released the statistics to the media. In September of that year, Campbell ended his two-decade career with the coroner's service. "I just woke up one day and thought, 'I can't possibly see another way of people dying that I haven't already investigated,'" he remembers. "I started getting bumps in the night from cases from years before." Campbell began to do some consulting work for the provincial government and the Police Complaint Commissioner, and he would go on to be shortlisted for the police chief's job in both Saskatoon and Vancouver. He also became a member of the Harm Reduction Action Society, formed by health care workers, activists, and drug users to lobby governments for change.

Around the same time, Donald MacPherson, city hall's drug policy coordinator, invited "a parade" of people from Germany, Switzerland, Amsterdam, and Australia to Vancouver to speak about harm reduction. Philip Owen asked MacPherson to write a drug policy paper that focused on the four pillars. The mayor wanted it written before the upcoming provincial and federal elections, hoping it would stir debate. MacPherson finished the initial draft in October 2000, and several hundred copies were made, but most would never be distributed. Although Owen's long-standing ruling party, the Non-Partisan Association (NPA), had a strong majority on Vancouver city council, his caucus revolted when they saw the report, complaining they had not been consulted properly on the radical new plan. "They tore a strip off me [and] Philip," MacPherson recalls. As Owen remembers it, "Don MacPherson and I were absolutely shattered. It was a stab in the back. It was just disastrous."

The councillors did not ask for any of the report's recommendations to be removed, but they wanted a few things added—like the mention of mandatory drug treatment for some users. They also requested that a couple of sections be changed around, such as moving the enforcement pillar to come before the harm reduction pillar. Philip Owen was a good mediator and finally got his council on side, MacPherson recalls. "My biggest fear was that they would pull the injection site stuff, or the free heroin stuff, but they didn't. And Philip held the line."

Council approved the edited draft report, entitled *A Framework for Action: A Four-Pillar Approach to Drug Problems in Vancouver,* in November 2000. The document was the culmination of more than two years of research, and it offered thirty-one recommendations for tackling Vancouver's addiction crisis at an estimated annual cost of $20 to $30 million. The four pillars were to be of equal importance, and they collectively supported a system-wide platform: prevention, which involved educating the public about the dangers of drug use, why some people become addicted, and how to avoid it; treatment, which consisted of a continuum of support programs that would allow addicts to make healthier decisions and move towards abstinence; enforcement, which targeted the organized criminals behind drug importation and dealing but advocated alternatives for marginalized users, such as drug courts; and harm reduction, the most controversial pillar, which called for new approaches to decrease the harm addicts face. Among the ideas discussed for the last pillar were safe injection sites, heroin maintenance programs, and the decriminalization of drugs. The report stressed that such initiatives did not condone the use of drugs but merely recognized that abstinence is not a realistic first step (or even final step) for many street-entrenched addicts. "[This] means accepting the fact that drug use does and will occur—and accepting the need to minimize the harm this has on communities and individuals," the report stated.

The goals of *A Framework for Action* were threefold: to jump-start Ottawa and Victoria into writing cheques and assuming responsibility for some of the problems in the Downtown Eastside, to bring some public order to Hastings Street by reducing the open drug scene, and to make people healthier by limiting the spread of HIV and other communicable diseases. The document did not mince words about the lack of action to date by senior governments, labelling existing treatment services "inadequate and poorly coordinated." It called for services to be more inclusive: more culturally sensitive for groups like Aboriginal people, more flexible for women with children, and more accepting that relapses would happen and did not constitute failure.

The city took a strategic chance by creating a draft copy of the report and then consulting with the public. More than two thousand residents participated in six public forums and thirty community meetings in early 2001. Advocates argued all four pillars were necessary to create a balanced drug policy, but many citizens wanted to cut down the harm reduction pillar. In fact, the report alienated some traditionally strong NPA supporters, like residents in Chinatown and business owners in Gastown, who quietly but persistently lobbied Mayor Owen to take a hardline abstinence stance instead. Richard Lee, executive director of the Vancouver Chinatown Merchants Association, argued that politicians should be providing fewer, not more, services for drug users in the Downtown Eastside. "One theme that keeps coming back as I talk to people is they say, 'I elect these people, but they only put themselves in the shoes of the addict,'" Lee told reporters. He also said his group believed any available money should go to treatment, not to things like safe injection sites.

Some citizens also argued the enforcement pillar of the plan wasn't strong enough. Even though overall crime statistics had been steadily falling across Canada, many Downtown Eastside proprietors and homeowners remained concerned about crime associated with drug use. The report acknowledged that "illicit drug dealing and prostitution have increased in the Downtown Eastside and surrounding neighbourhoods. The constant presence of drug dealing, drug use and the associated risks of discarded drug paraphernalia are extremely stressful for those living in these communities. Over time, this takes its toll on perceptions of safety and well-being." However, the document concluded that the answer to this problem was investing money into more clinics, not more cops.

At the public forum held January 29, 2001, at the Vancouver Public Library, a panel of legal, medical, and harm reduction experts, including Larry Campbell, fielded questions from the public. Campbell remembers that people on both sides of the issue were very vocal, and the so-called experts didn't have all the answers. The report was proposing something brand new for Canada. "We were going into unknown territory," Campbell says today. "It was like walking into a mine field. There was no book that said, this is how to do this. There was no perfect solution." However, Campbell says Owen's calm demeanour helped set the tone. Campbell told the crowd of 150 people at the library that unhealthy addicts were an immense expense to the community and argued that harm reduction would save money. "For every dollar we spend on treating addiction we save $7 in health and social costs," he explained. As for the prevention pillar, the province was doing a poor job of identifying children at risk of taking drugs in the future: the RCMP's vaunted, abstinence-focused DARE (Drug Abuse Resistance Education) program in the schools was a failure, the former Mountie argued. Campbell was frustrated by those opposed to the harm reduction pillar, because those measures would immediately reduce the health care crisis on the streets. He felt the report offered a "blue print" for all Canadian cities grappling with drug use problems.

The Vancouver Board of Trade, which had been pushing for solutions to the city's rampant drug problems, called the plan bold and enlightened, but they leaned more towards recommendations that were "firm" on abuse and on sentencing, rather than those that were "enabling" and could attract more users to Vancouver. Organizations like From Grief to Action, though, wholeheartedly backed the document on numerous talk show programs. During a presentation to B.C.'s new Liberal government, elected in the spring of 2001, Nichola Hall told cabinet ministers they could fund more treatment by diverting money from law enforcement; studies showed the cost of putting an addict into the justice system was 4.5 times higher than giving him or her treatment.

Bud Osborn, whom Owen had invited to participate in several of the community forums, believed the four pillars debates would help open the public's mind to harm reduction initiatives, but he was more skeptical about the end result. "To be honest, I was not optimistic about this document bringing about change," Osborn says today. He believes some components that address the root causes of drug addiction were missing from the report: housing, jobs, help for the mentally ill, and other initiatives to give people the incentive to change. "Often it feels, when you are a junkie out there, that your spirit is dead," he explains.

City council was set to vote on accepting the four-pillars plan as the future drug strategy for Vancouver in May 2001. According to Larry Campbell, veteran NPA councillor George Puil fretted privately that endorsing the plan would "kill" the NPA, but Puil told Owen he would support it out of respect for the long-serving mayor. Owen remained convinced the plan was good policy. "I said, 'I think I'm right. If I go down in flames, I go down in flames,'" Owen recalls. It was tense in council chambers the night of the vote. Several members of Owen's ruling party hesitated before the group unanimously voted in favour. It would soon become clear, however, that behind closed doors there was not unanimous support for the direction Owen was taking.

City hall was not the only institution proposing change for the Downtown Eastside, which at the time was home to 22,000 of Vancouver's 546,000 residents. Vancouver Coastal Health, a new super-sized health authority created by the B.C. Liberals in 2001 to amalgamate several smaller boards, continued the work of the now-disbanded Vancouver/Richmond Health Board, which had been lobbying for years for something that seemed an obvious way to help the neighbourhood: the transfer of addiction services from the Ministry of Children and Families to the Ministry of Health, which would allow detox and other treatments to be incorporated into the medical system. The provincial government eventually agreed, and by 2002 all drug treatment services had been transferred to the health authority. Coastal Health's Downtown Eastside point person, Heather Hay, remembers provincial officials sending her all their existing addiction services contracts. She examined them with interest, shocked at the paltry number of services they reflected. "There was [almost] no treatment there," she recalls. Sadly, very little had changed on the ground since the government review of 1998 that had concluded drug and alcohol services in Vancouver were "inadequate," listing problems with accessibility, scope, and the number of resources. In 2001, with an estimated 4,500 drug addicts living in the Downtown Eastside alone, the only treatment programs offered across the entire city were 54 residential detox beds (30 of them in the Downtown Eastside), 145 support recovery beds (40 of them in the Downtown Eastside), 58 residential intensive treatment beds, three-day treatment programs, 34 outpatient alcohol and drug counsellors, and home-based withdrawal management services for some seniors.

Vancouver Coastal Health continued to work on Heather Hay's integrated health approach plan, which had started in 1999 with immunization and housing initiatives. Before launching into the next step—better access to primary health care—Hay had to determine what services already existed in the neighbourhood. As it turned out, there were very few. Despite the "burden of illness" in the Downtown Eastside, Hay found residents there had no access to basic health care—something the majority of

Canadians took for granted. Other than crusading physicians like Dr. Stan de Vlaming, who had been dispersing methadone in the neighbourhood for years, there were almost no family doctors in the community. Statistics in 2002 showed that there was one physician for 1,170 patients in the Downtown Eastside, compared with an average ratio in the rest of Vancouver of one to 791. A health board survey of residents who received services from the Kettle Friendship Society's centre revealed that eighty-five per cent of them considered a St. Paul's Hospital emergency room physician to be their primary health care doctor. There was a shortage of family doctors right across B.C., and this group of people, with their complex illnesses, were the least attractive patients. Some general practitioners didn't think they had the expertise to address the mental health, addiction, and communicable disease issues of clients who might struggle even to provide an accurate medical history. But other doctors had more selfish reasons; one group of physicians in east Vancouver denied Hay's request to accept some Aboriginal clients because, she says, they felt those patients would have "ruined the milieu of their waiting room."

The health board's action plan proposed the establishment of four health centres that would provide doctors and treatment services, though it did not include the controversial safe injection site. The plan would be funded, in part, with $14 million from the new Vancouver Agreement, an unusual five-year pact among municipal, provincial, and federal governments to address health, housing, law enforcement, and other community issues in the Downtown Eastside. The idea was to create health centres with low barriers to entry, to establish creative harm reduction strategies to keep people alive, and to expand initiatives like needle exchanges. The health board held more than 350 community meetings to discuss the four new centres.

There were as many as five hundred protesters at some meetings—some of them bussed in, according to Hay, by those in the neighbourhood who feared the sites would attract more users and increase crime. People also expressed concerns that offering more social services in the Downtown Eastside would further ghettoize the area. "There was unbelievable opposition. Unbelievable," Hay recalls, shaking her head. "The development permit meetings [for the four sites] were very confrontational." In the end, however, the centres were approved.

The existing Downtown Community Health Centre was moved to Powell Street, and its hours were vastly extended. The drop-in clinic expanded its methadone services and added a new program to improve access to HIV/AIDS drugs. On the centre's first day open in its new location, residents started lining up at 3 AM to see a physician. "Folks were way sicker even than what we were anticipating," Hay recalls. Patient visits to the centre tripled from 18,000 in 1999 to 58,000 in 2002. The second facility was a new clinic that opened on Pender Street to provide similar services, as well as alcohol and drug counselling and a team to support patients who wanted to leave the Downtown Eastside. The clinic also served as a triage site for the most difficult-to-reach residents, who came in for respite from the street, to use a washroom, and to see a nurse. The third facility, the LifeSkills Centre, was designed to assist patients with multiple health, social, and economic challenges.

The fourth and most controversial initiative was the Health Contact Centre, a drop-in program on the ground floor of the Roosevelt Hotel at Main and Hastings, which opened on Christmas Day, 2001. The facility gave addicts a place to go even if they were high. It offered health services, food programs, referrals to other agencies, and social activities. Vancouver police were mainly supportive; they believed that if addicts had a place to go inside, dealers would be easier to target. However, members of the Community Alliance in Chinatown and Gastown feared the drop-in centre would make an already bad street drug scene even worse. And there were some problems inside initially, as fights broke out between people waiting to use the services. The centre was closed briefly, then renovated to better handle the crowds. In 2002, an average of seven thousand people per month signed in to use the centre; by 2004, the average would jump to eleven thousand a month.

Core health care services were also established outside the Downtown Eastside, so users who wanted out of the neighbourhood would have a place to go. This was crucial for other users, too, because drug addiction existed everywhere. In fact, the health board estimated that forty per cent of people who came to the Downtown Eastside to use drugs in 2000 lived outside the neighbourhood.

Proponents were buoyed by early signs that the health care situation in the Downtown Eastside was slowly improving. A September 2002 draft report by the health board, the *Vancouver Community Operational Addictions Plan,* reported that overdose deaths and HIV transmissions had dropped by half since the mid-1990s. The number of people swapping heroin for methadone had jumped from 1,300 in 1993 to 8,000 in 2002. And Hepatitis A had been nearly erased by the immunization program. The health board report acknowledged some of the most vulnerable addicted people, most of them in the Downtown Eastside, were still underserved by treatment and housing services: Aboriginal people, injection drug users, high-risk youth, women, seniors, and the mentally ill. "Across all these population groups in the area, many people are homeless or live in housing that is so substandard it is equivalent to homelessness (a complete lack of facilities such as kitchens and washrooms). The provision of health care for these people includes the need for amenities like toilets, showers, laundries and kitchens where people can help themselves in the most basic ways," said the document.

The health board report said "much additional funding" was necessary to implement long-term solutions, and it rejected common arguments that bringing more services into the Downtown Eastside would draw more users there or result in more public nuisance. Research in Vancouver, along with observations by police, suggested that users were drawn to the neighbourhood for the accessible drugs and the cheap housing, not the health care services. The report attempted to dispel a "perplexing myth" that the answer was for police to shoo the area's estimated 4,500 drug users out of the Downtown Eastside. "At the end of the day, regardless of where they are dispersed, these people will remain in the neighbourhood because they live here. Only through increased contact with health care will they be able to choose to live here in a healthier way, or make the choice to move out of the neighbourhood," the report said.

Following the report's release, the health board beefed up some services: Vancouver Detox in central Vancouver and Cordova Detox in the Downtown Eastside increased their residential programs. Outpatient detox, ambulatory detox, recovery beds for women, methadone services, and sobering programs were also expanded, though all at facilities outside the Downtown Eastside. Needle exchanges were opened in all Vancouver health centres, offering 24/7 access to clean needles.

Heather Hay says today that Philip Owen's four pillars plan complemented the direction the health board was taking. Although she admits she was disappointed health officials weren't asked for input when the city's *Framework for Action* document was being created, she now realizes Owen and Donald MacPherson had "the finesse" to sell such a plan, while health care bureaucrats were not as inclined to think about the strategies required to galvanize public support. "We were all on a learning curve," Hay remembers. "[The four pillars plan] needed Philip Owen to say, 'I'm on side, and this is what we're going to do.'"

Owen wanted to get Vancouver police chief Jamie Graham, who became the city's top cop in August 2002, on side. He knew Graham couldn't support elements of the plan that violated federal laws, though, such as safe injection sites and legalizing illicit drugs. So Owen made a pitch to Graham: instead of panning the entire report, the chief could support the recommendations that didn't violate his oath of office. Graham accepted the compromise, Owen says, and having even a partial endorsement from the chief was crucial.

But while Owen worked to rally support from officials and the public for the four pillars plan, he had failed to truly convince his NPA councillors or the people running the old-school party that had dominated Vancouver politics for so many years. Behind the scenes, their reservations took the form of an apparent coup against Owen, the mayor who had easily led his party to victory for three straight elections.

In early 2002, Philip Owen was wondering whether he should run again in the municipal election that November. He wanted to ensure his four pillars report was not shelved, but he also thought the NPA was suddenly being run in a "quiet, secretive way," he says today. One of the warning signs was a February visit to his office by two senior NPA members, Dale McClanaghan and party president Jamie Brown, who wanted to know immediately whether Owen planned to run or not. The next day the mayor received a letter from the NPA brass ordering him to decide within days whether he would seek a fourth term; he was also told he would have to compete for the nomination, something unusual for an incumbent politician. "Then it became clear to me that I was getting the cold shoulder from a lot of councillors," Owen recalls. Those in the anti-Owen camp complained the mayor was increasingly hard to work with, saying his focus was almost exclusively on drug policy, not on other city business.

Owen could read the writing on the wall, and he decided not to run again for the NPA, the party he had represented in various elected positions for twenty-five years. He says he later learned that Jennifer Clarke, a nine-year NPA councillor, had been holding secret strategy meetings with key members of the party and "relentlessly" lobbying to be the NPA's mayoral candidate herself. (Clarke, whose aspirations to be mayor were well known, denied repeatedly in media interviews in 2002 that she had pushed Owen out, maintaining she would have stepped aside had he decided to run.) Owen was riding high in the popularity polls, and he considered running as an independent. But people who had supported him for years were now turning their backs on him. He is convinced that the mutiny was the result of the proposed four pillars plan. "I think they thought this was too big a step, that it was fraught with danger and we shouldn't go there because there were very severe possible problems," he says today.

Larry Campbell also believes Owen's lobbying for the four pillars report led to his demise, calling certain NPA councillors "right-wing bastards" for supporting the coup. "It was quite amazing, because it changed the face of politics in Vancouver," Campbell says. "They had an incumbent mayor for nine years— not an exciting mayor, but the city was in good shape. It was political suicide for the NPA." The Downtown Eastside had plummeted into despair under Owen's watch, Campbell allows, but Owen was also the first mainstream political leader to advocate a radical new solution. "He laid all the ground work for it. He gave credibility to it. Here was someone who was seen as a very staid, conservative, blue-blazer guy who woke up and got it," Campbell says. "His position was that the major traffickers should be in jail, but the people who use are medically ill and should be treated as a medical problem. That was pretty revolutionary for the mayor of a big city at the time."

When Owen decided not to run for the NPA, supporters like Gillian Maxwell, by now involved with an advocacy organization called Keeping the Door Open (KDO), feared all the work that had been done to promote the four pillars plan would evaporate. "We were devastated, because we thought we had lost everything," recalls Maxwell. KDO, which organized public discussions about harm reduction and other substance use issues, aimed to educate people about answers to the health concerns in the Downtown Eastside and empower voters to demand change. The group, still active today, had a wide variety of members, including service providers, health officials, academic researchers, charities, public policy makers, drug users, city hall bureaucrats, and business owners. Larry Campbell, himself a member, says KDO was a trailblazer, "legitimizing people with no legitimacy." Maxwell, Campbell, and other KDO members had long discussions about what to do to keep drug policies on the public agenda now that their political flag-bearer was leaving Vancouver's dominant municipal party.

Campbell told Owen that if Owen ran as an independent for mayor, Campbell would support him by running as an independent councillor. Owen turned down Campbell's offer. "I think he felt so betrayed and so hurt by this whole thing. These were his friends. He had spent twenty-five years with this party. They all lived in the same neighbourhood," Campbell recalls. Campbell, who had never been even a member of a political party, next thought about running as an independent himself, but he didn't have the financial or political backing. He then went to see two officials with COPE (the Coalition of Progressive Electors), the city's left-of-centre political party. "They said, 'We'd like to have you run as a councillor.' I said, 'I don't want to be councillor; I want to be mayor,'" Campbell recalls, laughing. First, though, Campbell had to secure the support of two long-time COPE members who had declared their intention to run for mayor: Downtown Eastside activist Jim Green and environmental crusader David Cadman. Although disappointed about stepping aside, Green and Cadman both thought Campbell had a shot at rescuing their party from the political wilderness. There were, of course, inherent risks with the scheme: Campbell knew nothing about COPE's policies, and the public knew little of his stand on issues other than the four pillars plan.

When Campbell officially announced in September 2002 that he would run for mayor, he was far behind Jennifer Clarke in the polls. "I was pretty honoured that this whole nine yards was going down, and I was also pretty worried about my lack of experience. But I didn't actually think that I would get elected," Campbell says today; he just wanted to force the drug policy onto the campaign agenda. However, Campbell had a well-oiled group of strategists working with him, and he started building momentum one coffee meeting at a time. His strategists referred to him as the "un-politician," portraying Campbell as a hard-nosed, straight-talking, fun-loving leader with "a kick-ass attitude" that would inspire change. And Campbell didn't have the hang-up most career politicians do: the fear of alienating voters by taking controversial stands. "I never worried about that," he says. "I always said what I felt, and if you always do that you can't get caught up in misspeaking."

In the end, the NPA operatives had guessed wrong. The drug policies included in the four pillars document became the constant theme of the election. And they had not anticipated the popularity of COPE's mayoral candidate, a man who had seen it all, from street dealers and organized crime to thousands of dead bodies in morgues. From Grief to Action organized a mayoral debate on the city's drug policies in the final weeks of the campaign. No one in the packed church gym spoke out against safe injection sites. Instead, candidates were grilled on how they would ensure that at least one such site would open in Vancouver. The tide had not only turned but was now rushing towards the shore, carrying with it the public's demand for change.

12 | Canada's First Supervised Injection Site

JUST BEFORE THE VOTING BOOTHS closed on the evening of November 16, 2002, Larry Campbell slipped out of the hotel room where his campaign team and friends had gathered to watch the results roll in. He briskly walked to the Four Seasons Hotel, where he knew Philip Owen was having a quiet dinner with his family and close staff. Campbell simply wanted to say, again, that he was sorry for how everything had worked out: Owen was ending a career in politics, and Campbell was worried he was about to start one. Eleventh-hour polls had predicted a Campbell victory, and the neophyte politician was having last-minute pangs. When Campbell got back to his hotel, he was greeted by his handler, Stephen Leary.

"Get dressed. It's over," Leary said to Campbell, who was wearing jeans and a T-shirt.

"It can't be all over," Campbell replied.

"Larry, you're the mayor. It's all over."

The election marked a sea change in Vancouver politics. COPE had not only had its first mayoral candidate elected, but it now

dominated city hall, winning eight of ten council seats. The bois-
terous victory party was at the Vancouver Public Library, and
among the crowd of enthusiastic supporters was a trio of supervised injection site supporters from the Portland Hotel Society:
Dan Small, Liz Evans, and Mark Townsend. It seemed Vancouver's voters had finally endorsed the harm reduction strategies
the society had been preaching for so long. Evans cried that night.
"How did that happen? The entire city of Vancouver had supported the injection site. It seemed to be a sign that things could
change," she recalls today.

Dan Small sought out Campbell during the victory party,
gave him a card, and told him a secret only a handful of people
knew: the Portland group had already found a location for the
controversial project and had renovated the space. Campbell
had heard rumours a site was being prepared, but he didn't know
any more about it. Now he learned the site was ready to go, and
it would be up to the new mayor to get permission to open it.
Campbell believed the injection site would soon be operating,
either with or without Ottawa's support, but it was suddenly, he
recalls, "the most important thing on my plate."

As soon as Owen "got knifed," Dan Small remembers, he and
his colleagues at the Portland had gone looking for a building to
house the injection site, fearing a new mayor would not continue
to back the concept. No one had any idea at that time that Campbell would end up running. The group knew it would be difficult
to find a landlord willing to rent to them, and without any government endorsement or funding, it seemed unlikely that any of
the usual suspects—hospitals, churches, or non-profits—would
be keen to take the risk. Small and Mark Townsend were walking
one day in early 2002 along Hastings, just west of Main, when
they met a man sweeping the sidewalk in front of a sandwich
shop. For twenty years, the man said, he and his wife had run the
business. They had raised their two children in the second-floor

apartment above the shop, and they had rented out eighteen single rooms on the third floor to hard-to-house tenants. Small and Townsend thought the building was perfect and asked the man for a meeting. They showed him videos of injection sites in Frankfurt and Zurich, to convince him that such facilities improve the health and long-term fate of drug users.

Following that, Small and Townsend made the man an offer: the Portland Hotel Society would sign a lease for the building's main floor, with an option to eventually take over the top two floors. The society didn't yet have the funding to pay the rent or the legal permission to run such an operation, though behind the scenes Small says he had received assurances from senior regional health officials that the site would likely be given some money. Nothing could be put in writing, however, until Ottawa, Victoria, and the city of Vancouver were all on side. Small promised this brave man that he would personally take responsibility should anything go wrong and that the site would be shut down immediately if it wasn't working out.

The man thought about the proposition and, against all odds, said yes. He told Small he had been a silent witness to the neighbourhood's growing problems, and he decided to trust that the Portland would get the money somehow to pay the rent. He and Small toasted their new partnership over glasses of the man's hand-squeezed orange juice. "He told me, 'I've made my living off the people in the community for twenty years. It's time to give back,'" Small recalls today. "That was courageous."

The sandwich shop was closed, and the PHS spent thirty thousand dollars on renovations, installing six mirror-lined injection booths, some sinks, and low-level lighting. The 1,200-square-foot ground-floor space, code-named "the hair salon," had high, dark ceilings, white walls, an observation platform for staff, and a waiting room. The site was ready, but when Larry Campbell announced he would run for mayor, the group decided to back off its renegade plans to open the place on their own. Both Campbell and the NPA's Jennifer Clarke had said publicly that they endorsed a supervised injection site for Vancouver. It would be preferable, the Portland group knew, for the site to be properly funded and staffed with the appropriate number of health care workers. Ideally, the PHS also wanted their injection site to offer security to users, without the police bursting through the door at any minute. Eventually, Small says, they wanted it to be a full-service medical facility, too—one that could offer detox on demand and recovery beds. So the Portland put its plans on hold, betting that Campbell would win the election. If so, he would have both the personality to sell the idea and the panache from *Da Vinci's Inquest* to get it open. "It seemed like the battle was over," Liz Evans recalls of that time.

In the midst of election-night excitement, Campbell promised the crowd that the injection site would be open seven weeks later—by January 1, 2003. "It was naiveté on my part," Campbell now concedes; nothing moves that quickly in government. Nonetheless, shortly after he was sworn in as mayor, Campbell went to Ottawa with a delegation from Vancouver to discuss with Health Canada draft guidelines for opening supervised injection sites in the country. There were representatives at the meeting from five different cities, and Vancouver's large contingent included two senior police officers, regional and provincial health officials, VANDU president Dean Wilson, and Donald MacPherson, the city's drug policy coordinator. "It was very unusual that a politician would show up at a meeting like that," MacPherson says with a chuckle. "But Larry made it very clear to Health Canada that we were going to move ahead with this." MacPherson remembers the meeting going relatively well until two RCMP officers paid a surprise visit, explaining they did not think the site should be approved until the system for treatment was better funded. "Larry's blood started boiling," MacPherson recalls, and the second the officers were done talking, Campbell pounded the button that indicated he wanted to say something. "The people of Vancouver have spoken. They want this to happen," MacPherson remembers a frustrated Campbell blurting out. "'No' simply was not an option," Campbell recalls today. "We were going to open it. What would happen? I didn't know. Would I go to jail?"

Officials from Quebec at the meeting took the position that they didn't need Criminal Code exemptions to provide a safe place for addicts to shoot up. Campbell agreed morally with Quebec's position. However, the new mayor decided to see what the feds wanted in exchange for their approval, because he didn't get the sense that Prime Minister Jean Chrétien's Liberals were against the site. "We weren't a bunch of wack jobs, and I had just been elected with a huge, huge majority," Campbell says.

Ottawa eventually decided that it wanted rigid protocols around issues such as how used needles would be disposed of and what medical action would be taken in case of an overdose. The feds also wanted the Vancouver site to be a research project, and they agreed to pay $1.5 million over three years for the research. There didn't appear to be any deal-breaking issues, Campbell recalls. That the federal Liberal government would be relatively supportive of the contentious plan was also not that surprising. A national task force on reducing the harm associated with injection drug use had recommended to federal and provincial ministers of health in 2000 that they should consider a medical research project involving a supervised injection site.

Upon his return from Ottawa, Campbell confidently told Vancouverites that an injection site would open very soon— March, he thought. But the new mayor was getting a public crash course in politics. No longer a chief coroner who could make his own decisions, Campbell was at the mercy of multiple layers of government needing to reach agreement. Ottawa was not prepared to provide any funding beyond the research dollars, so the site would require the Liberal government in British Columbia to provide money for operating and capital costs through the health ministry. Premier Gordon Campbell had endorsed the city's first needle exchange in 1989, while he was mayor of Vancouver, and Larry Campbell says the premier needed no convincing to ante up funding for the injection site, which had a $1.4-million budget in its first year. "I never felt a sense of hesitation on Gordon Campbell's part. He could have easily said it was a federal issue, but he didn't. He saw it as a health care issue," Larry Campbell says today.

Heather Hay says that although she supported the concept of an injection site, Vancouver Coastal Health had little interest in endorsing the polarizing idea until Larry Campbell became mayor. In early 2003, the health board submitted an application to the federal government for an exemption from Section 56 of Canada's Controlled Drugs and Substances Act, allowing them, for the purposes of scientific research, to implement a pilot supervised injection site for three years. Another hurdle was winning over Jamie Graham, who had beat out several notable candidates—including Larry Campbell—to become Vancouver's police chief in 2002. Some members of the department, including union president Tom Stamatakis, vocally opposed the proposed site. The Canadian Association of Chiefs of Police had also raised concerns about the plan. Graham, who had chaired a police chiefs' mental health committee, understood the link between mental illness and drug addiction, but he didn't want to condone breaking the law, Campbell says. "All Jamie wanted was for it to be lawful, so until we got the Criminal Code exemption he stayed on the fence," Campbell recalls. "Jamie Graham was not a leader who was conflicted. He knew right and wrong."

Still more negotiations were required before Larry Campbell could fulfill the promise he had made to the electorate.

For example, there were disagreements over how the federal research would be conducted. Ottawa wanted users to fill out detailed forms about their histories to track who was using the facility. The Portland Hotel Society folks, who would be running the site, knew users wouldn't have the patience or the focus to fill out such forms, especially when they were on their way in to fix. So a compromise was reached. After being buzzed in through the locked door, any new users would be required to give a one-minute interview, which could be followed up on later with more in-depth questions. Since VANDU members got money from the Portland to sign people up in advance, the facility had a database of about a thousand names before it was ready to open its doors.

ALTHOUGH VANCOUVER was applying in 2003 to run the first supervised injection site in North America, it was not the first such facility in the world. Several sites had opened in the Netherlands during the 1970s. The Dutch had wanted to draw heroin users into treatment, but traditional drug services and an insistence on abstinence had demonstrated little success in reaching that population. So, the purpose of the supervised injection site was to provide users with an alternative to street drug use and to initiate contacts that might improve their physical and psychological health. The new facilities offered informal meeting places and basic health services. Users had access to medical care, counselling, food, and laundry; the sites also provided users with a syringe exchange machine (a precursor of needle exchange programs) and a facility in which to inject. Frankfurt followed the Dutch example, creating injection and inhalation rooms in the late 1980s for similar reasons. By 2000, there were sixteen sites in the Netherlands, seventeen in Switzerland, and thirteen in Germany. In all locations the goals were the same: to provide health services to a difficult-to-reach population and to reduce the public disorder associated with street drug use. In a 2006 article in the prestigious medical journal *Lancet,* two research-ers would report that supervised injection and inhalation rooms in Switzerland had "changed the image of heroin use as a rebel-lious act to an illness that needs therapy... Heroin seems to have become a 'loser drug,' with its attractiveness fading for young people." Polls of the Swiss population at risk have indicated a decline of more than eighty per cent in Switzerland since 1990, for reasons that appear to be at least partly attributable to the provision of injection and inhalation rooms.

Larry Campbell visited his first supervised injection site in Zurich in February 2003, while in Europe on a fact-finding tour of Olympic Winter Games sites. (Vancouver was competing to host the 2010 Olympics at the time.) Campbell was impressed by the site, which housed a restaurant that employed addicts, a laundromat, public computers, and a medical team to attend to overdoses and other ailments. The Zurich facility had an inha-lation room for addicts who smoked drugs, which Campbell wanted to replicate in Vancouver. In fact, such a room had been built in the back of Vancouver's injection site, complete with a negative-air circulation system. But getting permission to open the inhalation room would be a fight for another day. First things first: Campbell still had to get the injection part of the facility up and running, and there were new hurdles he needed to clear.

The new mayor had to respond to a concerted public backlash that followed a massive, unprecedented Vancouver police crack-down on the Downtown Eastside's notorious open drug scene on April 7, 2003. Triple the usual number of officers flooded the streets on horseback, on motorcycles, in cars, and on foot patrol as part of a three-month pilot program aimed at drug dealers, police said. Some business owners and homeowners supported the action as a move to protect their properties and community. The clampdown dispersed the dozens of people usually loitering in front of the Carnegie Centre, making it easier for non-users to get into the historic building. But advocates for the poor cried foul, saying police should have coordinated the enforcement action with medical, social, and housing experts. How was the police action going to change anything? they asked. Addicts and dealers were unlikely to quit using or selling just because there were extra officers around.

Larry Campbell saw his share of protesters at city hall, people who felt he had betrayed them by endorsing the crackdown. Enforcement was part of the four pillars approach, however, and Campbell says the police action was desperately needed to try to claw back the street scene along Hastings. Nonetheless, just days after it began, Mayor Campbell and city council told the public the police action was an experiment that would require time to fully evaluate, and they voted unanimously to deny Police Chief Jamie Graham's request for $2.3 million to extend the campaign for another six months. In mid-April, when Campbell reached out to community, social, and business groups to talk about the four pillars, he was heckled by a protester who accused him of already shoring up the enforcement pillar with the ninety-day police crackdown. Campbell was so exasperated he gave the finger to Dave Cunningham, a Housing Action Committee member who was a regular thorn in the side of city council.

Today, Campbell believes the crackdown did some good. "It was the right thing to do, because somehow you had to break that cycle of what was in front of the Carnegie. A few months later there was an event at the Carnegie, and this woman in her sixties, First Nations, came up to me and said she lived in a hotel near the police station. She told me that now she felt safe to come out of her SRO and go back to the Carnegie. Police were always saying people were afraid to come out, and I didn't believe it. But it was true. It was anarchy down there. People who weren't addicts were afraid to come out. It did break up some of the anarchy on the street."

A 2004 report prepared for the city of Vancouver by four professors at B.C.'s University College of the Fraser Valley concluded the crackdown had been successful in disrupting the open drug market, reducing social disorder, and increasing feelings of safety and security among people who lived and worked in the Downtown Eastside. It also found, however, that drug dealers had been displaced into other areas of Vancouver and into other cities, and police had not pursued them in their new temporary locations. The report determined the crackdown had made no significant impact on the price and availability of drugs in the Downtown Eastside, and the drug market had adapted to the police presence by moving from the public realm into private locations. There was no evidence, the report said, that the crackdown had interfered with the flow of stolen property into and out of the neighbourhood. The report's authors also said Vancouver police had not sufficiently communicated with Downtown Eastside agencies about their plan. They found no evidence that drug users had suffered more fatal overdoses or had greater problems getting access to health care services because of the increased number of officers in the area, although similar reports, like one by New York–based Human Rights Watch, had alleged that police crackdowns drove injection drug users away from the services set up to help them.

Even before the crackdown began, Ann Livingston was reading media reports about police plans to increase enforcement in the Downtown Eastside. She was angry about how it might affect users, and she was tired of waiting for a supervised injection site that didn't appear to be materializing. So she became involved in plans to open an illegal injection site—her third covert facility in eight years. (In December 2000, she had started a small injection room on Dunlevy Street, which ran for a few months before the landlord shut it down.) The new site "was to put pressure on the government to approve the official site," Livingston recalls. She found a location, at 327 Carrall Street, but was afraid if she rented it in her own name the business community would find out and shut her down. So her friend Dave Diewert, a religious studies instructor and community activist, put his name on the lease, she said. The next hurdle was getting money to run the place. That came to Livingston from an unlikely source: Christian Owen, a businessman, a highly successful fundraiser for municipal and provincial governments, and the son of Philip Owen. While Owen was mayor, he had often taken his adult son with him to speak to marginalized people living on the streets of the Downtown Eastside. "Christian heard that Ann was planning a safe injection site. He said, 'I'll raise the money,'" Philip Owen recalls.

The facility opened on April 7, the same day the police crackdown began. It had two injection booths, and it offered clean needles and sterile water to the fifty or so users who became regulars. Instrumental to the radical site was registered nurse Megan Oleson, who volunteered her time. Oleson taught drug users safer ways to inject, and she referred visitors to other services in the Downtown Eastside. (Oleson would win an international human rights award in 2004, presented by the Canadian HIV/AIDS Legal Network and Human Rights Watch, for her work at the injection site.) Larry Campbell remains in awe of Oleson, recalling that she ran the unsanctioned site professionally, continuously fending off police and others intent on closing it down. "She was young and tough, and, in hindsight, she was doing the work that others in power—like me—should have been championing," he says. "She was pushing the rock that I wasn't getting going. I admired her hugely." Campbell, who as mayor was also chair of the police board, said there were private discussions about police monitoring the site, but not closing it down. "At least we knew where it was, and there wasn't mayhem going on there."

The small operation on Carrall Street stayed open without legal approval or any funding or paid staff for nearly six months—until the official supervised injection site opened in September 2003, ten months after Campbell was elected. The former sandwich shop chosen by the Portland folks had been approved by health officials as the location for the government-sanctioned injection site, but the health board spent another $1.2 million to expand the number of injection booths with mirrors and sinks to twelve and to build a nursing station and a post-injection "chill out" room complete with a food bar. When the official facility, called Insite, finally opened its doors, it was an emotional event. "We were all in tears the day it opened. It was like we were in church, celebrating [the drug users'] right to life and liberty. In contrast to using the dirty alleys, the injection site really did offer a bit of hope," Liz Evans remembers.

VANDU president Chuck Parker had been lobbying for a long time for that day as well. Parker had been using drugs for thirty-seven years, and he hadn't been confident that he'd ever see an official injection site in his Downtown Eastside neighbourhood. "I never ever thought they would have a place for people to go, to safely inject, under the supervision of a nurse. No longer using a dirty old needle you hid under the shrubs one night. No longer using water dropping from a drain pipe to make my fix," he says today. On opening day, Parker stood with the other dignitaries outside Insite as the community celebrated this milestone. But even as he enjoyed "the sense of satisfaction," all Parker could really think about while officials spoke was: "Can I get inside there and shoot my dope?" When he finally sat down in one of the twelve booths inside, it wasn't history or the future Parker was thinking about. It was this: "I hope I don't miss my vein." Because if he did, where would he get the money for another hit? That was the reality for people trapped in addiction.

For Dan Small and the rest of the Portland crew, the biggest fear had been that no one would show up—that addicts would continue shooting up in their SROS or in back alleys in privacy, avoiding the watch of nurses. But six hundred people came through Insite on the first day. The number of injections rose to average between seven hundred and one thousand daily and was even higher on "Welfare Wednesdays," when the monthly social service cheques were dispersed.

Insite's large reception room had space for homeless people to park their grocery carts, which often overflowed with sleeping bags, clothes, and other worldly possessions. In the waiting room, the anxious and the agitated cooled their heels until one of the injection bays became available. When it was a user's turn, a staff member asked if he or she would be using up (cocaine) or down (heroin). Each user received a tray containing an alcohol swab, a vial of sterile water, a clean syringe, a spoon, a rubber tourniquet, and a "cooker" to liquefy the drug. When the user was done, the equipment was disposed of in a special hazardous-waste treatment unit.

A heroin overdose is a very quiet affair. So whenever someone appeared to be nodding off, a staff member would quietly walk over, pat the person on the back to wake him, and measure his oxygen. In dire cases, the nurses at Insite would administer Narcan, a drug that jerks the user awake by reversing the effects of the opiate. A cocaine overdose, by contrast, can produce a rapid and irregular heart rate or a seizure, even a stroke or heart attack in extreme circumstances. Benzodiazepines were sometimes used to slow heart rate and reduce anxiety. The medical staff at the site were employed by Vancouver Coastal Health, while the non-medical staff were hired by the Portland Hotel Society. Many of the latter had active drug addictions themselves. Not only could they relate to the clients visiting the site, but they received much-needed job experience and a regular paycheque—two things that could help to stabilize their lives.

A critical part of the initial funding for Insite was attached to a three-year, arms-length, scientifically rigorous evaluation of the facility by the B.C. Centre for Excellence in HIV/AIDS, which produced dozens of papers that were published in esteemed peer-reviewed journals. The research team looked at whether Insite reduced overdoses and studied the supervised injection site's role in lowering the transmission of HIV, Hepatitis C, and injection-related infections. Researchers also considered Insite's impact on public order and the extent to which the facility served to increase access to other addiction and health care services. The research findings were extremely positive.

At the time Insite opened, the former sandwich shop owner continued to live with his family on the second floor. Eighteen Downtown Eastside tenants, most of them addicts, still lived on the building's third floor. One of them was Chuck Parker, who would inject eight to fifteen times a day at twenty dollars per hit. It was handy having the site downstairs. But that convenience for Parker and his neighbours lasted only a year, because in 2004 the Portland Hotel Society took over the entire building to expand the site. The building's owner and his family moved out, and Dan Small promised the eighteen tenants that he'd find them temporary rooms until two coveted renovation projects were complete—Woodward's and the old Portland Hotel, which had been vacant since the PHS opened the new Portland Hotel in June 2000. The society fought to secure government funding for renovations and planned to reopen the old Portland under one of its previous names, the Pennsylvania.

With the tenants gone, the Portland Hotel Society built a twelve-bed detox unit called Onsite on the second floor of the Insite building, and on the third floor constructed an eighteen-bed recovery wing for people waiting to get into long-term treatment. The rooms were modern and clean and had private bathrooms—a luxury in the Downtown Eastside. There were legitimate questions about the appropriateness of putting a detox centre just above a legal shooting gallery. But Dan Small argued that detox should be located near "the eye of the storm": when addicts using Insite finally said they needed help, all they had to do was walk up the stairs.

George Chow, who had spent his high school years living in tiny apartments in the Downtown Eastside, was initially opposed to the concept of Insite. By 2001, Chow was an engineer with B.C. Hydro and had moved to a tony area of the city, but he maintained ties with his old neighbourhood. As a member of the Chinese Benevolent Association, he participated in marches and attended city council meetings to voice his objection to not only the proposed injection site but the health board's new Health Contact Centre for drug users. "I think we were concerned about the so-called honey-pot effect, attracting more drug people to the Downtown Eastside, and about more people congregating in front of these facilities," Chow says today. "There was a big philosophical debate, that still goes on, about whether Insite was promoting the use of drugs, and that there wasn't enough [law] enforcement." Chow had become a pillar in the Chinese community through his involvement with the Chinatown Merchants Association, and he feared the decline of that community would be hastened if facilities like injection sites were established. Chinatown residents were already suffering an economic downturn because people had stopped shopping there when more modern one-stop stores were established in the suburb of Richmond. A Chinese newspaper opposed to the injection site proposal ran a photo of Larry Campbell with a circle around his head and a big needle diagonally through it—mimicking the international symbol for "no."

Chow ran as an independent candidate for Vancouver City Council in 2002 on an anti-drug platform, and his campaign resonated with voters; independent candidates typically finish at the back of the pack, but Chow garnered a respectable 17,849 votes—though not enough to win a seat. However, seeing how citizens had turned out in droves to back mayoral candidate Larry Campbell and his harm reduction policies caused Chow to reconsider his position. He remained concerned about the health contact centre, but after Insite started operating, his fears about the supervised injection site were alleviated. It appeared to be professionally run, he recalls, and had not become a magnet for trouble. Instead, Chow says, he began to "support the notion that Insite was fulfilling its mandate to decrease public disorder and save lives, and act as a clearing house for people who need help." Chinatown merchants actually noticed a decrease in the number of people shooting up in alleys behind their stores. "I think the whole community evolved in its thinking," Chow says today.

After the long philosophical and legal battle to open Insite's doors, some Vancouver skeptics were starting to embrace the benefits of the facility. However, on the national stage, its future would remain uncertain.

13 | The Harm Reduction Two-Step

INSITE WAS A VICTORY FOR Vancouver's new mayor—a high-profile, controversial idea that Larry Campbell, the Portland Hotel Society, and other supporters had fought to bring into existence. But the office of mayor was not always a comfortable perch. It was impossible to keep everyone happy, Campbell found; he was forced to juggle the harm reduction approaches he believed in with the understandable demands of business owners who wanted city hall to clean up Vancouver's open drug scene.

Campbell had vowed on election night that Insite would be one of his top priorities, but there was another matter brewing in the Downtown Eastside that needed his immediate attention. Since the previous September, about sixty squatters had been living in a tent city on the sidewalks surrounding the old Woodward's building, protesting a lack of social housing in the neighbourhood. The weather was getting colder and damper, and the living conditions were harsh. Campbell wanted the city to buy the mothballed iconic building, which had been purchased in 2001 by the NDP provincial government under short-term premier Ujjal Dosanjh, after attempts by Fama Holdings to develop the site had failed. Campbell was among a group of like-minded people who envisioned the old department store becoming a vibrant residential/commercial complex that would include social housing, a project that would anchor and hopefully reinvigorate that turbulent stretch of Hastings Street. "People in Vancouver were sick and tired of that building sitting there and reminding them of failure," Campbell says today.

The new mayor got right to the point when Premier Gordon Campbell called him to touch base after the Vancouver election. "Gordon phoned to congratulate me. He said, 'What do you want?' I said, 'I want Woodward's.' He said, 'Well, I don't,'" Larry Campbell recalls with a chuckle. In late January 2003, the province sold the landmark building to the city for $5.5 million, even though it was assessed at $18 million. "We bought it for below market value," Campbell remembers, "and the province agreed to put money into one hundred social housing units. It wasn't easy figuring out what to do with Woodward's, but we knew we had to have it." The province was divesting itself of buildings at the time, though Premier Campbell said the fire sale price (roughly $16 million less than the previous government had paid for the building) reflected the need for all governments to work together to help the Downtown Eastside.

In the weeks before the sale went through, however, the newly elected city government had to figure out what to do about the squatters. Campbell says today there was general public support for the reasons behind the squat, and he recalls citizens coming by with food and water for the protesters. However, according to city hall housing advocate Judy Graves, the squatters were living in dangerous and unhealthy conditions by then. The squat had begun as a fairly calm occupation of the empty building, which Graves says was intended to last about a week, but protesters became enraged when "the cops, in their wisdom, busted it up at Day 6." The backlash had morphed into a permanent tent city along the sidewalks outside the 600,000-square-foot former department store. Protesters became riled whenever police tried to patrol the area, so the city sent Graves—who after twenty-four years of working in the Downtown Eastside knew many of the people on the streets—each day to monitor the situation. Protests like this "all start the same way," Graves says. "The first week it's Eden." During the second week, she says, people get tired and disillusioned, and anarchists take over in the third week. Then the water runs out, the food goes bad, and the porta-potties stop working; the tents get mouldy, the area smells like puke and pee, and people start to get desperate. Outside Woodward's, the sidewalks had turned into a refuse zone of tents, tarps, mattresses, blankets, shopping carts, clothes, and garbage. Wanting to protect their meagre belongings, many squatters were afraid to go to sleep at night, which created a perfect new market, Graves says, for crystal meth dealers. Until then, crystal meth—a potentially psychosis-inducing drug that does significant damage to some users—had largely been a party drug in Vancouver's more upscale neighbourhoods, but the synthetic stimulant was the perfect answer for some at the squat; rather than being hungry or sleepy, people stayed awake and aggressive. Crystal meth would go on to tear a destructive swath across the Downtown Eastside in the years to come.

Turf wars broke out among the squatters, who numbered 280 at the height of the protest. According to Judy Graves, those along Hastings and Abbott were the more prestigious group, controlling the makeshift kitchen that those camping on Cordova Street were not invited to use. But Graves also witnessed compassion and forgiveness at the squat. When a work crew building a parking garage on Cordova messed up, leaving the structure in danger of falling, Vancouver police sergeant Malcolm Cox ordered large city garbage trucks to be parked along the curve in front of the tents, so that if the garage fell the city vehicles would protect the protesters. The Cordova Street squatters finally agreed with requests by the police to move, and those along Abbott and Hastings made room for them.

On November 29, three days before mayor-elect Campbell and his new COPE team were to be sworn in, a B.C. Supreme Court judge granted the city the right to dismantle the tent city. Judy Graves passed out notices telling protesters that if they took their belongings to the Carnegie Centre they'd get a referral to a shelter and some food. But few budged. Jim Green, one of the new COPE councillors, filed an affidavit with the court asking for a short reprieve. The affidavit said that there were not enough social housing spaces or shelter beds to take in all the Woodward's squatters but that negotiations were underway with some nearby hotels for short-term accommodations. The siege ended two weeks later when city hall arranged for the protesters to be moved for four months into the privately owned, mostly empty Dominion Hotel on Abbott Street. The city paid the $200,000 tab and arranged for the Portland Hotel Society to manage the section of the recently renovated hotel where the squatters were to live.

With the protesters gone, city council began contemplating what to do with the new piece of real estate they would soon own. It was the mayor's job to buy the place, Campbell says, but he handed the rest of the responsibility over to Green, who held fast to his vision of maintaining as much of the original building as possible and filling it with a mix of housing, stores, and offices. Though some Downtown Eastside activists felt there was too little social housing planned for the building, Campbell, Green, and others wanted upscale condos in the project to subsidize the low-rent units—a model that would become more common as senior governments withdrew from social housing projects.

At the start of Campbell's time at city hall, contentious questions were also swirling around Vancouver's bid to host the

2010 Olympic Winter Games. Wouldn't it be better to spend all that money on social services? Would pre-Games development displace poor people, as Expo 86 had? Would there be any long-term benefit to the city's neediest citizens? The new mayor's response sent the backers of the bid into a tailspin: he announced a city-wide plebiscite to gauge public support. "It was important to me that the citizens had a say on how their money was spent," Campbell says today. "If I had had my way, the referendum would have been province-wide."

Campbell's plan was also strategic. His party's internal polling and his gut instincts made him confident the plebiscite outcome would prove Vancouverites were supportive—even though previous referendums held in Olympic-bid cities had ended with the majority voting "no." "I knew in my heart that it was going to be okay. I knew we'd win. We just needed to educate the people," says Campbell today. He also believed that the plebiscite would help seal the deal on Vancouver being chosen by the International Olympic Committee.

Olympic bid committee chairman Jack Poole was furious about Campbell's plan, and he made that clear when he asked to see the mayor-elect three days after the election. "It was a very tense meeting, because these guys had spent a long time on this thing," Campbell remembers. "Jack said if the referendum failed, he'd throw me down centre ice at GM Place with my ass hanging out. And I said, 'If we win, you'll have to kiss it.'" The provincial Green Party lobbied for a "no" vote in the referendum, as did a large citizens group called the No Games 2010 Coalition. But in the end, nearly two thirds of those casting votes said Vancouver should host the world in 2010. And in July 2003, the IOC announced that Vancouver was being awarded the Games, barely beating out Pyeongchang, South Korea.

If Campbell's Olympics flag-waving upset some Vancouver residents, his wholehearted support for the four pillars plan continued to scare other foes. At a two-day conference called Visioning a Future for Prevention: A Local Perspective, organized by city hall in November 2003, homegrown and international experts joined with citizens, including a high school student and the parents of a teenage addict, to discuss the prevention of problematic drug use. "If the people of Vancouver are serious about preventing harm from the use of psychoactive substances, we have to step back and take a hard look at the way we live, the values that we cherish in this city," Campbell would write in a report following the conference. "We must reflect on how we involve youth in our dialogue about drug use, and look beyond the traditional messages targeted at young people alone, and acknowledge that prevention is a life-long challenge and health priority in this community."

One presenter at the forum was Neil Boyd, who argued that the distinctions between legal and illicit drugs were arbitrary and had been defined not from a public health perspective but from a moral one. "Problematic use of prescription drugs—particularly among the elderly—is often overlooked, as prevention strategies tend to focus more on alcohol, tobacco, and illicit drugs," Boyd told the audience. He argued further that since each type of drug was different, each deserved its own regulatory framework, similar to the way airlines distinguish between alcohol and tobacco: you can have a glass of wine or two while on a flight, he said, but no longer smoke. Boyd pointed out that criminal prohibition of illicit drugs had clearly failed, since there was no shortage of them in Canada; the other extreme, allowing unlimited marketing and access, was also not appropriate. "I think the better responses lie in between the poles of prohibition and laissez-faire commercial promotion," Boyd said in his presentation.

By now, the issues facing the Downtown Eastside had begun to attract national and international attention, partly through screenings of a popular documentary. Larry Campbell's predecessor as mayor, Philip Owen, was featured in filmmaker Nettie Wild's FIX: *The Story of an Addicted City*, which had been released in 2002. The film chronicled the lives of Owen, VANDU coordinator Ann Livingston, and former VANDU president Dean Wilson as they fought for more enlightened drug policies in their neighbourhood. The story also followed the unlikely love story between Livingston, a social activist and non–drug user, and Wilson, a former IBM salesman and long-time addict. The film had received some funding from the B.C. Nurses' Union, and all the proceeds from Owen's farewell mayor's dinner were donated to the project as well.

Owen had granted Wild and her film crew unrestricted access during his final stretch at city hall, as the four pillars debate was unfolding, though some councillors were squeamish about the crew recording their discussions. Owen was excited when he saw the final documentary, he says today. "It kind of shocked me. It just revealed the rawness, the realism of it, the seriousness of it, the destruction, the law and order [issues]." He hoped the resulting publicity would shine a spotlight on the Downtown Eastside and spur politicians to make change.

Owen went on the road with Wild to promote the film during screenings in more than two dozen big cities and small towns across Canada. Wild always invited "experts" to answer audience questions after a screening, including Larry Campbell, a huge fan of the documentary. "The film made a difference because it put a real face on people," he says. "This was not just a fictionalized version of the Downtown Eastside." In Kelowna, veteran mayor Walter Gray refused to attend the screening of FIX, Owen says, because the topic was too controversial. But six months later, Gray phoned Owen to ask for help in crafting Kelowna's new drug policy.

The diversity of opinions on many municipal topics, not just drugs, amazed and frustrated Larry Campbell during the monthly Greater Vancouver Regional District (GVRD) meetings, where representatives from twenty-two municipalities discussed issues ranging from transportation to drinking water. At these meetings, Campbell encountered a political soul mate: Simon Fraser University professor Neil Boyd, who had just been elected councillor for Bowen Island, a small community off the coast of West Vancouver. "We sat beside each other, and I felt a kindred spirit there," Campbell remembers with a laugh. "Not just on ideas about prostitution and drugs, but on the question of joie de vivre, on 'How did I get here?' and 'What am I doing in politics?'"

Boyd had entered politics because he wanted to give something back to the island; he'd lived there for thirty years, and as a university administrator he'd learned that he liked the challenges of government and governance. Boyd also liked a competition, and when he topped the polls, a number of his fellow councillors suggested that he become the regional director for Bowen Island, replacing the incumbent mayor. Boyd weathered a stormy meeting with the mayor's supporters, and in December 2002 he took his place at the GVRD. Both Boyd and Campbell considered themselves socially progressive, but each of them had a more difficult time post-election with the self-congratulatory rhetoric of those on the left than with the more thoughtful pragmatism of the political centre.

As Campbell continued his time in office, there were more positive signs of change in the Downtown Eastside. The Pivot Legal Society, a group of socially conscious lawyers doing legal work for marginalized citizens, was starting to make waves. Bud Osborn remembers saying to Ann Livingston at a VANDU meeting in the late 1990s that no great change would ever happen in their community unless they "got lawyers involved," and they later linked up with activist lawyer John Richardson, who had worked as legal counsel for the Woodward's squatters and been arrested with them when police tried to end the initial six-day-old occupation. Other progressive lawyers got involved in the planning, and eventually Richardson and Livingston formed Pivot, which at first was little more than the two of them meeting with residents of the Downtown Eastside. As the legal society grew, it targeted increasingly high-profile issues affecting vulnerable citizens: sex work, child welfare, and housing.

Pivot's most volatile cause, however, was challenging the relationship between Downtown Eastside residents and Vancouver police. In a report entitled *To Serve and Protect,* published in October 2002, Pivot had presented fifty affidavits from residents alleging they had been mistreated by officers. An RCMP investigation substantiated eleven of those complaints, though the VPD concluded none were valid after reviewing the Mounties' report. (Nine VPD officers would eventually be disciplined for not co-operating with the RCMP review, and Chief Jamie Graham would be found guilty of discreditable conduct by B.C.'s police complaint commissioner in 2007 for not ensuring better participation by his members.) The report signalled Pivot's arrival as a major player in the law and politics of the Downtown Eastside; with the mainstream vindication of Pivot's comprehensively articulated concerns, Neil Boyd says today, it became clear that the organization not only would be taken seriously by all levels of government but would be looked to for guidance and leadership in matters affecting the neighbourhood.

Pivot's concerns notwithstanding, some VPD programs and some members of the department in particular were well attuned to the community. From the late 1980s onwards, the department had adopted one of the most liberal drug policies in Canada, with officers generally ignoring personal possession of drugs and individual drug use in the Downtown Eastside; there was no way they could arrest every person they saw shooting up in an alley. Instead, enforcement efforts targeted the dealers. In the 1990s, Vancouver police became the first police department in Canada to stop responding to 911 calls about overdose deaths, leaving that to the paramedics unless public safety was at risk, so that users would be more likely to phone for help when a companion was in distress. In 2004, the department also started working with the sex-trade worker support group PACE (Prostitution Alternatives Counselling and Education) to offer self-defence training to women in the Downtown Eastside. And while some officers remained law-and-order traditionalists, others embraced harm reduction as the only answer to the mayhem.

As part of a master's degree from Simon Fraser University, Inspector Kash Heed, whose twenty-nine years with the Vancouver police included leading the city's drug and vice unit, authored a study in 2005 that showed the majority of drug dealers in the Downtown Eastside were Canadians, shattering the myth that dealers were mostly Central American immigrants. Both Neil Boyd and Larry Campbell sat on Heed's thesis examining committee, and they gave his study rave reviews. Heed's conclusions called for harsher sentences for entrenched drug dealers with many convictions but advocated treatment for their young apprentices before they, too, became committed to criminal careers. In an article published the following year in a special Vancouver section of the *International Journal of Drug Policy,* Heed wrote, "There is an increasing consensus by our officers that drug dependency is primarily a health issue rather than a legal issue... However, these same officers are frustrated with the limited treatment resources and addiction services available, despite all the attention that has been given to the Four Pillars Approach."

Heed's article, "If Enforcement Is Not Working, What Are the Alternatives?," estimated that five thousand of the city's hardcore drug addicts were responsible for about half of the crimes committed in the downtown retail and business district, as well as in the Downtown Eastside. "However, the best way to protect society is not necessarily to increase enforcement," he wrote in the article. "If that were the right course of action, the police would begin by pursuing alcohol users who cause far more aggression and misbehaviour than any other substance, licit or illicit." The answer, he said, is that all four pillars need to be adequately funded, so that officers can refer addicted, mentally ill users to treatment services, not send them to jail. "We cannot arrest our way out of the drug problem. The best way to address the drug problem is to stop people before they start. If people are using drugs, we must try to make them stop, and if we cannot make them stop, we must try to reduce the harm that it is going to bring to them, and consequently to society. This means accepting and respecting the fact that addicts are people too. They are not a lost group. They have an identity, they have stories, and they can still lead useful lives." Heed would go on to become chief of the West Vancouver police in 2007 and then B.C.'s solicitor general, after being elected as a Liberal MLA in May 2009.

In 2004, B.C.'s attorney-general had asked the Street Crime Working Group, a coalition of judges, lawyers, police officers, and government officials, to study street crime in Vancouver's downtown core. A year later, the group of heavy hitters released a report revealing that in 2003–2004 about seventy per cent of adults committing street crimes were chronic repeat offenders. "Addiction and mental illness are often contributing factors to street crime, and homelessness contributes to visible disorder," said the report, entitled *Beyond the Revolving Door: A New Response to Chronic Offenders.* The report estimated there were more than 9,000 intravenous drug users and 11,000 people with mental health issues in the Metro Vancouver area, and between 600 and 1,300 homeless people. The statistics related to contact with the justice system were startling: between thirty-five and forty offenders with mental illnesses appeared in Vancouver Provincial Court each day; seventy-four per cent of drug addicts in the Downtown Eastside had criminal records, and sixty-one per cent admitted to regularly committing crimes to pay for drugs. The situation was due, the report said, to society's failure to address underlying causes. The working group also identified a paucity of responses available to judges when dealing with chronic offenders who committed relatively minor crimes, and inadequate resources for referrals to mental health, detox, and housing resources before or during the court process.

The Street Crime Working Group recommended "not a lenient approach to crime," the report said, "but a realistic approach to long-term protection of the public. It requires a more effective system of triage so that offenders are assessed to determine which ones should go to jail and which ones are willing and appropriate for treatment. Other jurisdictions have demonstrated that focusing on the underlying causes of street crime can lead to greater protection of the public than is currently being achieved in Vancouver." The study warned, however, that the approaches would succeed only with proper funding from all three levels of government.

The municipal, provincial, and federal governments had signed the Vancouver Agreement in 2000 while Philip Owen was mayor, and it continued under Larry Campbell's administration. Those behind the agreement issued a report card in 2005, listing some of the things the three levels of government had accomplished while sitting at the same table. The list included a new program that had found jobs for about 475 Downtown Eastside residents in programs funded by the agreement. The report found the Vancouver Agreement had also backed undercover operations that targeted fifty-four stores, hotels, and pubs, resulting in sixty criminal charges for drug trafficking and welfare fraud. There had been a reduction in the number of pawn shops and second-hand stores (both of which often sold stolen goods) from forty-seven in 2000 to eighteen in 2005.

There were also advances on the health care front from 2000 onwards. Heather Hay, Vancouver Coastal Health's representative for the Downtown Eastside, had discovered that despite an overwhelming need for detox beds, the Vancouver Detox facility was often only sixty per cent full, because managers were unable to reach those on the waiting list—most people didn't have phone numbers or, in many cases, a permanent address. So in 2005 the health board established Access One, a centralized phone line people could call to inquire about detox services at all facilities, as well as the D-Talks line for youth detox services. Also that year, in conjunction with Vancouver Coastal Health, the Portland Hotel Society opened a de facto mini hospital, just a block away from Insite, to treat drug users who had been discharged from St. Paul's Hospital but still required a medical facility for more care. The Community Transitional Care Team (CTCT) provided services for patients uncomfortable with traditional hospitals who needed, for example, extended intravenous antibiotics for serious infections. The clinic was necessary, Portland's Dan Small says, because the Downtown Eastside's most problematic addicts can overwhelm hospitals with their unpredictable behaviour. Some patients also leave mainstream hospitals against medical advice, only to be readmitted later with more serious conditions.

In order to evaluate its four new health clinics, Vancouver Coastal Health contracted the B.C. Centre for Excellence in HIV/AIDS to study the medical habits of four thousand people in the Downtown Eastside under the CHASE (Community Health and Safety Evaluation) Project. Although the centre's final report, published in May 2005, found a high volume of traffic in all of the health board's four facilities, ambulance calls remained high in the Downtown Eastside, and the St. Paul's Hospital emergency room had recorded a rising number of visits. The report also noted that services like needle exchanges had higher use than programs like detox or recovery houses, a conclusion echoing that of several earlier European studies. Suggesting that abstinence-based services might attract more participants if they had fewer rules, the report proposed more health care services that operated on a drop-in basis and additional harm reduction training for health care staff to end the "discrimination" often felt by injection drug users.

Although there had been fears at the outset among business owners and residents of Chinatown, Gastown, and Strathcona that the new facilities would attract more users and, therefore, more crime, the CHASE report said Vancouver police statistics showed no major spike in crime rates between 2001 and 2004. In closing, the CHASE report praised the health board for taking "some bold steps" with their "highly successful" new facilities but concluded, "It remains to be seen how effective these programs will be in reversing the adverse health outcomes that have been gathering momentum over so many years. Clearly, for many of the long-time residents, the challenges of addiction, mental illness, and chronic physical disabilities will not be reversed through the opening of new health facilities. However, through coordinated and innovative health and social interventions, health outcomes should improve over time."

The CHASE report in 2005 confirmed what many people familiar with the issues suspected or already knew, Neil Boyd recalls. Crack use was supplanting heroin use, with more adverse health outcomes for users; the mix of substance abuse and unstable housing in the Downtown Eastside was still not being adequately addressed; and much more outreach was required for those living with HIV and Hepatitis C. The new clinics had made progress, but there was a mountain of work still to be undertaken. The need for improvement was made starkly obvious in one set of statistics contained in the CHASE report: the death rate due to alcohol in the Downtown Eastside was seven times the provincial rate, death due to drugs was twelve times that in the rest of B.C., and death due to HIV-related diseases was more than sixty times the provincial average. Antiretroviral therapy was still underutilized by HIV-positive people in the Downtown Eastside, the study said, and some who were taking the AIDS cocktail couldn't sustain ongoing delivery because of the stringent regimen the medication required.

Donald MacPherson, the city's straight-shooting drug policy coordinator, issued his own report in 2005. It focused solely on the prevention aspect of the four pillars approach, which he and others agreed most needed shoring up. *Preventing Harm from Psychoactive Substance Use* called for, among other things, a strengthening of programs that eased reintegration into the community after treatment and modernized drug laws to reduce the harm associated with drug use. The report recommended loosening the rules around cannabis, tightening rules for the chemicals used to make crystal meth, and creating a system that offered safe heroin to addicts to reduce criminalization and health risks.

MacPherson acknowledged that some would find his report's recommendations contentious, and he emphasized the need to proceed with caution. He noted, however, that some jurisdictions (Australia, the Netherlands, and many countries in Western Europe and Latin America) were considering changing or had already changed their marijuana laws. "Jurisdictions that have decriminalized cannabis... have not noticed an increase in use and have reduced enforcement costs," he wrote. As the Le Dain Commission had argued thirty-three years earlier, the enforcement of laws against simple possession "would appear to cost far too much, in individual and social terms, for any utility which it may be shown to have." The report argued that changes to certain drug laws would also lower prison populations, cut down on property crimes, free up police for more pressing matters, and create fewer opportunities for organized crime. The decriminalization of marijuana would also allow teachers and authority figures to speak realistically to young people about the consequences of pot use, MacPherson wrote, as they were able to do with alcohol and cigarettes. Ultimately, the report said, it would require courageous political leadership to make change. "If this commitment towards preventing and reducing harm from the use of drugs is achieved, Vancouver will experience reduced individual, family, neighbourhood and community harm from substance use," he wrote. "Given the serious levels of harm from problematic drug use that continue to occur in our community, this is not the time for half measures but for bold directions and committed follow through."

Mayor Larry Campbell endorsed MacPherson's strategy, saying publicly that legalizing and regulating pot would allow officials to both control the supply and "tax the living hell out of it," with tax revenues being directed to the health care system. Vancouver city councillors from both ends of the political spectrum agreed in June 2005 that it would be better to legalize marijuana than to keep bulking up the wallets of organized crime, a radical recommendation that was part of the city's proposed twenty-four-point drug-abuse prevention strategy. Prime Minister Jean Chrétien and his December 2003 successor Paul Martin, also a Liberal, both spoke publicly about reducing penalties for the possession of small amounts of marijuana. But there was also tremendous opposition from some quarters, and Conservative leader Stephen Harper travelled to Vancouver in 2005 to announce that, if elected in 2006, he would scrap Liberal plans to decriminalize small amounts of marijuana as part of the Tories' policy to crack down on drugs.

Larry Campbell had never been shy about butting heads with those opposed to the four pillars strategy. As mayor, he spurred debate in 2004 by asking, "What's the impact? What's the big deal?" in response to complaints that marijuana was being sold illegally in some Vancouver cafés. Campbell didn't condone the practice, he said, but surely there were bigger issues for city hall to target. However, it was becoming clear to him that he might not remain in place as the "courageous political leader" MacPherson's report said was needed to usher in new drug policies. Campbell's popularity ratings continued to be high—those who didn't like him at least thought he was energetic and entertaining—and he loved being mayor. But he hated being a politician, dealing with the continual stress of balancing the hopes of the left and the tax-cutting demands of the right in one of Canada's largest and most polarized cities.

By now, Campbell got along with only three of the eight COPE councillors who had swept to power with him in 2002: Jim Green, Raymond Louie, and Tim Stevenson. The divisions widened between the more radical half of the slate, dubbed COPE Classic, and Campbell and his three allies, dubbed COPE Lite, until there was a permanent break. The biggest problem, Campbell says today, was that he was a centrist; he had been elected under the banner of a left-wing political party, but he was also comfortable working with those in positions of economic power, who were often the target of COPE's attacks. His own party was Campbell's Achilles heel; he felt they were not well suited to the task of governance, more a party of protest than a party that knew what to do with political power. According to Campbell, party members never really understood that COPE's success in the election had been an endorsement more of Campbell and his hard-won pragmatism than it was of the party's policies. "The wheels started falling off 'er pretty quickly," Campbell says today. "Clearly, the inability to keep the party together was my fault, my failure. I thought I had the managerial skills to keep it together, but I had no idea about the lack of discipline within that party, even considering that I sometimes have a lack of discipline myself." In December 2004, supporters of the mayor formed a group called Friends of Larry Campbell to raise money for his re-election in 2005, along with that of Green, Louie, and Stevenson. The fledgling organization conducted a poll that showed Campbell would have seventy-two per cent voter support if he ran as an independent.

However, for about six months in late 2004 and early 2005, as Campbell fought with his fellow councillors and made the nightly rubber-chicken circuit required of the mayor, he had been ignoring pains in his chest. In February 2005 doctors discovered he had a blocked artery, forcing him to undergo heart tests and to (temporarily) quit smoking. Five months later, Campbell decided not to run again for office. "I had accomplished what I wanted," he explains today. "I had been elected on three issues: Insite, the Olympics, and the rapid transit line to the airport. And I'd accomplished all of those." (Canada Line, a rail system connecting downtown Vancouver to the airport, was under construction for more than three years and is scheduled to be up and running well in time for the 2010 Olympics.) "I wasn't taking care of myself. I was smoking too much and staying up too much. I loved the job, but I was just not made for it, because things always move so slowly in politics. The solution is obvious, but you've got to go through all this 'yada, yada, yada' to get there."

Campbell was confident the changes he had started at city hall would continue. His friend and colleague Jim Green had agreed to run for mayor with the new Vision Vancouver party, while Louie and Stevenson would run for council under the same banner. Green didn't have Campbell's charisma, though, and some feared he was too far to the left politically and would be terrible with finances. The concerns about Green's monetary capabilities stemmed from the Four Corners Community Savings Bank, a financial institution Green and the former NDP government had established in 1996 so that Downtown Eastside residents would have a user-friendly place to keep their money. The bank was forced to close in 2003 after losing $6 million. Larry Campbell argued at the time that the bank had provided an essential service and wasn't given sufficient time to get into the black. Today, he says, it is hard to dispute Green's success at finagling and financing new social housing. "People were scared of Jim Green because they saw him as a socialist, but he's not. He's likely done more developing in this town than anybody, from the point of view of social housing. I was hoping he would continue the progressiveness at city hall."

But it was not to be. At the end of a hard-fought race, during which a mayoral candidate named James Green surfaced on the ballot, Jim Green lost on November 19, 2005, in a squeaker, to NPA candidate Sam Sullivan, a long-time city councillor. "It was truly one of the most emotional nights I've ever had, because Jim took it hard. Really hard," Larry Campbell says today. "I was shocked when he lost. I was absolutely stunned." However, Louie and Stevenson, along with Heather Deal, were elected as Vision councillors, putting the new party on the political map. George Chow, who had been wooed to run under the banner of the NPA party, instead opted to run for council with Vision, and he also handily won his seat. But Campbell and many other Vision supporters are still seething over Jim Green's defeat, arguing it was a direct result of James Green's name on the ballot. Jim Green lost to Sullivan by fewer votes than James Green got in the election, leading Campbell and others to speculate that the mystery candidate had been a ploy to confuse voters, especially those who spoke English as a second language. James Green's campaign office was in the same Plaza of Nations complex as Sullivan's. Sullivan adamantly denied arranging for James Green to get that office space but did confirm he called the landlord on Green's behalf after Green received an eviction notice. James Green maintained he was just an independent candidate with a coincidental name.

So what did the future hold for the Downtown Eastside, and Campbell's beloved Vancouver? "I wasn't worried about Insite," Campbell says today, "but I was worried about some of the social housing and mental illness plans, and about forging a better link with the feds and the province." Appointed as a Liberal senator in August 2005, which occasioned a new work life in Ottawa after Sam Sullivan was sworn in as mayor in December, Campbell became even more worried when Stephen Harper's Conservatives unseated the federal Liberals in January 2006. The Liberals, although cautious, had found a way to support Insite and initiatives like the NAOMI Project, a heroin maintenance trial established in 2005. With the Tories now ensconced in Ottawa and the NPA again in city hall, would the Downtown Eastside lose many of the meagre gains it had made for its most vulnerable citizens, including the addicted, the homeless, and the women still struggling to survive on the streets?

14 | Sex Work, Safety, and Sanctuaries

SERVICES FOR WOMEN IN THE Downtown Eastside were lacking; women in general, and Aboriginal women in particular, were statistically at higher risk for HIV infection and were more likely to die without ever receiving antiretroviral therapies, according to a 2005 report signed by the CHASE Project, which evaluated medical options in the neighbourhood. "Women appear to be consistently disadvantaged when it comes to health related services," the report said. In addition, women, though more likely than men to find relatively safe housing, had lower levels of education, used heroin and crack more frequently, and experienced more physical and sexual assault.

At the time the CHASE report was published, thirty-eight per cent of the Downtown Eastside's population was female, a figure including not just women involved in drugs and/or prostitution but also impoverished single mothers living in the area because of the availability of low-cost housing. The report recommended the creation of women-only medical facilities as well as women-only hours in existing services so that women were not anxious about bumping into dealers, johns, or pimps while going to their appointments. The Vancouver Coastal Health Authority's Life-Skills Centre had established a Women's Wellness program in 2004, offering literacy, leadership building, and mentoring programs, and Tuesday nights from 5:00 to 8:30 PM were already reserved for female clients only at the Downtown Community Health Centre, where women could get meals and a variety of services. But more needed to be done, the CHASE report said. "In order to make substantial changes to the environment of risk facing women in the Downtown Eastside, societal changes are needed to ensure equal access to education, employment, and income for women, and further efforts are required to address the multitude of gender-based abuses and human rights violations currently encountered by women, especially those living in poverty."

The Vivian, a unique social housing complex, was one of the projects in place in the Downtown Eastside at the time the CHASE report was released. The twenty-four-room Vivian was opened in 2004 by Triage for at-risk, chronically homeless women. It was the first low-barrier facility in Vancouver specifically designed for women with concurrent disorders, typically mental illness and drug addiction.

The building was named after Vivian Grace Ash, whose three sons donated money for the facility following Ash's death in 1999. Ash was born in 1933 with syphilis. She was taken from her prostitute mother to be raised in foster homes, where she endured physical and sexual abuse. As a teenager, Vivian Ash lived with a supportive foster family, and in her early twenties she married a rail worker, with whom she had her sons. For about fifteen years, Ash worked as a nurse's aide and maintained a happy family life, but her behaviour became increasingly bizarre, and she was eventually hospitalized with mental illness. She ran away, grew apart from her children, and ended up on the streets, dying alone in Halifax at age sixty-six. Despite her internal pain, Ash had a spirit that never gave up, her sons say, and they wanted to financially support other women in similar circumstances.

Myrah Anderson moved into the Vivian in March 2008. She was the first of nine children born in Winnipeg to an unstable Aboriginal mother, and all of them were taken by the authorities and put into foster care or adopted. Foster care, Anderson says, was "brutal." On one night when she was fifteen, she drank her first alcohol, smoked her first pot, and lost her virginity. At age eighteen, Anderson followed a friend to Vancouver, where she supported herself by working around Commercial Drive and Hastings Street on the mid-track, where healthy, attractive women could make decent money selling sex. At first life was good. Anderson could afford to buy nice clothes, and she lived in a condominium in Vancouver's trendy False Creek area. She had a pimp who was nice to her, got her pregnant, then supported her while she had the baby. They raised the boy together until he was seven. Then, she says, things changed.

First, Anderson checked herself into detox to battle a severe dependency on alcohol. When she found out from her young son that his father had had a baby with another woman, Anderson linked up with a fellow detox patient who had fallen in love with her—and with crack. She knew nothing about crack at the time, but today she is living proof of how it can ravage a human body. The man she met "caused me to end up with nothing," Anderson says. "Every possession, everything I owned was gone. Including custody of my son." For five years she was homeless. "Sleeping on the sidewalk, at churches, at women's drop-ins. I'd sleep under bridges, I'd sleep in buildings under the stairs," she says matter-of-factly. Anderson went back to hooking to make money, but this time on the low-track near Main and Hastings. "I've been raped lots of times," she says. "I was beaten, I was robbed. I kept myself going by knowing I needed to service my craving for that next hit." After a pause, she adds, "And by knowing that something better had to happen. Life couldn't all be bad."

Off and on, Anderson went to the Triage Shelter in the Downtown Eastside to spend a night or two. "I could eat there, get changed there, wash up there. They helped me get on welfare," she says. The shelter also helped her in a life-saving way—staff there found Anderson a room at the Vivian. For the first time in years, she had some stability in her life. She continued using and hooking, but she now had a private room in a place where she was accepted regardless of her lifestyle. "It's awesome," Anderson says in describing her new home. "It's not the cleanest room, it's not the best place in the world, but it's my little hole in the wall." In the lobby of the former SRO building, women can snooze on the couches or watch TV; in the back is a laundry room and a communal kitchen. "It's sisterly, almost. We have our fights, but we look after each other," Anderson says. More importantly, the Vivian is a place where Anderson can look after herself. "I have a little bit of stability. I have a safety spot. If I'm in danger, I can come here," she says.

The Vivian has a waiting list, but it lets women in based not on how long they've been waiting but on who needs a room most. "Residents represent the most marginalized people in the community. They are disproportionately Aboriginal, HIV-infected, survival sex-trade workers with untreated mental health issues and victimized by layers of past and present violence," says literature published by RainCity Housing and Support Society (which Triage changed its name to in 2008). With the aim of helping women to get stabilized, the facility allows drug use in the building and permits women to turn tricks in their rooms—a cleaner, safer alternative to the backseat of a car or a dark alley. The small bedrooms have bar fridges, and each tenant has a private locker inside the communal kitchen. Residents share the bathrooms on the upstairs floors.

A pharmacist comes by the Vivian several times daily to give tenants with HIV their antiretroviral cocktails. Other medications, the majority of which are for mental illnesses, are distributed by the Vivian's staff. A psychiatrist regularly visits the women, as do a couple of family doctors. Nurses and social workers run a three-hour evening clinic in the Vivian one night a week, which is the best time to interact with the tenants. "A lot of the women don't live in the nine-to-five world that we live in," says Amelia Ridgway, the Vivian's soft-spoken program manager.

Jodi Loudfoot, an outreach worker with Oak Tree Clinic, a B.C. Women's Hospital program specifically for women and families affected by HIV or AIDS, is also based in the Vivian. Loudfoot has contact with eighty to one hundred women a month throughout the Downtown Eastside, most of them homeless or in precarious housing. She and other outreach workers track women down wherever they are: in rooming houses, in drop-in centres, or on the street. During the first few meetings, workers try to determine what barriers need to be knocked down for a specific woman to start receiving treatment. Following that, outreach workers can provide counselling and housing help or refer women to other services, such as dentists, government benefits, and harm reduction initiatives. Workers also arrange rides for women to the Oak Tree Clinic, but outpatient services are problematic for unstable women because of challenges with transportation and keeping appointments, Loudfoot says.

The Downtown Eastside Women's Centre, one of the longest-running services for women in the neighbourhood, has been operating for more than two decades, and an estimated three hundred women and children use the centre each day. It offers hot meals, free clothing, washrooms, toiletries, counselling, haircuts, phone and computer access, and a secure mailing address—something many women in the area don't have. The centre also runs an emergency shelter with fifty spots for women with severe addictions and mental health issues, most of whom have been rejected by other shelters because of erratic behaviour. In an interview in 2008, when she was coordinator of the women's centre, Cynthia Low said that society needs to change its values about sex work; the trade does not define who women are, she points out, but is instead an economic necessity in their lives. In the 1960s and 1970s, Low says, working women were part of "the business, the culture, the growth of this neighbourhood." Today, women talk about turning five-dollar tricks and enduring horrific abuse. Low also says single mothers in the Downtown Eastside and elsewhere need better support so that they can keep their children, rather than seeing them taken by the government. Many of the sixty-four missing women on the Vancouver police poster were mothers, though few got to raise their own children.

The horrendous statistics that prompted the Vancouver Native Health Society to start the Sheway program in the 1990s—approximately half the babies born in the Downtown Eastside were affected by their mothers using drugs, and all of those children were apprehended by Social Services—have been improving over the last decade, says Native Health executive director Lou Demerais. Sheway helps women to make better decisions by offering parenting advice, health tips, lunches, bags of groceries, clothing, and baby formula. Vancouver Native Health also operates an early childhood development program to prepare vulnerable children for elementary school, in an effort to reduce extremely high drop-out rates among Aboriginal teens.

The 2005 Street Crime Working Group report, *Beyond the Revolving Door*, said that though it was difficult to get precise information, some estimates indicated up to ninety per cent of young people being lured into prostitution were Aboriginal. The report suggested a link between the fact that half the kids in foster homes in B.C. were Aboriginal and the finding that "youth in care seem to be over-represented as victims of sexual exploitation" at some point in their lives. The report described the trend in shocking terms: "Drug traffickers target some East-side [Vancouver] elementary schools, picking and 'grooming' young Aboriginal girls and supplying them with drugs in efforts to involve them in the sex trade." One Aboriginal court worker explained how young girls became trapped in the cycle of making money and spending it on drugs to feed their addiction. It was very difficult for them to break this cycle, he told the report's authors, because their peers and "boyfriends" pressured them not to leave the lifestyle.

Aboriginal outreach worker Jerry Adams knew two of Robert Pickton's victims, Mona Wilson and Sereena Abotsway, in the years before their disappearances in 2001, and it pains him to think of their loss today. "You could just see the deterioration of those two young women as they stayed in the Downtown East-side," says Adams, who is now executive director of the Native Friendship Centre on East Hastings. "They abused drugs and got themselves into dangerous situations." Adams recalls that there were challenging times for his people with rice wine and other cheap alcohol in the 1970s and 1980s, but he says Aboriginal people in the Downtown Eastside are even more vulnerable today, owing to drugs like crack and the escalating level of violence. "It's gotten worse, the killing of women. How could people not see that, whether they are Aboriginal or not?" he asks. There is not enough acceptance, Adams says, that for some women the survival sex trade is their only way to get cash. "They have no options. That's their livelihood. That's how they make their money. And then we have these disturbed men who abuse them."

While Adams laments the loss of a reserve-style family support network for urban Aboriginal people, he hopes to recreate something akin to a reserve within the city around the Hastings and Commercial Drive neighbourhood. The Friendship Centre and other Aboriginal services are located there, about a dozen blocks east of Main and Hastings. "I believe we can get those family values back. We've got the beginning of an Aboriginal community around here that is positive," he says. "So when people get off the bus, they don't go to Main and Hastings but Commercial and Hastings." Adams has been trying for years to get government funding to build an Aboriginal youth centre across the street from the Friendship Centre; through private donations, government dollars, and fundraising, the Urban Native Youth Association now owns three lots where the centre could be built. During the time Larry Campbell was mayor, the city donated $2 million towards the purchase of one of those lots.

By the 1990s, multiple service agencies had been offering direct support to women working in the sex trade in the Downtown Eastside. While these agencies worked towards one purpose—to make women's lives safer—they often disagreed about whether that goal would be best achieved by getting rid of prostitution or by making prostitution less violent for women to practise. WISH (Women's Information Safe Haven) began in 1984 as a drop-in centre for young men and women at St. Michael's Anglican Church in the Mount Pleasant area of Vancouver. In 1987, after losing its funding from the church, WISH was offered a lifeline by the First United Church in the Downtown Eastside. The organization moved there, where it provided dinner and other services to women only. Many of the women who went missing from the Downtown Eastside had used the nightly WISH drop-in, and former employee Elaine Allan knew five of the six women Robert Pickton was eventually convicted of killing. When the drop-in's doors closed at 10 PM, Allan said in an interview in 2007, she always worried about how the women would survive the dark nights. "Everyone knew that women were going missing," said Allan, who was a witness for the prosecution at Pickton's trial. "Every night when they walked out the door I would say goodbye and I would wonder if that was the last time I'd see them." In 2003, WISH received the annual $1-million Vancity Award to support a community project, and the organization began to prepare for a move from its cramped quarters at First United Church. WISH partnered in 2004 with another Vancouver agency, PACE (Prostitution Alternatives Counselling and Education), to operate a van that offered street-work essentials such as condoms, lubricant, sterile water, alcohol swabs, clean needles, and coffee, along with kind words, every night from 10:30 PM to 5:30 AM. Through its contact with 1,200 to 1,400 women a month, WISH was instrumental in collecting information for a "bad date" sheet and passing it around to working women. PEERS (Prostitutes Empowerment Education Resource Society), founded in Vancouver in 2001, hired former sex-trade workers to run drop-in programs and offered employment services and counselling to help women who wanted to leave sex-trade work. All three organizations favour decriminalization of the sex trade.

In March 2004, Pivot Legal Society released a report called *Voices for Dignity: A Call to End the Harms Caused by Canada's Sex Trade Laws*. The report, based on first-person accounts from ninety-one sex workers in the Downtown Eastside, called for decriminalization of the adult sex trade, arguing that existing laws violated the liberty, security, and equality of sex-trade workers. (Current Canadian law is confusing: prostitution itself is legal, but communicating, i.e., making the transaction to sell sex, is not.) The report caught the attention of Irwin Cotler, federal Liberal justice minister at the time, though its recommendations were controversial. Pivot's position, says executive director John Richardson, is that the sex trade is a reality, and until that changes the profession needs to be decriminalized to improve women's health and safety. Pivot lawyer Katrina Pacey took affidavits for the report from working women, and the central theme that arose was that the women were not integrated into society because their profession was against the law. "They are left on the margins with no protection," Richardson says. "These women are so vulnerable. There are people out there who want to hurt them, and it is so easy to do right now."

His experience as both coroner and mayor convinced Larry Campbell that the laws related to prostitution needed to be revamped. As things stand, he says, the city essentially condones prostitution by licensing body rub and massage parlours. "The city is already a pimp. We are licensing these escort agencies. We're complicit in this whole thing. We decide who is going to get protection and who isn't, in the general sense. It's the clash of morality versus reality. Instead, we could protect sex-trade workers and keep them alive and healthy." However, when Campbell met as mayor with several agencies who provide support to sex-trade workers, he found they could not reach agreement on which path to take. "It was not an issue that I could resolve or deal with as mayor," he says, still frustrated today. MP Libby Davies, who also supports decriminalization, says the prostitution debate has been harder for her to navigate, as a politician, than controversial drug policies like Vancouver's supervised injection site. Davies has been attacked personally for her views and has even battled members of her own NDP caucus in Ottawa. "People go after me and say I'm encouraging sex work, but it's a reality that prostitution is there, and decriminalization is a harm reduction approach. It's more complicated than just stopping sex work," she says. As Larry Campbell's successor, Mayor Sam Sullivan championed drug maintenance programs as a way to stabilize sex-trade workers' lives, rather than changing Canada's prostitution laws. "Fixing" a problem like drug addiction wasn't realistic, he told a *Vancouver Sun* editorial board meeting in 2006, but it could be managed by dispensing drugs or drug substitutes. A controversy arose, when Sullivan was elected mayor, as a result of earlier stories by the *Sun*'s Frances Bula, who reported that Sullivan, when he was city councillor, had given a young sex-trade worker forty dollars a day for three weeks in the late 1990s to fund her heroin habit; Sullivan had also bought crack for a drug user one night in 2001 and allowed the man to smoke it in his van. Sullivan blamed his political opponents, in particular Larry Campbell, for whipping up public concern about the incidents during the 2005 municipal election campaign. In a statement he provided in 2006 to the RCMP, which was reviewing his actions, the mayor said he had "been frustrated by the terrible harm caused to drug-addicted individuals and the communities that they live in" and that he was "committed to going further in following the path of harm reduction."

Pivot examined how the legal system would best work should the courts repeal the sections of the Criminal Code that make prostitution illegal in a 2006 report called *Beyond Decriminalization: Sex Work, Human Rights and a New Framework for Law Reform.* The document considered making sex work legal using the framework of labour laws, health and safety issues, municipal bylaws, taxes, immigration, human rights, parental rights, and welfare. The report's conclusions were reached after interviews with fifty-eight women and twenty-four men who worked for escort agencies, in massage parlours, and on the street. "Criminal law reform is the first step towards...a society where sex workers are empowered to create safe and dignified working conditions," the document said. Although those working the streets hesitated to make police reports when they were beaten or raped, the report said, there was no consensus among the sex workers interviewed by Pivot on whether a specific zone for sex work would be a good idea. Some said sex work should be located in the downtown core, near adult-oriented businesses like nightclubs and strip joints. Others advocated for a red-light district strictly for sex work, located in a non-residential area. All of the sex workers interviewed felt stigmatized by the illegal nature of their work, however, and they all faced discrimination when looking for housing, visiting the doctor's office, and applying for jobs. That situation would change with amendments to the law, the Pivot report argued, and law reform should be supplemented by social and economic initiatives designed to help those wanting to leave sex work.

The Pivot Legal Society filed a constitutional challenge to Canada's prostitution laws in 2007, and a similar Charter challenge was launched in 2007 in Ontario by law professor Alan Young of York University's Osgoode Hall. The subject is highly emotional, but John Richardson believes society has become more empathetic to doing something to help sex-trade workers. "I think so, given the Pickton trial and the increase in awareness of women's safety," he says. "I think we're fooling ourselves to think Pickton is alone."

In the fall of 2008, after prolonged negotiation with neighbourhood opponents, WISH moved into its own 3,500-square-foot space in a city-owned building on Alexander Street. The drop-in serves between 3,000 and 3,500 dinners a month to its clients and offers shower facilities, clothes, personal care items, and a safe place for respite from the streets. WISH also runs a literacy program, a health and safety program specifically for Aboriginal women, and a safety night every month before Welfare Wednesday. The organization now has the room to expand its services and its hours—when it can find the money to do so. The provincial government, citing financial pressure, announced in June 2009 that it would not renew the annual funding of $250,000 for the van WISH and PACE had operated for five years, distributing condoms, clean needles, and "bad date" sheets to forty to fifty women a night. Two months later, after widespread protests, the B.C. Ministry of Public Safety and Solicitor General and the Vancouver Agreement approved three more years of funding for the van, which offers the Downtown

Eastside's only all-night support service for sex-trade workers. While Kate Gibson, WISH's executive director, acknowledges there are multiple demands on taxpayer dollars, she says this type of service needs to continue. "My feeling is the level of violence on the street hasn't changed, or it's worse," Gibson says. "We shouldn't have the marginalized people in our community be the first to be hit." A similar service was cancelled after losing its government funding in 2006. DEYAS's Health Outreach van had been staffed by a nurse and had run nightly in the neighbourhood to provide wound care, pain medication, and other medical services. Manny Cu, who until July 2009 coordinated the DEYAS needle exchange vans, used to drive the health van, and he says the service reduced visits to the St. Paul's Hospital emergency room and calls for an ambulance. The nurse in the health van also treated injuries that sex workers might not otherwise have had anyone look at. "We saw some of the worst things that could happen to people," Cu recalls.

Retired Vancouver police officer Dave Dickson, who has served on contract with the Vancouver Police Department as its sex-trade liaison worker, said that the violence women in the sex trade are willing to accept is "incredible" because of the insatiable demands created by crack cocaine. Dickson is frustrated that six years after Robert Pickton's arrest, there is still no twenty-four-hour drop-in centre where women can go for help in the middle of the night. The WISH drop-in currently closes at 10 PM, another limitation Kate Gibson is hoping to resolve through more funding. Nurses attend the WISH drop-in three times a week, but that, the women-only Tuesday nights at the Downtown Community Health Clinic, and a new women-only pharmacy opened in the Downtown Eastside in July 2009 cannot meet the health care needs for survival sex workers who are on the job late at night.

A series of studies done in 2007 and 2008 by the Centre for Excellence in HIV/AIDS concluded that survival sex-trade workers (those who exchange sex for money, drugs, or shelter as a means of basic subsistence) are at high risk of being in poor health. A large percentage reported sharing drugs with clients, only a small number infected with HIV had sought treatment, and the majority had suffered physical and/or emotional abuse in their childhoods. In interviews conducted by the Pivot Legal Society, some women said johns would pay them more money if they didn't have to wear a condom. If women were desperate enough for the money, they would agree.

Larry Campbell and Neil Boyd share the view that the best approach to the sex trade would be to decriminalize the profession and create red-light districts—safety zones. The debate is not just about prostitution, Boyd argues; it's often about desperate women selling the last thing they've got—their bodies—to feed an overwhelming addiction to illegal drugs. By ignoring that reality and maintaining the legal status quo, Larry Campbell adds, "we are allowing these women to be prey." Campbell acknowledges the position of those who say that decriminalizing prostitution further exploits already vulnerable women. "By making it non-criminal, though, and putting in controls, we could give these women safety and hope that down the road, when they are ready, they can get into addictions treatment and counselling for abuse," he says. "There is a reason why this is referred to as the oldest profession. If there was no demand, there would be no supply. If prostitution could have been shut down, it would have been done centuries ago. It's like tilting at windmills. The question now is, what do we do to change the situation?"

In December 2008, Pivot Legal Society's hopes to rewrite Canada's prostitution laws were dashed when the B.C. Supreme Court rejected their legal challenge because it had not been brought by an active sex-trade worker. The challenge had named a non-profit society of prostitutes, the members of which wished to remain anonymous owing to fears of being arrested, and former sex worker Sheryl Kiselbach. "It's ridiculous that 30 years of experience in sex work, including criminal convictions, is not enough to give me the right to challenge the prostitution laws," Sheryl Kiselbach said at the time of the court's ruling. Added Pivot lawyer Katrina Pacey: "The court seems to fail to understand the risks that sex workers face in coming out publicly. This case is about how the laws marginalize sex workers, and it is ironic the court won't even let them through the door to make the argument." The situation highlights the need for action on two fronts, Neil Boyd says: first, a public inquiry into the disappearance of sex-trade workers in the province, and, second, another constitutional challenge to prohibition that would document the horrific consequences that criminalization continues to have for those working on the streets of the Downtown Eastside.

Many questions were left unanswered by Robert Pickton's trial, and there is general agreement that conditions have not improved for sex-trade workers in the Downtown Eastside. In March 2009, the B.C. Civil Liberties Association joined with Aboriginal leaders, community groups, and family members to demand that the provincial government hold a public inquiry into the women missing from the Downtown Eastside, as well as those missing or murdered along what has become known as the "Highway of Tears" in northern B.C., the stretch of Highway 16 between Prince George and Prince Rupert. "We feel it is critically important that this inquiry into the police actions, or inaction, on these files takes place now; we should not be forced to wait until all of [Pickton's] appeals are exhausted," Grand Chief Stewart Phillip of the Union of B.C. Indian Chiefs said at the time. Added David Dennis, president of the United Native Nations Society: "Our community sees what's happening along Highway 16 as exactly what happened in Vancouver's Downtown Eastside. We can't have this tragedy of ignoring these disappearing and murdered women repeat itself—we need to break this cycle." Their demands came six months after a group of Aboriginal activists completed a march from Vancouver to Ottawa, under the banner Walk4Justice, to lobby for such an inquiry. "We're walking for women across Canada. We've got a list of over 3,000 names of missing and murdered women from the past four decades," said walk organizer Gladys Radek, whose niece Tamara Chipman vanished along the Highway of Tears.

MP Libby Davies also backs a public hearing into the missing women case, arguing that the safety of sex-trade workers still does not get the attention it deserves. "The fear was that once the Pickton trial was over, people would forget, and that happened. We need a public inquiry into how the women in the Downtown Eastside went missing, and on the police failures, because the turf wars between the Coquitlam RCMP and the Vancouver police were huge with Pickton. The system as a whole saw the victims as write-offs." What such an inquiry would likely reveal, says Larry Campbell, is that different police jurisdictions weren't communicating well with each other—something police in B.C. had vowed years earlier would never happen again. "I think that the missing women suffered from exactly the same problem as in the Clifford Olson case," Campbell says today. (Olson pleaded guilty in 1982 to killing eleven children, whose bodies he concealed in various locations in British Columbia.) "Jurisdictions were not talking to each other. I don't think it was just municipal police versus the RCMP; I think even within the RCMP there was a lack of coordination. That's exactly what Olson fed on: take the body from here and put it there. But in the case of the missing women, it was even worse. Most of the time police didn't have a time or a date a woman had gone missing, and they didn't have a body. From a police point of view, this is the worse scenario. At the same time, one has to question how Pickton managed to stay under the radar."

The joint RCMP–Vancouver police Missing Women Task Force created in 2001 was mandated only to investigate the files on missing women that pre-date Robert Pickton's 2002 arrest. Even today, relatives must report a missing woman to the police agency in the jurisdiction where she was last seen, rather than to one central unit. Larry Campbell says communication between police agencies has improved since the creation of B.C.'s Integrated Homicide Investigation Team in 2003, and the B.C. Integrated Gang Task Force, created in 2005, has brought together RCMP and municipal departments to probe major crimes across Metro Vancouver. But Campbell still argues for the amalgamation of individual police agencies across Metro Vancouver into a regional police force. It is a concept that has been debated and rejected many times over the last decade. Neil Boyd agrees with Campbell, adding that while a regional police force would likely not save a lot of tax dollars, it would increase efficiencies and improve the effectiveness of police response. The Lower Mainland is the last holdout of Canada's three major metropolitan areas; Montreal and Toronto have already embraced regional policing.

Campbell and Boyd know their argument for the decriminalization of prostitution is not popular with relatives of some of Pickton's victims or with certain social service agencies, who draw immediate correlations between sex work and danger, abuse, and death. However, both men believe there would ultimately be more benefits to women from decriminalization. "The upside is you would have a trade that could be regulated from a health point of view and a safety point of view," Campbell says. "It would give sex-trade workers rights. I don't think a whole lot of people will come out of Grade 12 and say, 'I want to be a sex-trade worker.' But it will give people trapped in that life the opportunity to address it in a health care situation. What's the down side of the way it is now? People are getting killed, raped, mugged. People are continuing to have drug problems, and there is no safety. Any time you have a low stroll, it's an invitation to killers." Vancouver's missing women case is not an isolated one, Campbell adds. Northern B.C. and Edmonton both have unsolved, high-profile cases of prostitutes and other vulnerable women being murdered, possibly at the hands of serial killers.

For his part, Neil Boyd argues that our society's history with prostitution is quite similar to our history with illegal drugs. "You push it down here and you push it over there, but it never disappears. It pops up somewhere," Boyd says. "The harder we push, the more likely we are to drive it underground—and to put the most vulnerable women, and drug users, at risk."

Two Downtown Eastside residents, Lisa Alexson and Andy Desjarlais, take part in a massive picnic in Oppenheimer Park sponsored by several local agencies in August 2000. *Rob Kruyt/Vancouver Sun*

An unidentified woman shouts to friends on the street below from the window of a Downtown Eastside rooming house in January 2001.

Peter Battistoni/Vancouver Sun

Sharon Baptiste, originally from Alberta, shoots up heroin in a back alley in the Downtown Eastside in February 2001. *Ian Smith/Vancouver Sun*

After a toke of crack cocaine, a young female addict sits in an alley doorway off Main and Hastings in February 2001. *Ian Smith/Vancouver Sun*

At a Senate hearing on illegal drugs held in Vancouver in November 2001, Mayor Philip Owen holds the four pillars document, written by city hall's Donald MacPherson (*right*). *Ian Lindsay/Vancouver Sun*

During his campaign in November 2002 to become mayor of Vancouver, Larry Campbell hands out hot dogs to residents at Main and Hastings. *Glenn Baglo/Vancouver Sun*

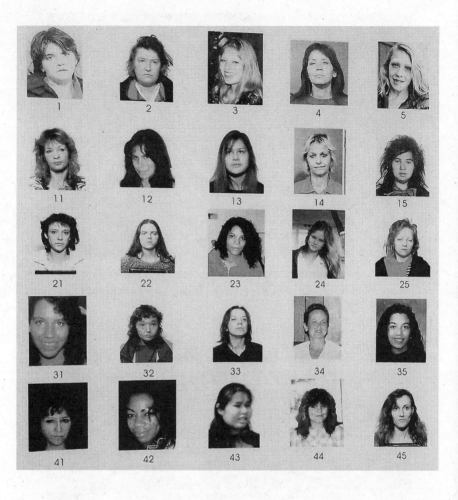

There were forty-eight faces on the police poster of missing women in
February 2002 when serial killer Robert "Willie" Pickton was arrested.

Bill Keay/Vancouver Sun

John Turvey is seen here in February 2003, while he was executive director of DEYAS, the Downtown Eastside Youth Activities Society.

Glenn Baglo/Vancouver Sun

Former VANDU board member Don Baker (*left*), former VANDU president Bryan Alleyne, and PHS's Liz Evans in February 2003, inside the injection site secretly built before government approval was received. *Peter Battistoni/Vancouver Sun*

People congregate in Pigeon Park. The unsanctioned injection site next to the park opened in the summer of 2003, after delays in getting Insite into operation. *Richard Lam/Vancouver Sun*

NDP MLA Jenny Kwan (*left*) and NDP MP Libby Davies discuss the lack of facilities for homeless people in the Downtown Eastside in December 2005. *Mark van Manen/Vancouver Sun*

Downtown Eastside residents share Christmas dinner at the
Salvation Army's Harbour Light centre on East Cordova in 2007.

Ward Perrin/Vancouver Sun

City hall housing advocate Judy Graves talks to a woman on the streets of Vancouver about health and housing in July 2007. *Don MacKinnon/Canwest*

D.J. O'Brien passes out popcorn to other female clients during one of the "beauty nights" at the Downtown Eastside's LifeSkills Centre in February 2008.

15 | NAOMI and the Fight to Save Insite

THE CITY'S FOUR PILLARS REPORT was "thrown to the wind" during Sam Sullivan's tenure as mayor of Vancouver, Larry Campbell says today. The ten-block stretch of the Downtown Eastside had been a Canadian leader in harm reduction, but Campbell says not enough was done under his successor to shore up the other elements of the four pillars plan. In an interview with the *Vancouver Sun* in April 2006, the new mayor explained he believed more should be invested in harm reduction than in the other three pillars—enforcement, treatment, and prevention—and mused about a program that would provide a wide range of free drugs to addicts as a way of reducing crime and public disorder. He supported more prevention and treatment, he told the *Sun*, "but I think we have to be honest with ourselves that that is not going to solve the problem." Larry Campbell, who was appointed to the Senate by the Liberals in 2005, dismissed Sullivan's approach as "simplistic," arguing that handing out drugs, especially potent stimulants, could not stabilize people without accompanying treatment and housing. Some advocates for sex-trade workers and drug addicts gave Sullivan's idea cautious support, applauding his political courage, but even they felt the concept would need to be accompanied by more support services. As he had done as mayor, Campbell also argued drug maintenance programs should be reserved for those addicts who couldn't be treated through more traditional programs.

In February 2007, Mayor Sullivan unveiled a plan called CAST (Chronic Addiction Substitution Treatment) that he said would focus on providing prescription drug substitutes to addicts. The InnerChange Foundation, headed up by former Conservative MP John Reynolds, was established to initiate clinical research trials into the CAST approach. Sullivan had attracted some heavy-hitters to the foundation's board, including doctors, businesspeople, and politicians of various stripes, and he said the organization would be seeking Health Canada approval to launch clinical trials that fall. But Sullivan's plans to provide crack and crystal meth users with more politically acceptable stimulants developed by the pharmaceutical industry were not well thought out, according to Neil Boyd; there was no evidence that such stimulant maintenance would work effectively and, most significantly, no credible data to suggest that users would abandon the quick highs of crack for longer-lasting pharmaceutical stimulants.

Campbell, Boyd, and Sullivan all supported a more focused project called NAOMI, however. Started in Vancouver in 2004, NAOMI was an experimental trial, the first of its kind in Canada, established to measure the impact of providing injectable heroin to addicts.

Dr. Martin Schechter of the University of British Columbia was the person behind NAOMI, the North American Opiate Medication Initiative. Schechter wanted to study whether giving heroin to entrenched drug users would be more effective than providing them with methadone, both in improving the psychological and social functioning of addicts and in reducing their involvement in crime. NAOMI was originally envisioned as involving six cities, three in Canada and three in the United States; however, all of the American cities later dropped out because they couldn't get funding for the controversial experiment. Montreal started its trials shortly after Vancouver's, but Toronto withdrew from the study because of timing issues and a failure to recruit a sufficient number of injectable heroin addicts. It was a slow battle to secure funding in Canada, but in 2002 the Canadian Institutes of Health Research provided $8.1 million. Schechter, who specializes in HIV/AIDS, addiction research, and the health of inner-city residents, expected his project would demonstrate what similar European studies had shown: that crime rates drop and addicts become more stable when they get heroin from a doctor instead of a dealer or a pimp.

Skeptics saw NAOMI as the next progression in a series of wacky harm reduction ideas: first you gave addicts needles, then you gave them a place to shoot up, and now they'd be getting their dope for free. The most vociferous opponents of NAOMI were the residents of a recently built, upscale development on Keefer Street, on the edge of the Downtown Eastside, that was home to the Chinese Community Policing Centre and other services for the Chinese community. These residents feared that a heroin maintenance program would create a honey-pot effect, bringing drug dealers and users into the neighbourhood, even though all heroin supplied would be used inside the project's clinic. But by mid-2005, the concerns of the new residents had disappeared; the presence of NAOMI had become a non-event, and it remained so until the trial's conclusion, Neil Boyd says.

One of the many procedural hoops researchers had to jump through to have the project approved was getting the go-ahead from the federal Liberals to hand out an illicit drug. The trials led by Schechter and nine other researchers were scheduled to run for three years, with final reports planned for 2008. The easiest part of the project, Schechter had assumed, would be finding addicts who wanted to participate, but the phone line researchers set up to take volunteers' names barely rang. Drug users, it turned out, were suspicious of the study, in particular the requirement that they make their medical histories available to researchers. There were also strict parameters governing the selection of participants, such as their not having responded in the past to any kind of drug treatment; being hard-core users for at least five years; having injected heroin every day for the previous year but not having recently used methadone; not being on probation or facing criminal charges; and living within 1.6 kilometres of the project's Downtown Eastside location. Three-quarters of the people who eventually signed up for the study didn't meet the guidelines, and it took a year longer than expected to get enough addicts on board to start the project. The total number of participants was also smaller than researchers had set out to find: 192 in Vancouver and 59 in Montreal, the Canadian cities with the most serious heroin problems.

An analysis of those accepted into the study found that, on average, they had been injecting drugs for 16.5 years. All used heroin nearly every day, commonly supplementing it by smoking crack cocaine. The participants had severe health and social problems, including precarious housing and regular unemployment. As the final assessment of the project would report, at the time of their initial involvement "participants [had] spent a median of 15 days involved in illegal activities out of the prior 30 days and spent a median of $1,500 on acquiring drugs in the same time period."

During staggered twelve-month testing periods, 115 people were given medical-grade heroin, a control group of 111 received oral methadone, and 25 subjects got injectable Dilaudid, a pharmaceutical sold as a very potent painkiller. Those receiving heroin and Dilaudid weren't told which drug they were getting.

Participants were required to show up two or three times a day at the newly opened NAOMI clinic at Abbott and Hastings to receive the drugs and were monitored before and after the injections. Those getting oral methadone came to the clinic once a day to pick it up. When necessary, research staff tracked down participants in jails and hospitals to keep them involved in the project. In response to neighbourhood concerns that the NAOMI clinic would create more street disorder, a hotline was established to log complaints, but it received not a single call. "Once people got stabilized by these treatments, they were very orderly," Schechter says.

Elsewhere in the Downtown Eastside, Canada's first supervised injection site had progressed from the starting-up pains of 2003 and 2004 to become a service that was an essential part of the health care system. The facility had seven thousand registered users by 2006 and recorded, on average, hundreds of visits per day. Staff nurses had intervened in hundreds of overdoses and provided other medical treatment. Clients had been referred to addiction counselling, hospitals, housing, and other services. Frequent referrals had also been made to Onsite, the detox facility on the building's second floor. The fact that clients frequently relapsed and had to go through Onsite multiple times was presented by critics as proof the program didn't work, but the Portland Hotel Society's Mark Townsend argued that Onsite's success rate was the same as, if not better than, that of other detox facilities, even those run by organizations that shunned harm reduction in favour of abstinence. Neil Boyd agreed. "He's right," Boyd said at the time. "That's what the best scientific literature tells us."

Vancouver's supervised injection site suffered a setback with the election of the new Conservative government in Ottawa in 2006, however. Insite's three-year exemption from Canada's narcotic laws, granted by the Liberals, expired on September 12 of that year, and it was only under duress that the Conservatives agreed to piecemeal extensions as they dithered about what to do. Prime Minister Stephen Harper's government fussed about the "enabling" nature of Insite, complaining the program was nothing more than a state-sanctioned drug den. The International Narcotics Control Board, a United Nations drug control agency strongly supported by the United States, urged the Conservatives to shut the facility down, arguing that Canada was flouting international drug control treaties by permitting illicit drug use at the site. According to Neil Boyd, the allegation was incorrect, because exemptions from criminal law for the express purpose of protecting public health are consistent with both domestic and international law. Nonetheless, the Conservatives cited the charge in voicing their objections.

Supporters rallied to the cause. Since its inception, Insite's allies had come up with creative ways to raise public awareness about keeping the site open—erecting hundreds of crosses in a park in 2006 to represent the estimated number of clients who overdosed at Insite but were saved by the medical staff and stopping traffic with five hundred protesters at one of Toronto's busiest intersections during the 2006 International AIDS Conference. Community activists, nurses' organizations, scientists, health researchers, and municipal politicians lobbied the Conservatives to keep Insite open. Vancouver mayor Sam Sullivan, himself a fan of Insite, argued that the city needed more facilities like it; to close Vancouver's only supervised injection site, he told reporters in 2006, would be a step backwards for the city's most needy citizens. Premier Gordon Campbell, a political ally of Harper's, in this case stood with those in favour of the controversial site, urging Ottawa not to close it, as did provincial health minister George Abbott. "[Insite] is part of the solution," the premier told the *Vancouver Sun* in October 2007. "I think that it's actually been a facility and a service that's made a difference."

Research on Insite had been published in the most prestigious peer-reviewed journals in the English-speaking world—the *Lancet*, the *New England Journal of Medicine*, the *American Journal of Public Health*, and others. The research was remarkable in its scope, pointing, among other things, to increased use of detox services in the year following Insite's arrival in Vancouver, decreased risk of HIV infection for Insite users, reductions in high-risk injection practices by those attending Insite, and reductions in drug injection in public places and the resulting street litter of syringes and other injection debris. These were all correlations, not actual demonstrations of cause and effect relationships, Neil Boyd points out, but they were suggestive of a positive pattern of change.

Not convinced by that impressive body of research, the Conservatives called in early 2007 for more research on the supervised injection site; they were particularly interested in assessing the impact of Insite on crime and public order. Neil Boyd put in a research bid, and the government's expert advisory committee recommended that his work be funded. The executive summary to Boyd's report on Insite, which was completed in February 2008, closed with the comment, "In sum, there is no compelling evidence to suggest that Insite has had a negative impact on public order, and, more specifically, there is no evidence to suggest that Insite has had any significant impact on either the rate or spatial distribution of criminal activity within the neighbourhood. There is evidence, however, that a clear majority of our sample of people who live and/or work in the neighbourhood view Insite as making a positive contribution to public order, and would like to see the service expanded, retained, or modified." Although Boyd's research was unequivocally supportive of Insite, using police data as its major source of information, the federal government stood firm in its resistance.

Faced with such uncertainty about Insite's future, the

Portland Hotel Society reluctantly decided in August 2007 to file a lawsuit against the federal government—a scary gamble, says Dan Small. The society and addicts Shelly Tomic and Dean Wilson said in their statement of claim to the B.C. Supreme Court that the closure of Insite would violate drug users' Charter rights to "security of the person" and said without it users would face "risk of death or serious harm to their physical and mental health." The federal government, for its part, argued that Insite should be closed for a variety of reasons, including that addicts' lives were endangered because they were injecting a harmful drug and that Insite created "a safe haven from the criminal law and undermine[d] its national objective and importance."

Justice Ian Pitfield's ruling in the B.C. Supreme Court on May 27, 2008—three days before the government's final Criminal Code exemption period was set to expire—was an unequivocal endorsement of the site, going further than the Portland Hotel Society had ever dreamed possible. Pitfield ruled that Canada's trafficking and possession laws were unconstitutional when applied to addicts using the site, and he concluded that the site should remain open for another year, even without an exemption from existing drug laws. During that year, Justice Pitfield said, the federal government should rewrite its laws to allow for the medical use of illegal drugs as part of a health care program. Pitfield made it clear in his decision that science and medical opinions were divided on how to treat addiction. However, he added, that didn't mean those who were addicted should be denied a form of health care treatment.

The Conservatives appealed the court decision, leaving Insite in limbo. Today, however, Dan Small says, Insite has even more vocal supporters than it had in the past, including politicians who initially did not endorse it. "This court ruling was a sea change," he argues. His colleague Liz Evans agrees, but she is frustrated that the fight for Insite must continue when there

are so many other battles to be waged in the Downtown Eastside. "It annoys me that there is so much work to do," Evans says,
"and here we are fighting to keep something open that we started
working towards in 1997. Most officials just don't understand
what life is like for addicts in the neighbourhood."

Although the Vancouver Police Department partnered with
the Portland Hotel Society and Vancouver Coastal Health to
establish Insite, the RCMP never supported the site. In October
2008, Pivot Legal Society released emails it had obtained through
freedom of information requests revealing that the Mounties had
commissioned and paid for negative studies on Insite, including
one produced by anti–harm reduction activist Colin Mangham
that concluded the facility had not reduced the number of overdose deaths, the level of public disorder, or the spread of disease.
Federal health minister Tony Clement's reference to Mangham's
report as evidence that scientific research was divided on the merits of Insite prompted eighty-five prominent Canadian scientists
to write a sharply worded open letter demanding the country's
political leaders stop misrepresenting the issues.

According to the B.C. Coroners Service, there have been
approximately fifty deaths from illicit-drug overdoses each year
in Vancouver since the opening of Insite in September 2003.
Those figures mean that while the annual number of fatal overdoses has not decreased since Insite opened, it has also not gone
up. Opponents of Insite point out that only about five per cent of
Downtown Eastside drug users are regular visitors to the supervised injection site and argue there is no evidence more lives are
being saved. Tom Stamatakis, president of the Vancouver Police
Union, believes that Insite is a "failed experiment." He has not
seen proof on the street that the site has meaningfully reduced
public disorder, Stamatakis says; marginalized people still "fix
thirty feet from the site." He also questions whether the stabilization of crime rates in the neighbourhood is a function of Insite or

of the extra Vancouver police officers that city hall agreed to pay for in 2003. After all, the way most addicts get their drugs is by breaking the law, Stamatakis argues, and a government-funded injection site seems to condone that behaviour by giving them a place to shoot their illegally obtained dope.

Stamatakis, who is also vice-president of the Canadian Police Association, agrees that drug addiction is a medical matter, not a criminal one. "We are not somehow going to arrest our way out of this issue," he admits, and he thinks some harm reduction is necessary to stabilize addicts before they can be effectively treated. However, he argues current medical research is not sufficient to conclude how many people have been helped by Insite and/or Onsite to get off drugs and says much more emphasis needs to be put on education, prevention, and treatment. For example, he supports legislative changes that would allow judges to sentence addicts to treatment instead of jail. The detox and recovery beds above the supervised injection site, Stamatakis says, aren't the same as long-term treatment, and new treatment centres need to be created outside of the Downtown Eastside; that way, when a recovered addict is released, the first person he or she bumps into isn't a drug dealer. "I'm not going to say Insite is the cause of all the problems, because the problems were here before it was. But it's a stretch to say [the site has] solved any problems," Stamatakis says.

Larry Campbell insists Insite was "never meant to be a silver bullet that would clean up the Downtown Eastside," and that even its small successes should be celebrated. If five per cent of the city's injection drug users frequent the site, he says, then that's five per cent fewer people sharing dirty needles or using toilet water to fix. And though more than four hundred people overdosed inside the site between its opening in 2003 and mid-2006, not one person died. Even one fewer death a year, Campbell says, is significant. For Neil Boyd, the figure of five per cent use speaks to a need for additional options—more facilities in the Downtown Eastside and elsewhere to increase the margins of safety for injection drug users. What many critics miss, Boyd says, is that the alternative to Insite is not abstinence. Without the site, its current clients would be joining the other drug users who are injecting beside dumpsters, overdosing without medical aid, and sharing needles—along with HIV and Hepatitis C—in rundown hotel rooms.

Campbell says that even if the appeal court ultimately rules in favour of the Conservatives, there is no reason Insite couldn't continue to operate without the Criminal Code amendment, especially considering that addicts aren't arrested now for openly injecting on Vancouver streets. "If you're not going to arrest the people shooting up in the alleys, why would you arrest them in a safe site?" Campbell asks. "What the Conservatives don't understand is that this is just one harm reduction tool we've got down here. It's just one element trying to keep people alive and disease free until, hopefully, they go into treatment."

Chuck Parker, one of the drug users who lived above Insite early on, believes the facility, as well as the detox and recovery beds upstairs, will lead to more success stories, because users will make better choices. "When you initially start using drugs, it's an action of choice," he says, "but that goes away with addiction, and then it becomes a medical issue. At times I didn't have that choice to put a needle in my arm." The long-time Downtown Eastside resident has seen fewer people injecting in the streets since Insite opened. He has also witnessed fewer incidences of dangerous practices like "jugging," which addicts typically resort to when their arms are too scabby or scarred for them to find a vein with the needle. "You no longer see people lying on bus benches, with someone else shooting directly into their jugular," Parker said, pointing to a penny-sized scar in the crook of his left arm that at one time was completely scabbed over.

Parker started taking methadone in 2006 to kick his heroin habit, and he believes Insite played a psychological role in helping him get more stable. But much more than a supervised injection site is needed to make his neighbourhood a healthier place, he says. "Not any single thing will fix it. But things like Insite will give people hope."

Another provider of hope, advocates argue, was the NAOMI project. The final report on the NAOMI study, entitled *Reaching the Hardest to Reach—Treating the Hardest-to-Treat,* was released in October 2008. The study measured both the retention rates of participants (whether they were still involved in the study after twelve months) and their treatment response (whether participants had reduced by at least twenty per cent their involvement in illicit drug use and criminal activity). The outcome was not surprising to anyone familiar with this kind of research, says Neil Boyd: the retention rates were higher (87.8 per cent) for participants receiving heroin than for those getting the oral methadone (54.1 per cent), as were the treatment response rates (67 per cent for those receiving heroin versus 48 per cent for those getting methadone). And 63.5 per cent of participants injecting heroin achieved both the retention and treatment response outcomes, while only 35 per cent of those getting methadone did. Generally, the physical and psychological health of all participants improved. Researchers were also intrigued that the results for the people taking Dilaudid were the same as for those getting heroin. Both maintenance heroin and Dilaudid stabilized participants' lives over the course of the study; to a lesser extent so did methadone, as long as it was prescribed in proper doses and with user-friendly rules. "A population of very severely affected people, who have not benefited from treatment in the past—what many might call the hardest core, whom society has dismissed as beyond help and write-offs—can get themselves into treatment and positively affect their lives," lead researcher Dr. Martin Schechter says today.

But while the results of the NAOMI project were encouraging, the final outcome was not. When the trial ended in June 2008, government funding stopped. Earlier that spring, Schechter had applied to the federal Conservatives for permission to continue to distribute heroin on a compassionate basis but was turned down. Following that decision, study participants were offered help with getting into treatment programs and/or obtaining methadone prescriptions. Some accepted; others did not. According to Martin Schechter, "Of the people who did not, the bulk of them relapsed into street life. It was tough for everyone, including the staff... They would see former clinic people not doing well while walking to work in the morning."

NAOMI's former clinic at Abbott and Hastings has been renovated, and Martin Schechter has approached the B.C. Ministry of Health for $1.5 million in annual funding to open the clinic on a permanent basis to provide two hundred people with proper doses of methadone. Many doctors currently give out watered-down methadone, Schechter says, because they fear it will take patients longer to get off the prescription otherwise, but the doses are so weak they don't suppress heroin cravings. Some doctors also withhold methadone if a patient tests positive for recent heroin use, which Schechter argues is the wrong tactic. If Schechter gets the approval he has requested from the B.C. College of Physicians, the new clinic could also prescribe Dilaudid as a form of heroin replacement, though first he'd like to see more trials conducted on the drug's effectiveness. Funding this type of clinic, which could offer access to the same support services given to the NAOMI participants—social workers, addiction counsellors, outreach teams, health care, and the dispensing of psychiatric and HIV medications—would save the provincial government money in the long run, Schechter maintains. By a conservative estimate, a heroin addict currently costs society sixty thousand dollars a year in medical, legal, and social costs. For two hundred addicts, that's a $12-million price tag, so a $1.5-million clinic would create "a ninety per cent savings," he says. Schechter has also applied again to the federal government for permission to distribute heroin, but he knows that will involve a long regulatory process. "I think I was a little bit more optimistic a few years ago, when there was more enthusiasm [about harm reduction] from governments. Now there is a bit of a chill," Schechter says. "But the pendulum swings. It's clear to most observers, I think, that what we're doing now isn't working. I think we *will* begin approaching this as a health problem."

16 | Housing Vancouver's Poor

AT ONE POINT IN HER LIFE, Theresa Myles was someone you might have seen sleeping in a doorway, a rain-soaked bag of belongings by her side. Those were the grim days, when Myles kept herself safe by staying up all night, watching her back so she didn't get robbed or attacked. A warm, open woman, Myles was born in Halifax to a heroin-addicted mother, but she went on to study at university, work in an office, and perform as a dancer. She battled with depression, though, and after moving to B.C. in the 1980s she lived in progressively worse places until she became homeless. "I slept in the daytime and roamed around at night. I slept in underground parking lots with heating and no security guards. I slept on the street. I was dead broke," the fifty-seven-year-old Myles recalls today. She didn't go hungry because of services in the Downtown Eastside that offered free meals, but there were other complications—like smoking more and more heroin. "I started chasing the dragon to get through it, and then it started chasing me. When you're doing good, you can handle it. But it's like quicksand when you're doing bad." Yet poverty is the true crime in the neighbourhood, Myles argues, not addiction.

In 2003, Myles moved into the Princess Rooms, a former SRO bought by Triage Emergency Services & Care Society in 2001 and renovated with a grant from the federal Liberals. Triage's goal was to provide rooms for forty-four chronically homeless people who were regularly in and out of its shelter but were too erratic for more traditional social housing. The investment made sense, the society believed, because such hard-to-house people were racking up big hospital, police, and shelter bills. "At the shelter, you saw people at the bottom of their cycle all the time," says Bill Briscall, who co-managed the Princess Rooms from 2001 to 2006. "At the Princess, you could see the change."

The low-barrier facility was staffed twenty-four hours a day by a team of health care workers who assisted the tenants physically, mentally, and emotionally. If residents were disruptive, staff tried to figure out what set them off—a psychosis? a drug-induced seizure?—to avoid a repeat of the situation. At times the solutions were so unusual they could never have been anticipated. For instance, some drug-addicted tenants picked away at the plaster in their rooms until they'd made massive holes in the walls, so six units in the building were given reinforced walls, and the plumbing and wiring were also protected. Still operating today, the Princess is not a castle, and it is certainly not ideal long-term housing. The rooms are tiny, the bathrooms are communal, and no guests are allowed in the building, in an effort to reduce the chaos inside. But the Princess Rooms gave Theresa Myles stability in the Downtown Eastside. "I love the neighbourhood," she says today. "I feel like these are the people I know. I feel like there's a pulse down here."

A year after finding housing at the Princess Rooms, Myles was selected by Headlines Theatre artistic director David Diamond to be one of six local residents to star in an interactive play, *Practicing*

Democracy, a means of using theatre to communicate with government. Myles was so determined to get the $550 gig that she lied ("Act? Sure, I've acted before!") on her application. The theatre company had been founded in 1981 by Diamond and other Vancouver artists including Nettie Wild, the filmmaker who later made FIX, out of their concern about the city's housing crisis. Headlines Theatre's first play, *Buy, Buy Vancouver*, captured the attention of then–Vancouver mayor Mike Harcourt (who would later become B.C.'s premier), and Harcourt arranged for it to be performed in Ottawa at a federal conference on housing. Theresa Myles played a sometime prostitute in *Practicing Democracy*, a story about how profoundly the real-life welfare cuts introduced by the provincial Liberals in January 2002 were affecting the poor. The government's rationale for the cuts was that the ministry was shifting its focus to getting welfare recipients into the workforce, but the sweeping reductions hit everyone hard, especially single parents, low-income seniors, and the homeless.

Practicing Democracy debuted in March 2004, and in keeping with the approach Headlines had developed, at each performance the play was done twice. The first round was performed by the actors, chosen because their own experiences mirrored the plot lines; during the second round, audience members were invited to replace characters in the play to help create solutions to some of the conflicts identified. The solutions arising from *Practicing Democracy* were summarized in a report sent to Larry Campbell while he was mayor, since city council had voted unanimously to consider them. "The outcome of the process will be a valuable contribution as we deliberate on future actions related to these issues," Campbell wrote in a letter to Headlines. Looking back today, he says, "We were continually looking at ways to engage people who were actually experiencing the difficulties." In the end, the group made ninety recommendations to council regarding housing, safety, and social services.

According to the Metro Vancouver homeless count, organized every three years by the Greater Vancouver Regional Steering Committee on Homelessness, the minimum number of homeless people in Vancouver doubled between 2002, when there were 630, and 2005, when there were 1,300. The estimates were reached by volunteers physically counting the number of people they encountered on the streets, in parks, in food lines, in temporary shelters, and at other locations. The numbers were considered conservative, because the volunteers couldn't possibly find everyone. Things were so bad by 2005, Larry Campbell remembers, that tent cities regularly popped up in parks or in vacant lots in the downtown area. Although there were some troublemakers in the camps, Campbell says the inhabitants were mainly unemployable, mentally ill, and addicted people. It was a conundrum: many business owners and other residents wanted the unsightly, potentially dangerous camps removed, but where was the city supposed to put these people?

"In Vancouver, housing has not kept pace with the need to provide stable and supportive housing for people with addiction problems," a 2001 Vancouver city hall report had found. "The social housing that has been built usually does not include funding for support services... Many of the hotel rooms are unstable and are clearly unsuitable for long-term accommodation... The health of SRO residents often deteriorates the longer they live under these conditions." While Larry Campbell was mayor, the city adopted the Homeless Action Plan, which identified the need to develop 8,000 units of social housing in Vancouver by 2015, including 3,800 units of supportive or transitional housing. During the time Campbell was at city hall, council also passed a bylaw requiring SRO owners to pay a fee of five thousand dollars per room if they wanted to demolish old hotels or convert them to tourist use. Although the plan riled hotel owners, who argued they shouldn't have to pay to change the focus of their own buildings, the city stood firm. Campbell says he would have made the conversion fee for SRO owners as high as forty thousand dollars per room if he could have increased it single-handedly; the higher fee would have meant the city could simply replace any SRO hotel they were losing by building a new one. Hotel owners could have afforded the higher fee, Campbell argues, because real estate values had skyrocketed in the area.

In June 2007, Vancouver mayor Sam Sullivan bumped the conversion fee for SRO owners to fifteen thousand dollars per room. Since his election, though, Neil Boyd says, Sullivan's plans for responding to homelessness were largely rhetorical and lacking in specifics. In November of 2006, Sullivan announced an initiative called Project Civil City, which he claimed would reduce crime and public disorder by cracking down on the open drug trade, "aggressive panhandling," and homelessness—which the mayor pledged to reduce by fifty per cent by the time of the Olympic Winter Games in 2010. Six months later, former B.C. Liberal attorney-general Geoff Plant was appointed as Project Civil City's coordinator. But the program was widely criticized for its emphasis on bylaw enforcement and other "crackdown" measures favoured by the Vancouver Board of Trade. Many individuals and organizations in the Downtown Eastside saw it simply as a move to get poor people off the street. "What kind of legacy is a year or two of bylaw enforcement?" asked David Eby of the Pivot Legal Society. "It's not a solution to the poverty issues down here. Increased enforcement is at odds with harm reduction initiatives." While the new mayor clearly wanted to address homelessness—it had been a critical part of his inaugural speech—he was pulled in many different directions, and he ultimately leaned towards the provincial and federal governments rather than making substantive commitments of his own, Neil Boyd says.

Various organizations in the Downtown Eastside continued to try to address the housing shortage. Among them was the

Lookout Emergency Aid Society, which had started in 1971 with a shelter for older, chronic street alcoholics. Funded by governments, service clubs, and donations, the agency later opened the Living Room Activity Drop-in Centre, which approximately 125 mentally ill people visited each day. From there, the society grew to operate 107 beds in its three emergency shelters, about 150 transitional housing rooms, and several long-term housing facilities, including the thirty-seven-room Jeffrey Ross Residence. Lookout opened fifty-six extra shelter beds in the winter, but demand remained so high that the organization routinely turned people away—several hundred a year in the 1990s, and several thousand a year in 2000 and beyond.

Triage Emergency Services & Care Society, which became RainCity Housing and Support Society in 2008, expanded to multiple locations with 350 shelter, transitional, and long-term beds. Bill Briscall, who today is RainCity's communications manager, was a student needing a job in 1991 when he started working in the neighbourhood, initially at the Lookout Emergency Aid Society. Back then, Briscall says, most of the people needing assistance with mental health problems had just been released from institutions or hospitals, and many were in an almost catatonic state from years of taking medications. Following their release, people became more erratic, their problems exacerbated by the shift many made from psychiatric medications or heroin dependency to crack cocaine and crystal meth. Today, the Triage Shelter has set up two outreach projects aimed at helping these desperate people: a concurrent disorders team that finds people in alleys, hooks them up with services, and routinely checks on their progress, and a housing team that tries to find space in SROs and other rooms to get people off the streets.

The comprehensive report on housing in the Downtown Eastside produced in 2007 by Jill Davidson, city hall's senior housing planner, showed that the number of SRO rooms in the downtown core had fallen from 13,412 in 1970 to 5,985 in 2007. During that time, her report said, one-person rooms in non-market buildings (better facilities run by the provincial government or non-profit agencies, many with crucial support services) had increased twenty-fold, from 256 to 5,386. Even with the new facilities, however, the total number of low-income single rooms available in the neighbourhood had dropped from 13,668 in 1970 to 11,371 in 2007. That loss of 2,297 units was significant, considering that the population in the Downtown Eastside had increased by 140 per cent between 1991 and 2007, many of the new arrivals vulnerable people searching for affordable shelter, services, or drugs. The vacancy rate in low-income buildings was at two per cent in 2007, the lowest it had been in recent history. According to Davidson's report, one reason for that low vacancy rate was an influx of students and employed single people (including construction workers building Olympic venues) filling rooms traditionally lived in by welfare recipients, a change driven by the low availability of rental housing elsewhere in the city and high costs in the conventional rental market. Another reason, Davidson wrote, was an Outreach pilot project run jointly by Vancouver city hall and the province. By June 2007, an estimated five hundred people had been plucked off the streets and given shelter, with a retention rate of about seventy-five per cent.

The woman behind the Vancouver Homeless Outreach Pilot Project was Judy Graves, coordinator of Vancouver city hall's tenant assistance program. Graves had come up with the idea after witnessing an explosion of homelessness that she traced not only to the lack of affordable housing but also to the B.C. Liberal government's January 2002 decision to both reduce the number of people eligible for welfare and increase the amount of time new applicants had to wait before receiving benefits. Subsequently, Graves says, there were two new groups of people on the street: those who had lost their jobs and couldn't get employment insurance, and those who had lost welfare and couldn't pay their rent. "In the summer of 2002, we saw homelessness on the streets of Vancouver like we'd never seen it before," she remembers. From there, things only got worse. There was initially no interest from Victoria in her idea.

The provincial Liberal government was no champion for the homeless during its first term in office, from 2001 to 2005. Gordon Campbell and Larry Campbell fought with each other over the issue in the media, with the premier saying the city had brought on its own homelessness problems by not enforcing bylaws that prohibited the conversion of SROs into market housing. The mayor fired back: "What the hell has [the premier] done to help the people who are suffering from mental illness? What's he done for those people who cannot find jobs? What's he done for the economy?"

But when the Liberals were re-elected for a second term in May 2005, there was a shift in some government policies, as Premier Gordon Campbell surrounded himself with pragmatic and more socially progressive cabinet ministers, such as Carole Taylor in finance and Wally Oppal as attorney-general. Judy Graves recalls getting a phone call that September from staff at the provincial housing ministry, asking if she had any suggestions for addressing the crisis in homelessness. Of course she did. She blew the dust off a proposal the Liberals had rejected two years earlier, and this time her Vancouver Homeless Outreach Project was accepted. Each weekday Graves would pick two homeless people, take them to the welfare office to get signed up for benefits, and find them rooms. The government, for its part, would fast-track those people back onto welfare and exclude them from the three-month wait for payments to kick in. Starting in October 2005, Graves and a volunteer met each weekday at 6 AM at a street corner where homeless people congregated. Many were too high by midday to take to the welfare office, Graves says, so she first fed them breakfast, which stabilized their blood sugar levels and made their behaviour less erratic. She started with the most needy, people who couldn't even manage to get cardboard underneath them while sleeping on the sidewalk. They could take a long time to wake, as they were often nearly hypothermic. Many of them had brain injuries and/or crystal meth addictions. But Graves, a diminutive woman, says no one was violent towards her. People were often skeptical, but they were at least willing to have her buy them breakfast. After getting the food, they'd usually agree to go to the welfare office. With people who firmly resisted, Graves would keep coming back until she changed their minds. After a while, homeless people started talking to one another about the mysterious lady who was helping everyone. "At first they were suspicious, but then I'd hear from people, 'I fell asleep last night praying you'd wake me up this morning.' The guys on the street were describing it as winning the lottery," Graves recalls, smiling. "At first it seemed like I was emptying the ocean with a bucket, but after a month I got to that corner one morning and there was no one there."

The solution wasn't ideal. At first, Graves was typically able to find someone a room in an SRO, though often not one with solid support services. But it became more and more challenging for her to find any vacant rooms at all. She worked off a list of one hundred low-income buildings, some of them dubious, privately owned establishments, but she'd negotiate with anyone to get people housed. Nonetheless, the number of available rooms continued to shrink. Vancouver was not alone in this, she says. In small B.C. communities like Vernon and Hope, former rooming houses had been turned into bed and breakfasts, leaving the poor with nowhere to go. "It was a federal issue right across Canada," Graves says, "and it still is."

The Portland Hotel Society expanded beyond the new Portland Hotel to manage several other facilities in the Downtown

Eastside; most were leased to the agency after the city or the province had bought the buildings and funded renovations. The list included three formerly notorious SRO hotels: the 84-room Washington, the 103-room Stanley/New Fountain, and the 52-room Sunrise. The Sunrise once had one of the worst drug-dealing bars in the city, but the space became home instead to a resident-run coffee shop and a co-op radio station. PHS also took over the Smith-Yuen Apartments, with 52 rooms for mentally ill people aged fifty and older. The society even branched beyond housing to operate other services for neighbourhood residents. It created the Potluck Café, a small restaurant that prepared whole-some, inexpensive food and received free rent from the Portland in exchange for serving the hotel's tenants one meal a day. And in 2004, PHS opened Pigeon Park Savings, a bank that operated with some assistance from Vancity credit union, so that mar-ginalized people could cash their welfare cheques and do other banking. The society also opened the Interurban Art Gallery, which displayed artwork created by Downtown Eastside resi-dents, and started a community garden on a rough patch of land sandwiched between two buildings, where residents could grow vegetables to be used in a neighbourhood lunch program.

Between 2007 and 2008, the B.C. government bought seven-teen SRO hotels in the Downtown Eastside area, an investment that represented more than one thousand rooms and tens of mil-lions of dollars in capital costs. The seventeen buildings would be renovated, the province announced, and be run by non-profit agencies based on the maximum welfare shelter rates of $375 a month. Most of the new SROs were to offer desperately needed support services to people with HIV/AIDS, at-risk youth, women, the mentally ill, and the addicted. Vancouver police would part-ner with the non-profit agencies managing the buildings to reduce 911 calls and criminal activity through initiatives like assigning specific beat officers to each hotel, the government said. A few of the seventeen Downtown Eastside hotels were empty when purchased by the province. The majority were still in operation, however, so although the end result was expected to be better, safer rooms for vulnerable residents, there would be few new rooms to address the homelessness crisis, and the units in the renovated buildings would be too small to be ideal as long-term housing.

In December 2007, the province and the city of Vancouver also agreed to expedite up to 1,200 new social and supportive housing units with private kitchens and bathrooms, to be built on twelve city-owned sites, three of them in the Downtown Eastside. The province agreed to pay pre-development costs for the sites, but capital costs will have to be covered by money from the province, the federal government, and corporate and private donors. The non-profit agencies selected to lease and manage the sites will be exempt from paying property taxes for sixty years. In March 2009, two months before B.C.'s provincial election, the Liberals announced more than $172 million in funding for six of the projects, though construction start dates were not specified. At the time of writing, the federal government had not stepped up with any money, and the future of the six remaining sites—plus two more the city wanted to add to the list—remained unclear as Vancouver and Victoria squabbled over funding and preparing the properties for construction.

The 2007 report by city housing planner Jill Davidson identified twenty-one non-market projects (with 1,347 rooms) under construction or planned for the downtown core. Half were slated as new rooms for homeless people, and half were pre-existing rooms in SROs undergoing renovation. Davidson's report predicted that by the end of 2010 new non-market units in the downtown core would offset SRO losses, with 700 more low-income housing units in the neighbourhood than there had been in two decades. In response, the Carnegie Community Action

Project, a group that focuses on improving housing and income in the Downtown Eastside, produced its own report, *Disappearing Homes: The Loss of Affordable Housing in the DTES*, in 2008. Researcher Jean Swanson and her team found that of ninety-seven privately owned SRO buildings, forty-six per cent were out of reach to people on welfare: the buildings were charging rents above the welfare shelter allowance of $375 per month; were letting rooms by the day or week, which is more expensive than monthly; had adopted student-only policies, since the number of private education facilities located downtown was on the rise; or were closed or in danger of closing.

The conclusions in the group's report applied only to privately owned SROs, not the affordable non-market housing run by governments or non-profit agencies. Nonetheless, the trend was worrying. According to the Carnegie report, sixty-seven per cent of Downtown Eastside residents are "low-income," and since the total monthly welfare benefit for someone deemed able to work is only $610, higher rents eat into the meagre $235 left over for food and all other expenses. Welfare rates haven't kept up with inflation, Swanson points out, so people living on social assistance are much poorer now than they were in the 1970s. A follow-up report by the group in June 2009, *Still Losing Hotel Rooms: CCAP's 2009 Hotel Survey and Report*, suggested the housing situation in the neighbourhood was continuing to deteriorate for low-income residents. It found an increase in SRO rooms renting for more than $375 per month; a rising number of hotels renting rooms daily or weekly, presumably to tourists; and an escalation of "double bunking," when two people share a tiny SRO room—both using their shelter allowance for rent—just to make ends meet.

Swanson has advocated tirelessly to end poverty since she began working with Libby Davies and Bruce Eriksen at DERA in the 1970s. Between 1982 and 1993, she says today, an average of

664 new units of social housing were built every year in Vancouver; between 2001 and 2007, Swanson adds, that average sank to only 85 new units annually. The numbers started to fall off after the federal government stopped funding social housing in 1993, Swanson says, and they plummeted when Gordon Campbell and the newly elected B.C. Liberals, in a 2002 cost-cutting move (and in addition to that year's welfare cuts), cancelled a provincial housing program. Unlike the city hall report, both Carnegie reports predicted the number of affordable low-rent units would continue to decline. "With the Olympics coming in 2010 and hundreds of thousands of visitors expected, it is reasonable to expect that some of these hotels and others may try to evict permanent residents in favour of tourists who can pay more," the 2008 report said.

A provocative 2008 study commissioned by the B.C. Ministry of Health, *Housing and Support for Adults with Severe Addictions and/or Mental Illness in British Columbia*, suggested that providing social housing for every homeless person would actually save B.C. taxpayers money. The study, by five professors from Simon Fraser University, the University of British Columbia, and the University of Calgary, calculated that each homeless person costs the government $55,000 a year in health, corrections, and social services costs. That's an annual total of $644.3 million, said the report, and yet providing sufficient housing and support would cost the system just $37,000 per person per year. A capital investment of $784 million would provide adequate housing for the estimated 11,750 people across B.C. without stable homes; a further $148 million per year would need to be allocated for housing-related support services. After removing what the province is paying now for health care, jail, and shelters, and spreading the capital costs over several years, the report said, taxpayers would stand to save nearly $33 million annually. It would not be a quick fix, but it could be a lasting one. The study also estimated that fifty to seventy per cent of homeless people have a dual diagnosis, suffering from both a mental illness and a drug addiction. "Research has shown that people with SAMI [severe addictions and/or mental illness] who are homeless, once believed to be unreachable and difficult to serve, can be engaged into services, can accept and benefit from mental health and substance use services, and can remain in stable housing with appropriate supports," the study said. Its authors estimated that 130,000 people in B.C. have a severe addiction and/or a mental illness; about 26,500 of those people are "inadequately housed and inadequately supported," including the 11,750 who are "absolutely homeless." At the time the study was written, there were 7,741 supported housing units in B.C. for people with mental illness and/or addictions, so the report concluded an estimated 18,759 vulnerable people were at "imminent risk of homelessness." The report's authors blamed "rapid gentrification" related to the 2010 Winter Olympics for part of B.C.'s growing homelessness crisis.

While some, including Larry Campbell, don't agree with the gentrification label, Jean Swanson of the Carnegie Community Action Project argues that's exactly what's driving developments in trendy Gastown and in parts of the Downtown Eastside. Swanson believes "the political will isn't there" to respond to studies like the one the five academics produced. "Everyone down here is petrified that poor people will be driven out, and the Olympics increases those worries," says Swanson. She contends little has improved since DERA first made good housing the organization's central target. "I have a callous on my head from banging it against the wall," Swanson says. "It's gotten worse. Thirty-five years of work, and it's gotten worse."

The housing debate has turned fractious in the Downtown Eastside, especially among social service organizations: do you jump into bed with large-scale developers out of necessity or

shun them as corporate leeches intent on gentrifying the neighbourhood? More and more new construction projects in the
land-starved downtown core, which is surrounded by water on
three sides and by east Vancouver on the fourth, contain a mix
of market housing and government-subsidized social housing,
with retail and commercial space on the ground floor. The most
high-profile example is the old Woodward's building, where private developer Westbank began construction in 2006 to build
536 market units (which sold out in twenty-four hours during
pre-sales, for a total of $200 million), space for retail shops and
services like child care, and 200 social housing units (including 30 units of alcohol-and-drug-free addictions-supported
housing). The social housing units, funded by the three levels of
government, will be managed by the Portland Hotel Society. Pro-
jected to open in late 2009, the project will also include Simon
Fraser University's School for the Contemporary Arts, which
will offer programs in dance, film, music, theatre, and visual
art, as well as the massive W2 Community Media Arts Centre.
Jim Green, who fought for the building for decades, is comfortable with the mix of uses in the iconic former department store,
which will sport a replica W on its roof when construction is
complete. The fact the unique project sold out in less than a day
proves the rich and the poor can cohabit, he argues, even in a
traditionally low-income area. "Woodward's broke that myth.
It shredded it," Green says in his trademark emphatic, take-no-
prisoners tone. Combine that, he adds, with the fact that about
fifty Aboriginal street youth employed by the Downtown Eastside BladeRunners office worked on the construction site, and
the project should become the formula for future growth in
other cities.

Larry Campbell agrees, noting that the two hundred non-
market units in the Woodward's development will be new
social housing, providing rooms for roughly ten per cent of

Vancouver's homeless people. The mix of market and low-income housing will inject activity into an area that is currently stagnating, he says. "As soon as you ghettoize poor people, then there is no social interaction, no drive to move up in life. The people who bought the market housing down here know this is not a dangerous community, but it has edgy things going on. You don't expect to move to the Downtown Eastside and wake up the next day and all of a sudden you're in yuppie Yaletown." Campbell says there is only so much a city government can do (it gets eight cents of every dollar of taxes collected) when senior governments are not committed to ending homelessness with their ninety-two per cent of the taxation pie.

Activist Bud Osborn has his own perspective on gentrification in the Downtown Eastside. He was walking in an alley with a friend when he discovered that Trader Vic's, a long-time greasy spoon on Main Street, was under renovation. The place may serve better food in the future, Osborn says, but it will be at prices out of reach for the area's poor residents. "People think that [kind of development] is a good thing, but that guy I was walking in the alley with, he and I will never go in there. We have lost that space," he says. However, Osborn is convinced his neighbours will band together, as they have in the past, to protect portions of the Downtown Eastside for the poor and to fight for sufficient housing and services. "I don't know of any other place where an inner-city, low-income neighbourhood was left to be completely wiped out but remained a community. There is just such resistance here," he says.

17 | The Road Ahead

SAM SULLIVAN LOST THE SUPPORT of his party during his time in office, and the NPA ran long-time city councillor Peter Ladner as their candidate for mayor in the November 2008 civic election. Vancouver voters were looking for a change, however, and a scandal about the city's involvement in the funding of the $1 billion Olympic village took centre stage in the final days of the campaign. Vision Vancouver's Gregor Robertson, a businessman and former NDP MLA, won the mayor's seat handily, bringing along with him seven Vision Vancouver councillors. Two COPE councillors were elected as well, with NPA representation limited to the lone remaining council seat.

Tackling homelessness would be his first priority, the new mayor announced to a cheering crowd on election night. But homelessness and the other problems facing the Downtown Eastside are challenges not just for that neighbourhood or for the city of Vancouver. They are problems that all levels of government—municipal, regional, provincial, and federal—must tackle, and all of them will have to come to the table if meaningful solutions are to be found.

Ending Homelessness

Homeless people continue to die on the streets of Vancouver. In December 2008, a forty-seven-year-old woman known only as Tracey burned to death in a cardboard shelter she had erected over her shopping cart on an unusually chilly Vancouver night. She had lit some candles in a feeble effort to keep herself warm, and her body was found smouldering in the cart just before dawn. Judy Graves, the city's housing advocate, told the *Vancouver Sun* that Tracey had probably opted to stay on the streets during the cold snap because most shelters will not allow homeless people to bring their shopping carts inside. And there is not always a place to stay, regardless of the weather: the Triage Shelter routinely turns away four to six hundred people a month because it is full. Lookout and other shelters report a similar situation.

Most experts agree that Vancouver currently has at least two thousand homeless people, the vast majority of them in the Downtown Eastside. *Still on Our Streets...*, the 2008 report by the Greater Vancouver Regional Steering Committee on Homelessness, estimated that the median age for homeless people was forty-one and that 153 of the homeless were eighteen years old or younger. Almost half of the people surveyed had been homeless for at least a year. Increasing numbers of them had several health conditions and/or a drug addiction, and Aboriginal people were overrepresented in the group. Forty per cent of those counted had slept in some type of shelter the previous night, while the rest were on the street. Some people had been turned away from full shelters, but many said they didn't like shelters anyway, complaining of bed bugs, dirt, noise, theft, restrictions on the length of stay, and rules against bringing in pets or shopping carts full of possessions. Of those in shelters, a quarter had part-time jobs and eleven per cent had full-time jobs. Forty-three per cent of homeless people were on welfare but either couldn't find or couldn't afford housing.

When asked why they were homeless, those interviewed cited a range of answers: lack of income (twenty-five per cent), cost of housing (nineteen per cent), addictions (seventeen per cent), abuse/family breakdown (ten per cent), poor conditions in the housing available (eight per cent), no available housing (seven per cent), health problems (seven per cent), and eviction from their last home (five per cent). The report attributed the slight decline in homelessness between 2005 and 2008 to successful programs run by non-profit agencies like RainCity and services offered by city hall, which put employees on the street to help specific people find housing. "While many of the drivers of homelessness such as mental illness, addiction, and lack of affordable housing remain, there has been some progress since 2005 in helping street homeless persons in particular gain access to housing through outreach teams," said the report. However, the authors added, "the number of new permanent supportive housing units built has clearly not been adequate to meet growing demand."

The Metro Vancouver region needs a supportive housing plan for all of its twenty-eight municipalities, Larry Campbell and Neil Boyd believe. Every city has challenges with drugs and homelessness, and the problems can't be defined by the borders of a municipality. A coordinated approach, Campbell and Boyd say, should be overseen by a regional council on homelessness and run by veteran bureaucrats from city halls; mayors and councillors often have polarized views, and they usually serve only one or two terms in power. Some of the new social housing needs to be in the Downtown Eastside, close to services for the marginalized; some needs to be outside that area, for the working poor and recovering addicts. A coordinated policy will also be needed to deal with NIMBYs, the two men say, the not-in-my-back-yard people who don't want social housing on their residential streets, despite the reality that the folks affected could have grown up in their neighbourhoods.

The first day after being sworn in as mayor in December 2008, Gregor Robertson announced that as a short-term solution to the city's homelessness crisis, Vancouver would establish five new emergency homeless shelters in the city. The Homeless Emergency Action Team created by Robertson was responsible for the low-barrier shelters, which had more relaxed rules about pets, possessions, intoxication, and other behaviour than most traditional homeless shelters. The new shelters, which housed an average of 450 to 500 people each night, led to a decrease in mental health calls, street disorder, and aggressive panhandling, Robertson told the media in March 2009. Funding for the shelters came from the province, the city, and the Streetohome Foundation, a community group launched in February 2009 to ensure that all Vancouver residents have decent housing by 2015. (The new foundation has an impressive board of directors, which includes Vancouver police chief Jim Chu, the chief justice of the B.C. Supreme Court, lawyers, developers, bankers, and other community leaders.) B.C. housing minister Rich Coleman told reporters that the temporary shelters would provide homeless people with safer places to stay while the province renovates existing housing and builds new projects. In June 2009, the provincial government agreed to provide $8 million to keep four of the shelters open until April 2010. The fifth shelter, which drew multiple noise and safety complaints from neighbours in trendy condominiums, was closed. While the city's new temporary shelters provided limited welcome relief, what the Downtown Eastside needs is not more shelters, everyone agrees. The goal, Campbell and Boyd say, should be more supported units run by non-profit agencies who specialize in this work, stalwarts like RainCity and the Portland Hotel Society.

RainCity executive director Mark Smith estimates that Metro Vancouver needs three thousand new social housing units to put a dent in the homelessness crisis. "Most people here [in the neighbourhood] are from outside the Downtown Eastside, and the ghetto creates an atmosphere that encourages drug use. It also makes it tough to take stock of life and pursue options. It would be healthier to create accepting communities, but first we need a cultural shift in society to make these people accepted," Smith says. Successful social housing must be geared to providing proper long-term accommodation with private bathrooms and kitchens. Most buildings will need ongoing medical and social support systems, according to Smith, because many future tenants will be mentally ill and/or addicted people who have been abandoned by the system for so long that they have little hope of ever leading so-called normal lives. "Do we think any of these folks are going to get to a point where they get a job and commute in from the suburbs each day? No, that's never going to happen. The population we see are so isolated and entrenched in addiction," Smith says matter-of-factly. "They are owed supportive housing by all of us, because in many respects we put them where they are today." It may sound audacious, but Smith also believes homelessness can be wiped out. "We could end homelessness if there was the will and the resources there. And we have the resources in this country. It's just a matter of where we want to spend our money: in Afghanistan or in the Downtown Eastside?"

When the federal Liberals were defeated in 2006, they left a $17 billion government surplus. The Conservatives diminished that surplus by a third in order to shave 1 per cent off the GST. Even half of that 1 per cent cut—$3 billion—easily would have funded the construction of enough supportive housing to fill the need right across the country, Larry Campbell and Neil Boyd say. "The Harper Conservatives aren't the compassionate Tories of the Stanfield era," Boyd points out. "They don't seem to believe in the provision of social housing by government, particularly for those they view as deserving their fate—the drug-addicted mentally ill."

Many people believe that if we are determined to end homelessness and ease the burden on the medical system caused by entrenched drug users, we need a countrywide housing strategy that requires the provinces to match federal funding and cities to provide the land for the developments. As a Liberal senator, Larry Campbell works with the Federation of Canadian Municipalities and big-city mayors on the issue of homelessness, but he says progress like that envisioned by Vancouver's 2005 Homeless Action Plan, adopted under his watch as mayor, is stalled under the Stephen Harper government. Campbell acknowledges that it was the federal Liberals who sacked the national social housing program, in 1993, and who presided over the disarray in the Downtown Eastside for many years. But he argues the Liberal Party today recognizes there is a crisis, while the Tories dismiss homelessness as a problem for cities to deal with. "Now we're seeing Vancouver cough up land and the province getting involved, but it should be the three levels of government looking at this. Homelessness is hugely expensive. For a federal government that says it's business-oriented, the Conservatives just don't get it," says Campbell, who has been active over the years on the boards of Downtown Eastside agencies such as RainCity Housing, the Lu'ma Native Housing Society, and the Aboriginal Mothers Centre Society.

With the TSX, the Toronto Stock Exchange index, losing almost half its value between 2008 and early 2009, and government deficits soaring, a national housing strategy may seem further away than ever. But Campbell and Boyd both believe it is crucial to begin building, even in an uncertain financial environment. Supportive housing and treatment resources will cost a tremendous amount, they admit, but those services will ultimately save society money by reducing the high cost of people revolving repeatedly through the justice, health, and social service systems. Once people are in a home and stabilized, there will be opportunities for some to get off welfare and to work and pay taxes. Job skills training for basic labour could also be offered as part of addictions treatment. "There's no sense in getting someone into treatment and then putting them back out into the conditions they came from. Many people who are addicted have skills and the ability to be contributing citizens. They need a roof and a door that locks, treatment, counselling for abuse, and then a future plan. Otherwise, we go back to the same pattern: you're poor, you've got nothing, and you self-medicate again," Campbell says. "You don't have to be an NDP supporter to see that this kind of change is needed; it just makes business sense."

There are currently a few signs that the three levels of government see it as important to work together. For example, the three shared the funding for renovations of the twenty-three-unit Jackson Avenue Housing Co-operative in the Downtown Eastside, for low-income single people and families, which opened in April 2009. But a national plan is critical, Campbell insists. "Everyone in Canada should care about this. So many people are one paycheque away from having their financial security crumble. And even if that's not you, or your family, or friends, you should care because it's happening in wealthy cities in your country. Whose responsibility is homelessness? It's everyone's responsibility. We have a responsibility as taxpayers, as citizens, to take care of everyone. It can be done." Libby Davies, the NDP MP for Vancouver East, called for a similar strategy in early 2009 with the introduction of a private member's bill in the House of Commons that describes housing as a human right. The bill would require the government to create a national housing strategy with provincial and municipal partners. "We're the only industrialized country now that doesn't have a national housing plan," Davies says.

For individual housing developments, Larry Campbell believes strongly that the Woodward's model makes economic and social sense. Most new buildings in Vancouver's downtown core, he says, should include market housing for people who can afford to pay full price and want the convenience of living close to where they work; less expensive co-op housing for the working poor and families; subsidized and supported housing for those needing assistance; and a mix of services like daycares, medical clinics, office space, and stores. The full-price units in a development help to fund the rest of the building, bring people from different walks of life together, and end the confinement of marginalized people to one area of the city, Campbell says. "We know what happens when we put poor people in a tower. It just increases ghettoization and violence. It increases all the bad things in society."

An upscale 160-unit building at 58 West Hastings being constructed by Concord Pacific, a giant development company, has sparked an uproar among Vancouver housing advocates, who fear such projects will drive poor people out of the neighbourhood. The city's official Downtown Eastside plan calls for both more social housing and more market housing for the area, but the Carnegie Community Action Project says its statistics show housing is being built in the neighbourhood at a rate of three market units for every unit of social housing. Sandy Cameron has concerns that if land values continue to escalate, and the demand for pricey downtown condos returns under an improved economy, then it will be the area's longest established residents and the stores that serve them that will get squeezed out. "Some people can't abide poor people living on land that someone else could make a whole lot of money with. They talk about cleaning up the streets, but these are people we're talking about," Cameron says. He adds, however, that the neighbourhood isn't likely to wave the white flag of surrender. "There is such an admirable spirit of struggle here. Who knows what's going to happen?"

While Larry Campbell is sympathetic to calls to protect social housing, he doesn't see firms like Concord Pacific as the enemy. He notes the developer provided $3.6 million for the old Portland Hotel renovation by purchasing rights under Vancouver's heritage density transfer program. Renovated to transform seventy tiny rooms into forty-four rooms with private baths, the hotel reopened in early 2009, complete with a replica of the 1920s neon sign flashing one of its previous names, the Pennsylvania. The $11-million restoration was funded by all three levels of government. Sometimes, Campbell argues, a compromise can benefit a neighbourhood, too. "We always use this term 'gentrification,' but I think we should face the reality that a city is a living, breathing being. Good cities never remain static. I think we can keep some of the streetscape and do something positive with mixed housing. People moving into the Downtown Eastside must realize this is an experiment, a new way of living. And if you already live in the Downtown Eastside, this should be your home."

Neil Boyd is more cautious, arguing that development will need to be closely monitored to ensure that the newcomers to the Downtown Eastside don't push established residents out. "It can be very subtle," Boyd says. "New stores and new restaurants, places that are outside the experience and the comfort zone of those who live there now. If you add to the mix a group of newcomers who, knowingly or not, push for what we might call a yuppie lifestyle, you can ultimately create displacement, even if that was never your intent." Boyd adds, however, that there is something to be said for dispersing the problems of mental illness and addiction. "Most of the people on the streets of the Downtown Eastside came from other communities," he says. "In Switzerland, for example, there has been a recognition that each community must do its share for its more vulnerable citizens. We still appear to be some distance from that kind of commitment."

Jean Swanson points out that it was Downtown Eastside residents themselves who fought to get trees planted on their streets and a green space that was named Crab Park. "This neighbourhood is going to stay by hook or by crook," says Swanson, adding that the world will be watching in 2010. Looking on the bright side, she sees the coming Olympics as a tool the community can use to lobby for more resources. "That gives me hope," she says. "But when you look at the forces working against the neighbourhood, it starts to look bleak again."

Darrell Burnham of Coast Mental Health says he is optimistic, though also a little unsure about the future. Burnham worries that the attention focused now on homelessness and mental health is related to the Olympics coming to Vancouver and could fall off the agenda in 2011. "It's the 2010 hangover I worry about: what's it going to be like?" It's a legitimate concern for folks in the Downtown Eastside—will the construction of supported social housing developments, for example, suddenly stop after the Olympics bandwagon pulls out of town? At a press conference MP Libby Davies and the Impact on Community Coalition called in March 2009, Davies said that commitments by Olympics organizers to create a "housing legacy" for Vancouver were "falling dramatically behind." Davies called on the federal government "to implement recommendations from a recently tabled United Nations report on housing that raises concerns about the potential negative impact of the Olympics on the homeless."

Campbell and Boyd, for their part, don't believe the upcoming Winter Olympics will be a catalyst for the displacement of Downtown Eastside residents. As the mayor who helped to bring the Olympics to B.C., Campbell doesn't think the kind of displacement seen during the six-month-long Expo 86 will repeat itself during the 2010 Winter Games. He argues that Hastings Street hotel owners will not turf tenants out, slap on a coat of paint, and jack up the rent on their rooms for an event in which the largest number of visitors will come for just sixteen days. And, Campbell notes, a portion of the athletes' village being constructed for the Olympics will be used for social housing post-Games. "The main thing is that the Olympics must live up to what they promised: that the Games are going to be a net benefit to the Downtown Eastside," he says.

Improving Treatment for Mental Illness and Addictions

A recent study undertaken by the Mental Health Policy Research Group of Toronto's Clarke Institute of Psychiatry found that more than two thirds of the homeless in Canada have a lifetime diagnosis of mental illness, and a full eighty-six per cent of those people have a substantial history of dependence on alcohol and/or illegal drugs. Only six per cent of those on the street had been released from a psychiatric facility during the previous year; by contrast, thirty per cent had been in either police cells or prison within the same time period. But with all of the bed closures in psychiatric facilities, people with both mental illness and difficulties with substance abuse are now more likely to find themselves in contact with the criminal justice system than with psychiatric institutions. For the past two decades, police have been handed a task that is sometimes akin to social work, responding to the problems of people who have rarely, if ever, been hospitalized.

In February 2008, the Vancouver Police Department released a shocking report that found forty-nine per cent of police calls for service in the Downtown Eastside involved a mentally ill person. The number of people apprehended by Vancouver police across the city under the Mental Health Act had jumped from 360 in 1999 to 1,744 in 2007. A lack of mental health services meant officers often arrested people who might hurt themselves or others, knowing that jail at least offered a warm place for the night and access to a nurse and food, said the report's author,

Detective Fiona Wilson-Bates. The situation had reached crisis proportions, police said, created by the "perfect storm" of mental health institutions closing, cutbacks in government funding for social housing, inadequate welfare payments, and the ready availability of drugs like crack that induce aberrant behaviour. The police report called for more housing, mental health, and medical services. An estimated forty per cent of the drug addicts in the Downtown Eastside, said the report, are also mentally ill.

"We should be ashamed of ourselves," then–Deputy Chief Bob Rich said during a walking tour of the Downtown Eastside when the report was released. It was increasingly difficult to find homes for people, Rich said, and some may be safer on the street than inside the worst low-rent hotels. The privately owned Backpackers Inn on West Hastings, for example, could only have been described as a hell hole at the time. The linoleum on the floors was ripped, and graffiti decorated the walls. A vile stench—likely from the hotel's common washroom—filled the air. The back stairs were covered with dead and live rats, used needles, and so much trash that Rich couldn't get the fire-escape door open. The pipe under one tenant's sink had rotted off, forcing him to use buckets to stop the water from rushing onto the floor when he turned on his taps. Despite that, the tenant was upset that he and fifty others were being evicted by the hotel's owners, since the place was preparing to close; he didn't know where else he could find to live.

Darrell Burnham of Coast Mental Health sees the 2008 VPD report as proof that many vulnerable street people haven't been supported properly for years. "I think there's a ton of people who need help, but they are sent to jail or a shelter or sent to a soup kitchen," says Burnham, whose organization receives funding from all three levels of government to provide services and housing. As a solution, Burnham champions new social housing—including so-called wet buildings, which allow drug use and methadone treatment—built outside the Downtown Eastside to get vulnerable people away from victimizers and opportunists. Some suburban cities, like New Westminster and North Vancouver, offer facilities for the homeless, and Surrey mayor Dianne Watts is taking that city in a more socially conscious direction. But some municipalities have balked. The growing city of Richmond, for example, caved in to community protests in 2008 and turned down a proposal from RainCity Housing for a badly needed thirty-two-bed drug-recovery and supportive-housing facility, with some dedicated rooms for women with children. Larry Campbell is amazed poor decisions like that are still being made fifteen years after former chief coroner Vince Cain's report showed that a new approach was needed. "The Richmond decision is an egregious example of how society still isn't embracing one of Cain's most important recommendations: to increase residential recovery and detox facilities, especially those that allow women to bring their children along, to avoid mothers checking out early to be with their kids again," Campbell says.

Darrell Burnham says many mentally ill people in the Downtown Eastside today don't even have a diagnosis. Those with an active addiction or who are "rough around the edges" are often excluded from existing mental health services. The Strathcona mental health clinic in the Downtown Eastside is more inclusive, Burnham says, and does wonderful work, but the staff there are overloaded, seeing an estimated 125 clients a day. The psychiatric ward for dually diagnosed people at St. Paul's Hospital is "always over one hundred per cent capacity," said Dr. Richard Pico, who oversees the program, in an interview in 2008.

The province opened the hundred-bed Centre for Mental Health & Addiction in 2008 in the nearby city of Burnaby to treat some of the most difficult-to-reach people on the streets. The facility's beds were filled instantly through referrals from

Insite, outreach teams, and the LifeSkills Centre, and turnover is not high because residents are expected to stay an average of nine months. The new facility is a start, Larry Campbell says, but many more long-term beds are required to stabilize people before they can move into supportive housing. Much as some people might shudder at the suggestion, Campbell says, the quickest way to get hundreds of people off the street and into care would be to reopen Riverview, which is now almost empty as remaining patients are being transferred to newer, smaller mental health facilities across the province.

"When I was a Mountie," Campbell says, "if someone was mentally ill you arrested them and took them to the hospital for assessment, then drove straight to Riverview. I think there's still a need for a place like that, for the people who are causing the most severe disorder: people who wander in traffic, break into houses, and are incoherent. People who, for their own good, need treatment immediately—many of the chronics, for example, identified by the Vancouver police report. In many cases now they are treated and back out in a short time with medication. And nobody gets abused more on the street than the mentally ill. The conundrum is civil rights. But as a society, we should be able to pick up people beyond help and take them to a safe place. If that safe place is Riverview, so be it." Such an approach, of course, would only be an answer for those willing to accept help once they got to a place like Riverview. Forced institutionalization will never work, Campbell realizes.

The provincial government argues that significant improvements to the system have been made in recent years for those struggling with addictions. In 2008, the treatment beds available for drug users across the province included 154 adult and 48 youth detox beds; 708 adult and 53 youth residential and support recovery beds; 305 beds in addictions-supported housing;

and 35 sobering/assessment beds. Vancouver Coastal Health estimates there are 12,000 injection drug users in Vancouver alone, with 4,600 of them living in the Downtown Eastside. The health authority funds eighteen residential detox beds for women, forty-one for men, and twenty-two for youth, as well as a variety of outpatient programs best suited to people with established support and stable housing. More than forty needle exchanges have been established in the city, with a total of three million needles exchanged annually. "Do we need more? Oh my god, we need so much more," says Heather Hay, the health board's director of addictions, HIV/AIDS, and Aboriginal health. "We could use one thousand more treatment beds."

People struggling with addiction issues complain of being turned away by crammed hospitals, being told to get clean before they are accepted at mental health clinics, and being told to get off medical prescriptions before they can receive treatment for illegal drugs. At a detox facility run by the Salvation Army, a veteran agency in the Downtown Eastside, administrators lamented in 2008 that the average wait to get into one of their detox beds was four to five days—far too long for vulnerable people who need immediate access when they finally decide to seek help. For those who make it through detox, there is a dearth of stabilization beds, places to stay during the several-week wait to enter a treatment centre. That gap is also far too long for people with poor housing and no support system to remain clean.

In May 2008, the federal Conservatives promised one-time funding to create twenty new transitional or stabilization beds for women in a Downtown Eastside SRO, where clients could stay for up to six months as they withdraw from drugs before going to supported housing or a treatment centre. The money is only for a pilot program, and Heather Hay fears the funding was politically motivated—since the Conservatives oppose Insite,

Vancouver's supervised injection site, they want to be seen as supporting other treatment alternatives. But regardless of the motivation, Hay says, the beds are badly needed.

"Overall, we're still a long way from where we should be on demand treatment," Larry Campbell says. "If drug addiction was any other disease, like cancer, we would be all over this like a rash. We probably have five to seven thousand people on methadone programs in B.C., but that's not treatment." Critics argue the reason addictions treatment hasn't expanded is because of harm reduction measures like Insite and needle exchanges, but Campbell says most government money is going into law enforcement, and harm reduction measures are only band-aid solutions until treatment is properly funded. "All we're trying to do is keep people alive long enough for someone to wake up and put real money into this," he says. Treatment also needs to include a wide range of options, since the same solution will not work for every addict, and be situated within a system that is easy to access and non-judgemental. Neil Boyd adds that there must be sufficient detox beds for drug users to be admitted the same day they make the request, and the system must be tolerant enough not to reject people who need to go through detox five, ten, or twenty times before it sticks. Critics must remember how often smokers try to butt out or drinkers try to sober up before they are successful, Boyd says; those with drug addictions are no different. Once patients have gone through detox, there must be many more transitional beds where marginalized people can stay while waiting to get into long-term recovery programs. The system also must continue providing treatment beds specified for women and youth. And for those who are diagnosed with both a mental illness and an addiction, Boyd says, we need treatment services that address both challenges at the same time.

Repeated recommendations over the years for the province to stagger the issuing of welfare cheques, so that they are not all released on the same day, have been ignored, and Welfare Wednesday continues to create a dangerous Mardi Gras atmosphere on Hastings Street. There are few places to take people when they need help on those days, Larry Campbell says.

At an inquest Campbell presided over as coroner in 1985, he recommended that people with severe alcohol poisoning be sent to hospital, yet an inquiry held in 2007 and 2008 into the 1998 death of Frank Paul showed that Vancouver police dragged the severely intoxicated man out of a cell and left him in an alley, where Paul died of hypothermia due to acute alcohol intoxication. Campbell suggests that some detox facilities could be made into triage centres to deal with people in this condition. "The police are constantly forced to make decisions about whether this person is mentally ill, how intoxicated is this person, what should I do with him or her? Police are not trained for that. They have gone from being peace officers, in my day, to becoming medical health care workers, social workers, and triage workers on the street," he says. Both Boyd and Campbell testified at the Paul inquiry, which recommended in February 2009 "a civilian-operated program for attending to chronic alcoholics who are incapacitated in a public place," "a civilian-operated sobering centre," and "the provision of permanent low-barrier housing."

Also in February 2009, the Vancouver Police Department produced a well-regarded report, *Project Lockstep*, that called for the hiring of a Downtown Eastside "czar"—one person who could oversee the severe problems afflicting thousands of the community's residents and orchestrate solutions. While there have been major efforts to improve the state of affairs in the Downtown Eastside, Chief Jim Chu told the *Vancouver Sun* upon the report's release, many have failed. The following month, the police department dropped a controversial measure that had increased by twenty per cent the issuing of bylaw tickets in the Downtown Eastside in an effort to reduce street disorder and had called for beat cops to ask four people in each block for their names and identification. Opposition to the measure had been widespread: advocacy groups complained loudly about the quotas, describing them as offensive; Pivot Legal Society attacked the overreach of the ticketing campaign; and Mayor Gregor Robertson openly questioned the utility of targeting the vulnerable through bylaw enforcement. The persistent criticism, Neil Boyd says, apparently prompted Chu and the VPD to change course.

Embracing the Four Pillars—Prevention, Treatment, Enforcement, and Harm Reduction

The Downtown Eastside no longer has the worst rate of HIV infection in the Western world, as Dr. Julio Montaner had declared in 1997, but the situation remains dire. Vancouver Coastal Health recently pegged the death rate from HIV-related diseases in the Downtown Eastside at thirty-eight times greater than that in the rest of B.C. Other studies have offered even higher estimates. The medical system still doesn't serve the community's marginalized population, Montaner says, and in his opinion continuing to ignore that is "genocide"—the deliberate extermination of a specific group.

Although there is still no cure for AIDS, Montaner says the spread of the disease can be controlled if vulnerable patients get the right medical treatment. A pregnant woman with HIV, for example, will not infect her baby if she's taking the proper drugs. "But there's a problem," the outspoken doctor says. "There's a reservoir of individuals who are not accessing treatment because they have other competing priorities." It's tough for people to make time to get to an AIDS clinic, Montaner says, when they are consumed with other more pressing matters: "Where am I going to sleep tonight?" "What will I eat today?" "How am I going to get money?" "How can I stop the abuse from my dealer/pimp/john?" "How can I function when my mental illness is fogging clear judgement?" "I could numb all this pain with heroin or cocaine. The HIV doesn't hurt; it's the least of my worries." As Montaner insists, "We need to address this community's needs. We need to bring them into the health care envelope on their terms, so we can make HIV treatment relevant to their lives... Failing to do that ensures we have a consistent and active reservoir of HIV that is preventing us from controlling HIV in our midst." The solution starts, he says, with better housing, better social services, and better mental health support. Montaner commends Premier Gordon Campbell for "getting out of his comfort zone" and funding harm reduction–focused housing and treatment services. But he remains frustrated by the federal government's unwillingness to back measures like Insite and the NAOMI project that could stem the spread of HIV. "We don't know [everything about] how to deal with the Downtown Eastside," Montaner says, "but if we find something that works better than the status quo—which means the continued neglect of these individuals—then we have an obligation to implement what works better. That's where the federal government is totally misguided."

Philip Owen is disappointed that Vancouver's four pillars report, produced while he was mayor, has not elicited more action from senior levels of government. In May 2008, Owen joined representatives from Vancouver's health board, city hall, the police department, the medical research community, and non-profit agencies at a meeting in Ottawa of the House of Commons Standing Committee on Health. Owen was given just five minutes to speak about Insite and other harm reduction matters, so he got right to the point. People start using drugs for a variety of reasons, he said, so we need a variety of services, including supervised injection sites, to encourage them to stop. Current drug laws won't get us there; drug users require medical help, not more criminal and moral penalties. Unfortunately, it didn't much matter what Owen had to say. Tony Clement, who was then the health minister, was absent from the room the entire time the six speakers from Vancouver were giving their presentations. "We weren't asked one question by the minister of health. He came in late and read from a prepared speech. It was a charade," recalls Owen. Clement indicated in his prepared statement that he believed there should only be three pillars: prevention, treatment, and enforcement.

Philip Owen disagrees vehemently with the Conservative position. Harm reduction should be the first rung on the ladder, he argues, the support a vulnerable person most requires before any other move is possible. "I'd see some sixteen-year-old girl all bent out of shape, and her pimp was on one side of her and the dealer on the other, and they were slowly killing her," he recalls. "Now she can go to Insite and can be directed to detox, and have a place to go to get away from the pimp and the dealers, to have a cup of coffee. To have Insite portrayed as just a centre to consume illegal drugs—they [its opponents] just don't understand it at all. Ten years ago when we were down there, there were these broken bodies between the ages of fifteen and twenty. Where are those people now? They are either dead or lost in the whole system. We had a new group of fifteen-year-olds there in 2008. And in ten years we'll have a new generation down there, who are in kindergarten right now." Unless we break it, Owen says, "the cycle will go on and on and on."

Donald MacPherson, author of the four pillars report and still city hall's drug policy coordinator, is also disappointed the blueprint he drew up hasn't resulted in more change. "Basically, we should be farther ahead on all of the pillars. We need more harm reduction, we need a couple more injection sites, we need more treatment. Prevention almost isn't even on the map. It's stunning how slow change has been, considering the public support," MacPherson says today. Over the years, he says, society has let a deeper and wider hole be dug in the Downtown Eastside, and the advancements made have been grains of sand, not the truck-loads of dirt required to fill in the crater. "People in charge knew there were things they could do and didn't do them. Haven't we failed miserably?" It's wonderful the province bought seventeen SROS in 2007 and 2008 to renovate, MacPherson says, but it should have been done years ago, and it will be difficult to repair the years of damage for thousands of people living on the streets.

MacPherson argues that the delivery system for programs needs to be better organized for coordinated change to happen. For example, he says, Vancouver Coastal Health should put addiction treatment and mental health services under the same umbrella so that the two areas are funded more evenly. "Mental illness gets all the money," he says, "and addiction is the little sister. We need a much more coherent approach to concurrent disorders. No one is driving the bus at the higher level, so it's a higgly-piggly system here, and we have a crisis, a disaster on our hands." Even so, MacPherson concedes, things are not nearly as bleak in 2009 as they were in the 1990s. "Having the premier on side and interested and willing to take action is really crucial. And maybe the Olympics have finally galvanized people, I don't know—perhaps the Games have finally gotten people talking about the Downtown Eastside. I think we are digging ourselves out of the hole."

Larry Campbell has been asked to speak across the country about Vancouver's four pillars concept, as other jurisdictions struggle to address their burgeoning drug problems. At first, he says, there is always apprehension around the harm reduction pillar. "I tell people, 'Don't be frightened by those who say harm reduction is just enabling drug users. Services like needle exchanges won't make your drug situation worse, and we just can't justify the money we have been spending on enforcement.'" In Vancouver, Campbell says, the prevention pillar has never been properly constructed either. High school teachers, for example, can identify many at-risk students, and Campbell would like to see straight-talking programs in schools that educate those kids about the decisions they are making and address root issues like poverty. Instead, Campbell says, the schools are inundated with the RCMP's DARE program, which is ineffective with its naive "Just Say No to Drugs" theme. When Campbell has raised these issues in the Senate, he's been told by Conservatives that money is already being spent on prevention and treatment. Not, however, Campbell insists, at the same level as the money going into enforcement. Neil Boyd notes that the DARE program rarely places alcohol and tobacco in the same category as illegal drugs, despite the fact that medical statistics show both alcohol and tobacco are more likely to kill users. An effective drug education program, Boyd says, wouldn't make such arbitrary distinctions or present a message that is both unrealistic and judgemental.

Neither Campbell nor Boyd believes that Insite, Vancouver's supervised injection site, will be shut down. Even if the current Conservative government won't grant exemptions for the operation of supervised injection sites, the two don't think the courts will turn down requests for exemptions that are clearly health-care based. It doesn't make sense, they say, to close down a facility where people are injecting drugs with sterile equipment under the watchful eyes of health care professionals, when for years they've been permitted to shoot up in dark alleys with dirty rigs. But the issue will remain a controversial one. The strongest support for the federal Conservatives comes from rural traditionalists, while harm reduction measures are mainly endorsed by urban residents who witness the dire effects of current drug policies every day. "This is almost an us versus them situation," Campbell says. If Liberal leader Michael Ignatieff and his party form the next federal government, Neil Boyd says, Ottawa's objections to Insite will almost certainly disappear. Though an

Ignatieff government would likely move cautiously and slowly in embracing further changes, Boyd adds, harm reduction would no longer be a dirty word in federal corridors.

Campbell and Boyd advocate a future drug policy that supports a continuum of care for people, serving everybody from the person who can quit by simply abstaining to the person who can get stable only if a doctor is prescribing him or her heroin. "If abstinence-based treatment worked for everyone, we wouldn't even be having this discussion," Campbell points out. To move towards a harm reduction strategy, say Campbell and Boyd, it's imperative to remove the stigma from addiction, which is now a crime. Legalize marijuana, says Campbell, and tax it, with the money collected going into treatment programs for those addicted to harder drugs. Even something as logical as regulating cannabis, though, Boyd says, will not be easy. It's a problem that requires a global revolution in approach—a dismantling of the framework of criminalization. At the moment, even in the Netherlands, the marijuana industry is not regulated; adherence to UN conventions requires instead that police simply make a decision not to enforce. Changes in the approach to heroin, ironically, might be a little easier to effect, Boyd suggests; heroin could be regulated, as it already is in Switzerland and the Netherlands, without running afoul of UN conventions.

The NAOMI project in Vancouver and Montreal and countless trials in Europe have demonstrated that heroin prescribed by a doctor to entrenched addicts can lead to improvements in both the rates of crime and the physical and mental health of users— all without allowing supply to migrate into the illicit market. The onus, Boyd says, is now on senior governments to support heroin maintenance through Criminal Code exemptions and funding. Neither Boyd nor Campbell endorses cocaine or amphetamine maintenance programs at the moment, but both feel that carefully controlled trials could determine whether there might be merit in programs of this kind. In Boyd's opinion, Ottawa needs to clamp down on people buying, distributing, and/or mixing the precursors for crystal meth; but even with crystal meth, there is no good argument for prosecuting users. "There's been a change in the public's attitude over the past thirty years around drugs. We've gradually moved towards considering the problem as a public health issue," Boyd says. "If you know about Insite today, if you are informed, you have to be hard-hearted to think it's a bad idea. It is so clearly about protecting the health and lives of very compromised people."

Public opinion is one thing, but official responses to drug policy are another. The astronomical increases in jail populations in the United States during the past twenty years can be traced almost exclusively to illegal drug use and distribution, Larry Campbell says. The rates for violent crime have been falling, but the jailing of drug offenders is fuelling a booming prison industry. "The U.S. is the big elephant in every room," Campbell says. "You would think that after Prohibition they would have learned a lesson, but they haven't. One in one hundred people in the U.S. are in jail. It's a growth industry. There's no room in state jails, and people are there longer. They act out because they have no hope. You can't jail your way out of this." But the Harper Conservatives seem intent on repeating the mistakes of the United States, Neil Boyd says; in 2009 they put forward Bill C-15, legislation that could place the grower of a single marijuana plant in jail for a minimum of six months.

Community activist Ann Livingston says that many Downtown Eastside citizens with chronic problems are already clogging provincial jails and remand centres, places that are poorly equipped to deal with their issues and that are extremely expensive forms of housing. "There is very little public discussion about how the legal system completely breaks down for people living outside, in extreme poverty, addicted to drugs. Pre-trial is not a proper prison, has no programming, and is maximum security, with lots of violence," she adds. Drug courts and community courts have been touted as a solution to the problem, and Neil Boyd says they are certainly better than a direct route to jail. But the approach has many drawbacks, in his opinion; a drug court is still employing a criminal justice response to addiction, something best recognized as a public health problem. "Drug courts can use criminal penalties to punish failures with addiction, an approach that would seem bizarre in any other public health context—with tobacco and alcohol addiction, for example," Boyd says. Drug courts have sprung up across North America, including in Vancouver, "but the moral judgement hasn't disappeared from the drug court," Boyd says. "Maintenance solutions are generally frowned upon, and the big stick of further criminal penalties is always looming in the background." In addition, the resources required to respond to an addict's needs are rarely adequate and are almost always constrained to some degree by prohibition, Boyd points out. "Are drug courts a terrible failure? No. They do represent a tiny step forward, but the problem is that they have too much power to punish and too little in the way of resources that might assist the addicted."

Gillian Maxwell of the citizens' group Keeping the Door Open says prohibition laws cause the most harm of all. "The globalized world is such a small place," says Maxwell, who has addressed the United Nations about the need to regulate drugs. "That's why I think these things will shift and change, but not immediately. This is just another version of women getting the vote and African Americans getting equality. I think we'll see it in our lifetime."

Another shift many harm reduction advocates support is the decriminalization of prostitution. It is a controversial stance, reviled by some service agencies and family members who argue public action should instead be directed towards arresting johns and getting women out of prostitution altogether. But Larry Campbell and Neil Boyd, along with some Aboriginal leaders and many community activists, argue that women forced into the survival sex trade need safer working conditions until they can get out, and targeting johns only makes a potentially dangerous sexual transaction disappear further into the shadows. Although the B.C. Supreme Court rejected the Pivot Legal Society's challenge to existing prostitution laws in December 2008, an appeal has been launched, and other cases are ongoing. A constitutional challenge in Ontario points to criminalization as a violation of Section 7 of the Charter—the right to life and liberty and security of the person, Boyd says. As the argument notes, the law permits the pursuit of prostitution but creates "legal prohibitions on the necessary conditions required for this type of work to be conducted in a safe and secure setting, thus exposing the sex worker to an increased risk of physical or psychological harm." As Simon Fraser University criminologist John Lowman has often noted, the hypocrisy of the existing law lies in its tolerance for prostitution and its concurrent prohibition of solicitation.

In 2008, a diverse group of Vancouver sex-trade workers led by Susan Davis got an unusual approval from the B.C. government to incorporate themselves as a co-operative. The West Coast Co-operative of Sex Industry Professionals is developing plans for several arts and business initiatives, including opening a legal brothel in time for the 2010 Olympics. Davis, a long-time advocate for working women who has written about prostitution on a website created jointly by sex workers and Simon Fraser University, believes a brothel would create a safer environment for the sex trade. "Everyone is affected by the trial," she said shortly after the verdict was handed down in the Pickton case. "And the workers, they don't want to die. We are looking for one opportunity to demonstrate the impact of bringing the sex trade in off the street." A co-operative brothel could also benefit the larger community, Davis says, because sex acts would take place and used condoms would be disposed of behind closed doors. Before the proposed brothel can open its doors, however, the new co-operative will have to overcome a large obstacle: convincing the federal government to grant the brothel amnesty from the Criminal Code provisions regarding adult prostitution.

Rick Frey, whose daughter Marnie was among the six women Robert Pickton was convicted of killing, finds the idea of a legalized brothel scandalous, saying women are forced into prostitution to support drug addictions and therefore need help to get clean, not to turn more tricks. "To think of prostitution as a job and treat it as such is ridiculous," Frey says. "What we need are facilities to get women off and away from drugs and keep other young girls from this horrible lifestyle by helping them when they are still young." In agreement with Frey are agencies like Vancouver Rape Relief and Women's Shelter, which for thirty-five years has advocated for an end to violence against women. Prostitution is "part of a continuum of violence against women that includes rape, wife assault, and incest," argues the group. In May 2008, Rape Relief hosted an international conference for transition-house workers who are united against the brothel idea and any other efforts to decriminalize the sex industry in time for the 2010 Winter Games. Suzanne Koepplinger, executive director of the Minnesota Indian Women's Resource Center, said during the conference that there is anecdotal evidence from social service agencies in Salt Lake City that many sex-trade workers were imported into Utah for the 2002 Winter Olympics there. No studies exist to prove exactly how many, however, and reports produced by pro-decriminalization groups here indicated that large events do not affect sex work in this way. Other speakers at the Rape Relief conference came armed with studies arguing that regulated prostitution in countries like Germany, Austria, and the Netherlands promotes sex trafficking, does not increase safety, and forces some women—those who do not want to submit to mandatory health checks, for example— to work an even more underground low stroll on the streets. Instead of decriminalization, conference participants called for more social services for working women.

Neil Boyd disagrees that something like a legal brothel will encourage women to enter the sex trade; ideally, he says, such an entity would provide better health and social services to those already in the industry. In some European countries, police have been proactive in their efforts to protect prostitutes, Boyd says, particularly vulnerable street workers. The "tippelzones" in the Netherlands are areas in which police and medical workers co-operate to provide a somewhat regulated environment for sex-trade transactions; closed-circuit television cameras are often used as a means of protection, as are police patrols of the geographic space.

Another supporter of the legalized brothel idea is Libby Davies, the veteran Member of Parliament for Vancouver East. Davies, who sat on a special federal government subcommittee that examined Canada's prostitution laws, favours taking sex work out of the Criminal Code and using other provisions in the law to deal with violence and sexual assault. "My sense is that life is not much better for sex-trade workers today than before Pickton was arrested," she says. She argues that a brothel like the one the Vancouver sex-trade workers have proposed would make it easier for women to lodge complaints against violent clients. "They are trying to develop something they believe will create a much safer environment that they will control," Davies says. "No one is talking about legalization. No one is talking about setting up some sort of state-sanctioned commercialized sex trade." Davies hopes prostitution laws will change one day, as they have for same-sex marriage, but says that may have to happen through the courts before any government is brave enough to tackle the thorny issue.

Improving Aboriginal Health and Well-Being

The Positive Outlook clinic at Vancouver Native Health has the same number of staff today as it did when it opened in 1997—Executive Director Doreen Littlejohn, four outreach workers, two intake workers, two drug and alcohol counsellors, and a nurse. Now, however, the clinic has 1,500 clients, nearly four times the number with which it started. Most clients are mentally ill and/or are injection drug users with no stable home. About 400 are HIV-positive, though for a variety of systemic reasons only 130 are receiving life-prolonging antiretroviral AIDS drugs. "That's pretty poor," Littlejohn says. "Our death rate is still unacceptably high at our clinic. It is still ten per cent each year, similar to sub-Saharan Africa." Aboriginal people, she says, are still becoming infected at the highest rate in Canada, despite all the harm reduction advancements that have been made. The overall HIV/AIDS infection rate did finally start to decline in 2007, and Littlejohn isn't enduring the procession of funerals she did in the late 1990s, but she still attends her fair share.

One of Littlejohn's clients, Frank McAllister, died at the age of thirty-seven on a frigid evening in December 2005 in a Downtown Eastside alley, lying next to his wheelchair. Earlier that year, McAllister had belonged to a music group at Outlook that produced a CD called *The Circle of Songs*. McAllister composed the first track, "Frank's Song," and sang the lyrics while playing his guitar. Littlejohn keeps a copy of the CD in her tiny office and smiles as she listens to it, surrounded by the hundreds of photos of clinic patrons taped to her walls. McAllister, she says, was an HIV-positive Aboriginal man with a mental illness who had been raised by foster parents. His behaviour at times was so manic he wanted to play his guitar in the middle of busy Hastings Street. Littlejohn struggled to get him connected with the proper mental health services. McAllister was on a long waiting list for subsidized housing; he couldn't get into an SRO room because he kept spending his welfare cheques on drugs and didn't have enough left over for a damage deposit. McAllister likely would have been rejected by landlords in his final months, Littlejohn says, because he was often filthy from being on the streets. At the same time she was contemplating having him re-certified for his own safety, some of McAllister's friends called 911 after finding him sick on the street during the first snowfall of the year. He reportedly told paramedics he didn't want to go in the ambulance, and no one called the Vancouver police's dedicated cruiser with an officer and a nurse on board. It turns out McAllister had bronchial pneumonia, a high fever, and end-stage AIDS. "They left him to die on the street," Littlejohn says, tears welling up in her eyes. "His death really hit me hard."

Another Outlook client, a schizophrenic First Nations man with advanced AIDS, was kicked out of his hospice in 2005. A nurse explained it was because the man was not yet considered palliative, but Littlejohn suspects it was because he smoked crack and was disruptive. The man was sent to a rundown SRO, and when Littlejohn went to visit, she found bugs swarming the room and the sink full of the man's feces. She took the man to St. Paul's Hospital, where he was given a blood transfusion and sent to the Dr. Peter Centre, a unique twenty-four-hour care residence for people with AIDS, where he lived until his death two months later. "It's constant social justice issues down here, and it doesn't appear to be getting better," Littlejohn says. "It's always about budgets, but not about people who die on the street."

However, Doreen Littlejohn has also seen success stories. In September 2007, a forty-one-year-old First Nations man named Sam limped into the clinic. Sam suffered from a brain injury he'd received in a beating. Although he was not being treated for HIV, Littlejohn could tell from his thinning hair and the psoriasis patches on his skin that he was HIV-positive. The homeless man, it turns out, had extremely high viral loads and thrush, a mouth infection. Sam confessed to Littlejohn he had tried to kill himself by overdosing on pharmaceuticals. "I told him, 'You can't kill yourself until we find out if we can save you,'" she recalls. Littlejohn fought an uphill battle, since other service providers dismissed Sam as "untreatable." However, she finally got him into housing, and he came daily to the clinic to take his antiretrovirals. "Today he's clear mentally, he's not trying to commit suicide. He comes into the clinic, he talks, he's in good humour. His infection level is undetectable," Littlejohn says proudly.

Today, Positive Outlook offers acupuncture and massage sessions, along with music and art therapy programs, and the clinic has a liaison social worker on the HIV wing at St. Paul's Hospital. In 2007, Outlook served more than thirty-one thousand free meals and had almost 3,400 visits from clients. It runs a weekly food bank and a rent supplement program. The clinic receives funding from various levels of government and through private donations, but it is funded to provide full-throttle assistance to only half of the 130 AIDS patients it supplies with antiretroviral drugs. It's surviving on a proverbial wing and a prayer. When Littlejohn needed to fix the towel dispenser in the clinic's bathroom (a client pulled it down in a rage), she begged a construction crew across the street to give her a large board. When her request for a ventilation unit was turned down, she installed a couple of fans to keep air moving in the tiny common room where hundreds of very sick people congregate daily to eat and mingle. Littlejohn's boss at Vancouver Native Health, Lou Demerais, is realistic about the situation, though he confesses to being an eternal optimist. "The AIDS thing notwithstanding, the Hepatitis C notwithstanding, the lousy housing that has been allowed to be perpetuated notwithstanding," he says, Aboriginal people in the Downtown Eastside are healthier today than they were when he helped start the Vancouver Native Health Society clinic in 1991.

Jerry Adams of the Native Friendship Centre in Vancouver has faith in his people, and he hopes to spend more time playing basketball with the younger generation than analyzing problems. "We want to play with our kids," he says, "rather than social-work them to death." According to Adams, many teens coming into the Friendship Centre today have a maturity and a determination to make the future brighter. "They have some understanding of what needs to be done that I didn't have when I was in my twenties," he says. He believes that some of the wounds from residential schools are healing, and Canadians have a better understanding of the horrors many Aboriginal people battle internally. "Our situation now is a legacy of more than a century of bad public policy we had no control over. Somehow we survived—that in and of itself is worth celebrating," Adams says. "I think there's a lot more empathy for our people."

As a senator, Larry Campbell continues to lobby for funding that would allow the Native Friendship Centre to construct an Urban Native Youth Association building. The idea, first proposed during the years Campbell was mayor, would give Aboriginal teens a safe place to hang out. "When a group of Aboriginal people wants to make a difference," Campbell says, "we should be there to give them support. We haven't been doing that. We can help by creating a board of directors and finding some funding for this centre and similar projects. There's a huge issue with Aboriginal youth and gangs in Winnipeg. Vancouver will have that problem unless we help youth move in a better direction." Campbell notes the success of Vancouver's Friendship Centre, which has been serving Aboriginal families for decades. "I spent a lot of time in the Friendship Centre when I was coroner.

It fascinated me, because it was a place where good things happened. You could go down there and see young kids playing, see people learning languages and learning crafts. It was a good cross-representation of First Nations adults who, for all their struggles, were engaged," he recalls. "You can't minimize the effect residential schools had on Native people. I think the next generation is coming through that, although I don't know when it will get to be sunshine and roses."

Strengthening Community Pride

A twenty-six-page information bulletin released in early 2008 by Vancouver Coastal Health, *The Downtown Eastside: A Neighbourhood in Recovery,* found that two fifths of the area's 16,000 residents (6,400 people) were doing well or very well, one fifth (3,200) were getting by, and the rest (6,400 people) were living marginal lives and needed more support. Of the latter group, 2,100 people were "not adequately served," research by the health board showed, which meant they had no permanent housing, behaved erratically, had significant addiction and mental illness problems, and were not linked to health care services. Nonetheless, the document referred to the neighbourhood as "one of the most capable communities in Vancouver." More people had been immunized there than in the rest of Vancouver, the Carnegie Centre had the busiest library in the city, and an increasing number of people had jobs and were involved in volunteer activities.

Among the many successes in the Downtown Eastside, the most striking has been the ability of marginalized people to organize and advocate for themselves. DERA, VANDU, and various Carnegie Centre groups have accomplished much over the years. The staff at non-profit agencies, as well as nurses and outreach workers who have committed their lives to supporting the area's residents, have also brought energy to the neighbourhood.

However, in July 2009, a neighbourhood icon was shut down by health authorities: DEYAS, launched two decades earlier by the late John Turvey, was closed amid allegations of mismanagement and financial improprieties. The sad development means DEYAS's vans will no longer patrol Downtown Eastside streets to dispense much-needed clean needles, condoms, and counselling.

Over the years, in-fighting has dogged the Downtown Eastside's many social service agencies, there has been constant jockeying for scarce funding dollars, and organizations have often disagreed on the best direction for change. Bud Osborn, though, has noticed more unity in recent years, and he points optimistically to a new batch of young advocates, like Wendy Pedersen from the Carnegie Community Action Plan and lawyers from Pivot Legal Society, who are committed to collaborating for the common good. "I know if there is any hope to sustain this as a community, we need to work together," Osborn says, "and we need allies." Larry Campbell agrees. Campbell was frustrated to see agencies working at cross-purposes in the past, and he argues that by combining efforts and funds, groups could effect lasting change. "If someone could pull all these groups together under one umbrella—housing, social services, and legal—that would make much better use of the money, and eventually you'd end up with a cohesive group that is going in the same direction," he suggests.

Mark Townsend is proud of the work he and his partner, Liz Evans, have done at the Portland Hotel Society, but he's frustrated that everything has been "cobbled together" on a shoestring budget. "I feel like we've provided some bread and butter, but with nothing else on it—and there likely never will be," Townsend says. He and Evans seem committed to their demanding jobs, even though a regular nine-to-five gig would make raising their two school-aged children a lot easier. "This is a community," Townsend says, "and people do care about each other in big ways.

The prostitute looks after the old guy in his room, in exchange for nothing. She's got kids she never cared for, but she's caring for him. I find people here are more connected, more honest, more human in the real way. Lots of people would say that's crazy, but people in the main system are screwed up, too. I now realize the people here are just like me; they're just like us. And it would all be okay if other people realized that. It's complicated, but it could be successful."

There is an unmistakable sense of community in the Downtown Eastside, from the celebration of small milestones in a struggling person's life at the Portland Hotel to the athletic, academic, cultural, and entertainment programs run out of the Carnegie Centre. Since 2004, the popular Heart of the City Festival has annually featured artists and activists from the neighbourhood. In late 2009, the W2 Community Media Arts Centre is scheduled to open in the renovated Woodward's building, offering arts programs and creative resources for Downtown Eastside residents. The neighbourhood held its first health fair in 2008 in the alley between the Carnegie Centre and the Health Contact Centre in the Roosevelt Hotel. Residents walked through the narrow space, getting a free hot lunch and speaking to nurses and other health workers at the booths. There was information about mouth cancer from the Portland Clinic, about treatment and support services from the B.C. Persons with AIDS Society, and about a fresh fruit and vegetable program offered through Vancouver Native Health, along with warnings about bedbugs in poorly run SRO hotels.

MP Libby Davies, as a long-time advocate and political representative for the community, remains impressed by the continued resistance in the neighbourhood. Attempts by business and government over the years to break up the Downtown Eastside have never worked, she says. Businesses took their awnings down so that homeless people wouldn't loiter in front of shops to get out of the rain; pay phones were removed so that addicts couldn't call dealers to get their next fix; "no camping" signs were posted in parks to keep the tent cities out. "But this community has been so resilient," Davies marvels. "The Downtown Eastside took a different path because the people there fought back. The fundamental question that faces the neighbourhood today, as it did forty years ago, and maybe does in the future, is that it occupies land that is the most expensive in the city, other than in the downtown [core]." Although the community needs more social housing, and residents would benefit from a more coherent drug policy, Davies is amazed at the accomplishments—including North America's first supervised injection site—in the Downtown Eastside over the last decade. "I think it is remarkable that in ten years there has been a fundamental shift. I think we should be proud," she says.

Bud Osborn is confident about the future of the neighbourhood, which he calls the "spiritual heart" of Vancouver. "I was doing a poetry reading recently," Osborn recalls, "and a young Native fellow said to me, 'I came to the Downtown Eastside because I wanted to die, because I thought it was death, despair, and disease. I hated my life. But since I came here and joined some groups, I really want to live now.' To me, that is the essence of a community—from what seems impossible, as his life seemed to him when he came down here ready to die, he instead found a reason to live." Osborn had a similar experience a few years ago after some serious health complications from fibromyalgia, spinal arthritis, and Hepatitis C. He convalesced at a friend's home in another community for many months. He felt like "his spirit was dying," however, so he returned to the Downtown Eastside, found a spot in the Four Sisters Co-op, and had friends like *Carnegie Newsletter* editor Paul Taylor bring him food each day. "I was very fortunate, because this is my community, and I had never known what a community was, or a family," Osborn says. "This is the first place I didn't feel out of place."

The challenge, people agree, will be to keep the Downtown Eastside a community but make it a healthier one in the future. All levels of government and every caring citizen should want to participate in that vision.

> Sunshine
> On downtown eastside sidewalks
> Glows fresh crimson
> Like rose petals fallen
> From ransacked gardens of the broken-hearted
> —BUD OSBORN, "Down Here"

Sources

CHAPTER 1: The Early Years

Boyd, Neil. *High Society: Legal and Illegal Drugs in Canada.* Toronto:
Key Porter, 1991.

Boyd, Neil. "The Origins of Canadian Narcotics Legislation: The Process
of Criminalization in Historical Context." *Dalhousie Law Journal* 8, 1984.

Cameron, Sandy. *Fighting for Community: Stories from the Carnegie Centre
and the Downtown Eastside.* Vancouver: Carnegie Community Centre
Association, 1996.

City of Vancouver Planning Department. *Downtown East Side.* Vancouver
City Hall, June 1965.

Giffen, P.J. *Panic and Indifference: The Politics of Canada's Drug Laws.* Ottawa:
Canadian Centre on Substance Abuse, 1991.

MacFarlane, Brian A., Robert J. Frater, and Chantal Proulx. *Drug Offences in
Canada, Third Edition.* Toronto: Canada Law Book, 1996.

Vancouver Public Library, Carnegie Branch. Downtown Eastside Special
Collection. (Miscellaneous newspaper clippings, magazine articles, and
letters, including letters between Dr. Stewart Murray and the Carnegie
librarian, July 15 and 23, 1940; *Vancouver Sun* article, September 27,
1968; *Muse News* magazine published by the Vancouver Museum, April/
May 1994.)

CHAPTER 2: We Call It the Downtown Eastside

Boyd, Neil. "The Question of Marijuana Control: Is De Minimis Appropriate, Your Honour?" *Criminal Law Quarterly* 12, 1982, pp. 212–32.

Campbell, Larry (presiding coroner). *Verdict of Coroner's Jury: Robert Grant Laws.* Vancouver: B.C. Coroners Service, December 1982.

City of Vancouver. *A Report on Residential Hotels and Rooming Houses in the Core Area of the City of Vancouver.* Vancouver City Hall, 1979.

Griffin, Kevin. "When Skid Road Became Home." *Vancouver Sun,* October 20, 2005.

Le Dain, Gerald. *Final Report, Commission of Inquiry into the Non-Medical Use of Drugs.* Ottawa: Queen's Printer, December 1973.

Shafer, R.P. National Commission on Marihuana and Drug Abuse, *Marihuana: A Signal of Misunderstanding; First Report.* Washington, D.C.: March 1972.

Still, Larry. "Ex-lawyer Tells Us Nothing New about Famous Drug Bust." *Vancouver Sun,* October 1, 1988.

Vancouver Sun. "Bruce Eriksen, Champion of Skid Road Poor, Dies at Age of 68." *Vancouver Sun,* March 18, 1997.

Vancouver Public Library, Carnegie Branch. Downtown Eastside Special Collection. (Miscellaneous newspaper clippings, including *Vancouver Sun,* November 14, 1975; *Vancouver Sun,* December 4, 1975; *Vancouver Sun,* April 18, 1978; *Vancouver Sun,* September 14, 1979; *Vancouver Sun,* January 25, 1980.)

CHAPTER 3: Lethal Heroin, Killer Coke, and Expo 86

Brandt, Michael David. "Opening the Casket: An Analysis of Alcohol and Heroin Overdoses—Myths, Misattributions, and Misunderstandings" (master's thesis, Simon Fraser University, 1996).

Cameron, Sandy. *Fighting for Community: Stories from the Carnegie Centre and the Downtown Eastside.* Vancouver: Carnegie Community Centre Association, 1996.

Campbell, Larry (presiding coroner). *Verdict of Coroner's Jury: Kenneth Hodgins.* Vancouver: B.C. Coroners Service, May 1991.

Green, Jim. *Housing Conditions and Population in the Downtown Eastside.* Vancouver: Downtown Eastside Residents' Association (DERA), March 1985.

Hume, Mark. "Older Fire Escapes Felt Traps." *Vancouver Sun,* March 18, 1986.

Jessup, John, Project Director, et al. *Downtown Lodging Houses and Tenant Profile.* Social Planning Department, City of Vancouver, October 1983.

Pemberton, Kim. "Sister Decries Robber's Violent Death." *Vancouver Sun,* May 3, 1991.

Sarti, Robert. "Senior Calls Eviction Move Horrible." *Vancouver Sun,* October 27, 1988.

Sarti, Robert. "Solheim Place Rises with Faith in Future." *Vancouver Sun,* December 18, 1991.

Vancouver Sun. "Alcohol Deaths Constant, Says B.C. Coroner." *Vancouver Sun,* December 30, 1987.

CHAPTER 4: The Cain Report

Aird, Elizabeth. "Heroin Deaths Blamed on Lack of Political Will." *Vancouver Sun,* March 7, 1996.

Cain, Vince, Chief Coroner of B.C. *Report of the Task Force into Illicit Narcotic Overdose Deaths in British Columbia.* Victoria: B.C. Ministry of the Attorney-General, 1994.

Darke, Shane, and Deborah Zador. "Fatal Heroin Overdose: A Review." *Addiction* 91 (12), 1996.

Engler, Gary. "Deputy Police Chief Supports Legalizing Drugs." *Vancouver Sun,* October 8, 1997.

Hall, Neal. "Typical Local Bank Robbers Are Supporting a Drug Habit." *Vancouver Sun,* January 4, 1991.

Hall, Neal, and Kim Pemberton. "Coroner Seeks 'Social' Fix for Drug Epidemic. *Vancouver Sun,* January 21, 1995.

Millar, Dr. John S. *HIV, Hepatitis, and Injection Drug Use in British Columbia— Pay Now or Pay Later?* Victoria: Office of the Provincial Health Officer, B.C. Ministry of Health, June 1998.

Pemberton, Kim. "Fight against Drug Overdose Deaths Still 'At Mile Zero.'" *Vancouver Sun,* July 17, 1997.

Teichroeb, Ruth. "Killer Coke 'Alarming.'" *Vancouver Sun,* July 13, 1986.

Vancouver Sun. "Cain Report a Good Start on a Tough Problem." *Vancouver Sun,* January 24, 1995.

Wigod, Rebecca. "Doctors Criticize Heroin Proposal: Stick with Methadone Program, Three Experts on Drug Abuse Say." *Vancouver Sun,* January 26, 1995.

CHAPTER 5: Woodward's

Armstrong, John. "Poet Had a Choice of Gutters: Emerging from a Terrible Childhood, Bud Osborn Has Managed to Get It Together at Last: Privilege for a Poet to Be Part of Community." *Vancouver Sun*, April 6, 1996.

Boyd, Denny. "When Ripley's Leather and Hats Goes, Another Piece of Vancouver Is Lost." *Vancouver Sun*, February 4, 1994.

Bula, Frances. "Eastside Groups Vow to Ensure Woodward's Has Social Housing." *Vancouver Sun*, April 7, 1997.

Bula, Frances. "Profile: Jim Green—Mean or Serene? Bad-boy Candidate Doesn't Understand Why He Gets Criticized." *Vancouver Sun*, October 8, 2005.

Constantineau, Bruce. "On a Knife Edge." *Vancouver Sun*, April 25, 1987.

Constantineau, Bruce. "Woodward's Considers Moving Downtown Outlet to a New Site: Woodward's Ponders New Site for Costly Downtown Store." *Vancouver Sun*, December 16, 1988.

Edelson, Nathan. *A Program of Strategic Actions for the Downtown Eastside*. Community Services, Vancouver City Hall, July 1998.

Laviolette, Tom. *On Hastings Street: 30 Years of Retail History in Vancouver's Downtown Eastside, 1970–2000*. Vancouver: Carnegie Community Action Project, 2000.

Mackie, John. "Journey into Fear Illuminates 100-Block West Hastings." *Vancouver Sun*, September 16, 2002.

Sarti, Robert. "Culture Gap Leading to Health Gap as Seniors Start to Shop in Chinatown." *Vancouver Sun*, October 23, 1992.

Sarti, Robert. "In Poor Neighbourhood, Adequate Housing Is the Delicate Balance Beam for Survival: Housing Loss Called Cause of Sickness." *Vancouver Sun*, April 16, 1996.

Sarti, Robert. "Social Housing, Retail Complex Goal of 'Battle for Neighbourhood.'" *Vancouver Sun*, October 23, 1992.

Stainsby, Mia. "Travelling in Time: Once the City's Cultural Core, Dowdy Hastings Is Humming Again to a Beat of Its Own." *Vancouver Sun*, January 12, 1990.

Vancouver Sun. "Woodward's Co-op Housing Supporters Stage Sit-in Protest." *Vancouver Sun*, April 16, 1997.

Ward, Doug. "Profile: An Act of Re-invention: Green Brings Wealth of Experience to His Spot on Council." *Vancouver Sun*, November 25, 2002.

CHAPTER 6: Homeless and Mentally Ill

Baldrey, Keith. "Mental-health Care in 'Crisis,' NDP says: Riverview Closing to Worsen Tight Bed Supply." *Vancouver Sun*, December 2, 1987.

Davidson, Jill, Senior Housing Planner. *2007 Survey of Low-Income Housing in the Downtown Core.* Vancouver City Hall, July 2007.

Edelson, Nathan. *A Program of Strategic Actions for the Downtown Eastside.* Community Services, Vancouver City Hall, July 1998.

Hanna, Dawn. "Riverview Halts Plans to Close More Beds." *Vancouver Sun*, October 15, 1991.

MacQueen, Ken. "B.C. to Spend $125 Million to Get Mentally Ill Off Streets: Health Minister's 7-year Initiative Includes Replacing Coquitlam's Riverview Hospital with Smaller Facilities across the Province." *Vancouver Sun*, January 21, 1998.

Millar, Dr. John S. *HIV, Hepatitis, and Injection Drug Use in British Columbia— Pay Now or Pay Later?* Victoria: Office of the Provincial Health Officer, B.C. Ministry of Health, June 1998.

Pemberton, Kim. "Mental Homes Wretched, Lobby Group Says." *Vancouver Sun*, March 9, 1989.

Sankar, Celia. "Shelters Organize More Beds for the Homeless." *Vancouver Sun*, December 23, 1998.

Vancouver Coastal Health Authority. *Vancouver Community Operational Addictions Plan: A Proposal in Support of the Vancouver Agreement Strategies* (draft discussion and feedback document). Vancouver Coastal Health Authority, September 19, 2002.

Vancouver Sun. "A Crisis Situation: Riverview Decision Belatedly Realizes That Mentally Ill Had Nowhere to Go." *Vancouver Sun*, editorial section, February 24, 1996.

Young, Mary Lynn. "Panhandler Sank in City's Depths." *Vancouver Sun*, August 22, 1991.

CHAPTER 7: Vancouver's HIV/AIDS Epidemic: The Worst in the Western World

Culbert, Lori. "Decriminalize Street Drugs, City Police Officer Says." *Vancouver Sun*, April 22, 1998.

Culbert, Lori. "Funding Focus of AIDS Rally: People on the Downtown Eastside Say Those in the Area Who Are HIV-Positive Are Being Forgotten by Government." *Vancouver Sun*, December 2, 1996.

Engler, Gary. "Deputy Police Chief Supports Legalizing Drugs." *Vancouver Sun*, October 8, 1997.

Millar, Dr. John S. *HIV, Hepatitis, and Injection Drug Use in British Columbia— Pay Now or Pay Later?* Victoria: Office of the Provincial Health Officer, B.C. Ministry of Health, June 1998.

Parry, Dr. Penny. *Something to Eat, a Place to Sleep, and Someone Who Gives a Damn.* Victoria: B.C. Ministry of Health, September 1997.

Pemberton, Kim. "Drug Overdose Victims Remembered as Lobby Pushes Easier Heroin Access: Scourge of the Eastside Cited as more than 1,000 Crosses Are Placed at a Rally." *Vancouver Sun*, July 16, 1997.

Skelton, Chad. "Some Get It, Some Don't: The AIDS 'drug cocktail' is meant to be available to anyone whose viral count has reached a threshold level. Yet the new wonder drugs have passed by many in Vancouver's poorest neighbourhood. It's not because they haven't asked for it, outreach workers say, but because their doctors won't give it to them." *Vancouver Sun*, April 3, 1999.

Strathdee, Steffanie, et al. *Needle Exchange Is Not Enough: Lessons from the Vancouver Injecting Drug Use Study.* AIDS, vol. 11, July 1997.

Strathdee, Steffanie, et al. "Barriers to Use of Free Antiretroviral Therapy in Injection Drug Users." *Journal of the American Medical Association*, August 1998.

Whynot, Dr. Elizabeth. *Health Impact of Injection Drug Use and HIV in Vancouver.* Office of the Vancouver Medical Health Officer, May 1996.

CHAPTER 8: Harm Reduction: A Grassroots Struggle

City of Vancouver. *Background Paper on Treatment Needs in Vancouver.* Social Planning Department, July 1998. Available at vancouver.ca/commsvcs/ socialplanning/initiatives/alcohol/background.htm.

Culbert, Lori. "Rehab Centre Could Save Lives: Coroner." *Vancouver Sun*, August 15, 2000.

Engler, Gary. "Ottawa Ducks Issue of Giving Heroin to Addicts: The Justice Minister and the Health Minister Each Say the Drug Issue is a Problem for the Other's Jurisdiction." *Vancouver Sun*, September 30, 1997.

Kerr, Thomas, et al. *Responding to an Emergency: Education, Advocacy and Community Care by a Peer-driven Organization of Drug Users—A Case Study of Vancouver Area Network of Drug Users (VANDU).* Ottawa: Health Canada, December 2001.

MacPherson, Donald. *Comprehensive Systems of Care for Drug Users in Switzerland and Frankfurt, Germany.* Social Planning Department, City of Vancouver, June 1999.

Millar, Dr. John S. *HIV, Hepatitis, and Injection Drug Use in British Columbia—Pay Now or Pay Later?* Victoria: Office of the Provincial Health Officer, B.C. Ministry of Health, June 1998.

Mulgrew, Ian. "End War on Drugs, Conference Concludes: Health-care specialists gathering at the first international meeting on Preventing Heroin Overdose agree that cities must turn their focus to the needs of users and expand 'harm-reduction' strategies." *Vancouver Sun,* January 17, 2000.

Munro, Margaret. "Decriminalizing Drugs Wrong, Experts Argue: 'Destigmatizing' illegal drugs will only encourage more young people to use them, says a report to politicians and health officials." *Vancouver Sun,* February 4, 1998.

Munro, Margaret. "Vancouver's Raging HIV Epidemic Most Rampant in Developed World: Nearly Half the 6,000 to 10,000 Addicts in Downtown Eastside are Infected, AIDS Expert Says." *Vancouver Sun,* October 2, 1997.

CHAPTER 9: *Da Vinci's Inquest*
Beatty, Jim. "The Demon Barber: Sober, he's a successful businessman who plays the stock market. Drunk, he's a predator who may have killed as many as 10 women. Now Gilbert Paul Jordan is out of jail and says he can't predict what he may do next." *Vancouver Sun,* November 4, 2000.

Di Fiore, Alan, Chris Haddock, and Esta Spalding. "Episode 14—A Cinderella Story," *Part 1. Da Vinci's Inquest* script, July 1999.

Edelson, Nathan. *A Program of Strategic Actions for the Downtown Eastside.* Community Services, City of Vancouver, July 1998.

Haddock, Chris. "Episode 1—Hard Rain, Part 1." *Da Vinci's Inquest* script, February 1998.

Haddock, Chris. "Episode 2—Hard Rain, Part 2." *Da Vinci's Inquest* script, February 1998.

Haddock, Chris. "Episode 3—Hard Rain, Part 3." *Da Vinci's Inquest* script, February 1998.

Rose, Chris, Kim Pemberton, and Robert Sarti. "Bodies in the Barber Shop." *Vancouver Sun,* October 22, 1988.

CHAPTER 10: The Missing Women

Bolan, Kim. "Memorial for a Missing Woman: Family, Friends Remember Sereena Abotsway." *Vancouver Sun*, March 12, 2002.

Culbert, Lori. "Lives Remembered: A troubled child who once won a trip to Holland eventually wound up on the streets of Vancouver. The *Sun's* Lori Culbert writes about that life, and those of two other women, cut tragically short." *Vancouver Sun*, January 13, 2007.

Culbert, Lori. "Mountie Tells How Stalled Investigation Was Renewed: For a time, they believed the disappearances had ended." *Vancouver Sun*, January 23, 2007.

Culbert, Lori. "Never to Be Forgotten: *Vancouver Sun* reporter Lori Culbert looks at the lives of three women whom Port Coquitlam pig farmer Robert (Willie) Pickton is accused of killing." *Vancouver Sun*, January 12, 2007.

Culbert, Lori. "Troubled Lives: Almost four months after the start of Robert (Willie) Pickton's first-degree murder trial, the focus of the mammoth hearing has moved to the six women he is accused of killing." *Vancouver Sun*, May 11, 2007.

Culbert, Lori, Lindsay Kines, and Kim Bolan. "Investigation Turns Up Startling New Numbers: Police to announce expanded probe; Women have history of drugs, prostitution and links to Downtown Eastside." *Vancouver Sun*, September 21, 2001.

Kines, Lindsay, Kim Bolan, and Lori Culbert. "How the Police Investigation Was Flawed: Too few officers, police infighting and lack of experience undermined first probe into disappearances." *Vancouver Sun*, September 22, 2001.

Kines, Lindsay, and Kim Bolan. "Two Former Police Officers Join Call for Investigation." *Vancouver Sun*, March 16, 2002.

Rossmo, Kim, ed. *Criminal Investigative Failures.* Oxford: Taylor & Francis, Inc., 2008.

Ward, Doug. "Sereena Abotsway Once Joined Missing Women March: Now She's among the Dead Honoured." *Vancouver Sun*, February 15, 2007.

CHAPTER 11: Four Pillars

Bula, Frances. "Pioneering Drug-Addict Centre Proves Too Popular: 'Overwhelmed' Quarters Undergoing Renovation." *Vancouver Sun*, February 22, 2002.

Bula, Frances, and Chris Nuttall-Smith. "Sounds Like a Plan: Reaction Is Favourable to the Mayor's Strategy on Drugs and the Downtown Eastside—but It's Not Unanimous." *Vancouver Sun*, December 1, 2000.

City of Vancouver. *Background Paper on Treatment Needs in Vancouver.* Social Planning Department, July 1998. Available at vancouver.ca/commsvcs/ socialplanning/initiatives/alcohol/background.htm.

MacPherson, Donald. *A Framework for Action: A Four-Pillar Approach to Drug Problems in Vancouver.* City of Vancouver, April 24, 2001.

Vancouver Coastal Health Authority. *Vancouver Community Operational Addictions Plan: A Proposal in Support of the Vancouver Agreement Strategies.* (draft discussion and feedback document). Vancouver Coastal Health Authority, September 19, 2002.

CHAPTER 12: Canada's First Supervised Injection Site

Dandurand, Yvon, et al. *Confident Policing in a Troubled Community: An Evaluation of the Vancouver Police Department's City-Wide Enforcement Team Initiative.* University College of the Fraser Valley, September 1, 2004.

Human Rights Watch. *Abusing the User.* New York: May 6, 2003. Available at www.hrw.org/en/node/12330/section/1.

Lee, Jeff. "Injection Site Should Be for Locals Only, Mayor Says: ID Requirement Would Pressure Other Cities to Open Their Own Sites." *Vancouver Sun,* January 8, 2003.

Lee, Jeff. "Prescribe Heroin, Cocaine to Addicts, Mayor Says: Larry Campbell Believes It's an Option when Methadone and Abstinence Fail." *Vancouver Sun,* January 9, 2003.

Read, Nicholas. "Injection Site Not Ready for Addicts: Reporters Tour East Hastings Site before It Opens Next Week." *Vancouver Sun,* September 16, 2003.

Stevens, Alex, (editor). *Crossing Frontiers: International Developments in the Treatment of Drug Dependence.* Brighton: Pavilion Publishing, 2008.

Wood, E., T. Kerr, J.S. Montaner, S.A. Strathdee, A. Wodak, C. Hankins, M.T. Schechter, and M.W. Tyndall. "Rationale for Evaluating North America's First Medically Supervised Safer-Injecting Facility." *Lancet—Infectious Diseases* 4(5), May 2004, pp. 301–306.

Wood, E., M.W. Tyndall, J.S. Montaner, and T. Kerr. "Summary of Findings from the Evaluation of a Pilot Medically Supervised Safer Injecting Facility." *Canadian Medical Association Journal* 175(11), November 2006, pp. 1399–1404.

Wood, E., M.W. Tyndall, C. Lai, J.S.G. Montaner, and T. Kerr. "Impact of a Medically Supervised Safer Injecting Facility on Drug Dealing and Other Drug Related Crime." *Substance Abuse Treatment, Prevention, and Policy* 1, May 2006, pp. 13–16.

Wood, E., M.W. Tyndall, Z. Qui, R. Zhang, J.S.G. Montaner, and T. Kerr. "Service Uptake and Characteristics of Injection Drug Users Utilizing North America's First Medically Supervised Safer Injecting Facility." *American Journal of Public Health* 96(5), May 2006, pp. 770–773.

Wood, E., T. Kerr, E. Lloyd-Smith, C. Buchner, D.C. March, J.S.G. Montaner, and M.W. Tyndall. "Methodology for Evaluating Insite: Canada's First Medically Supervised Safer Injection Facility for Injection Drug Users." *Harm Reduction Journal* 1, November 2004, pp. 9–13.

Wood, E., T. Kerr, W. Small, Kathy Li, D.C. Marsh, J.S. Montaner, and M.W. Tyndall. "Changes in Public Order after the Opening of a Medically Supervised Safer Injection Facility for Illicit Injection Drug Users." *Canadian Medical Association Journal* 171(7), September 2004, pp. 731–734.

CHAPTER 13: The Harm Reduction Two-Step

B.C. Centre for Excellence in HIV/AIDS. CHASE *(Community Health and Safety Evaluation) Project.* Vancouver, May 2005.

Bula, Frances, and Petti Fong. "Police Withdraw Bid for Crackdown Funds: More Evidence Needed on Effectiveness of Downtown Eastside Project, Mayor Says." *Vancouver Sun,* July 9, 2003.

Bula, Frances, and Doug Ward. "Rival Councillors Agree on Legalizing Pot: They Say It's Better Than Letting Organized Crime and Dealers Benefit." *Vancouver Sun,* June 9, 2005.

Campbell, Larry (foreword). *A Dialogue on the Prevention of Problematic Drug Use: A Summary of the Proceedings from the Symposium "Visioning a Future for Prevention, A Local Perspective."* Vancouver, February 2004.

Hansen, Darah, and Brad Badelt. "Drug Dealers Mostly Canadian Born, Not Immigrants, New Study Says: Vancouver police inspector also says most street traffickers have previous records for drug offences." *Vancouver Sun,* May 16, 2005.

Mackie, John. "Woodward's Squatters Say They'll Move to Dominion: Homeless will stay at hotel for four months, then move to more permanent digs." *Vancouver Sun*, December 14, 2002.

MacPherson, Donald. *Preventing Harm from Psychoactive Substance Use.* City of Vancouver Drug Policy Program, November 2005.

Pivot Legal Society. *To Serve and Protect: A Report on Policing in Vancouver's Downtown Eastside.* Vancouver, October 2002.

Street Crime Working Group. *Beyond the Revolving Door: A New Response to Chronic Offenders.* Vancouver: Commissioned by the B.C. Ministry of the Attorney-General, 2005.

Vancouver Agreement. *The First Five Years; 2000–2005 Progress and Highlights.* Vancouver, 2006.

Wood, Evan, and Thomas Kerr (guest editors). "Cities and Drugs: Responding to Drugs in the City of Vancouver." *International Journal of Drug Policy* 17(2), Elsevier, March 2006, pp. 55–60.

CHAPTER 14: Sex Work, Safety, and Sanctuaries

Arthur, Joyce, and Tamara O'Doherty. "A 2010 Deadline for Prostitution: Decriminalization and a Sex Worker Cooperative in Time for the Games Would Provide Safety and Equal Rights." *Vancouver Sun*, December 6, 2007.

B.C. Centre for Excellence in HIV/AIDS. CHASE *(Community Health and Safety Evaluation) Project.* Vancouver, May 2005.

Bula, Frances. "Mayor Tells Police Why He Bought Drugs for Addicts: Official Statement Blames Opponents for Controversy That Led to Investigation." *Vancouver Sun*, May 2, 2006.

Bula, Frances. "Prostitutes' Problems May Have to be Managed, Not Solved: Mayor: Red Light Districts Not the Answer, Says Sullivan." *Vancouver Sun*, January 27, 2006.

Culbert, Lori. "Family Wrestles with Street's Death Grip; Advocates Struggle for Solutions to Help Women Conquer Demons of Downtown Eastside." *Vancouver Sun*, February 28, 2008.

Culbert, Lori. "Lives Remembered: A troubled child who once won a trip to Holland eventually wound up on the streets of Vancouver. The *Sun's* Lori Culbert writes about that life, and those of two other women, cut tragically short." *Vancouver Sun*, January 13, 2007.

Culbert, Lori. "Odds Stacked against Women Trying to Recover; Treatment Available, but for Those Heading Down New Road There Are Few Places to Go." *Vancouver Sun*, February 27, 2008.

Culbert, Lori. "Walkers Seek Justice for Missing Women." *Vancouver Sun*, June 21, 2008.

Culbert, Lori, Neal Hall, et al. "Emotional End to Pickton Trial; Relatives and Police Had Wanted First-Degree Murder Convictions." *Vancouver Sun*, December 10, 2007.

Culbert, Lori, Neal Hall, et al. "'She Stays Alive in All of Us'; Victim Impact I Family Members Overcome by Emotion as they Remember their Loved Ones." *Vancouver Sun*, December 10, 2007.

Fowlie, Jonathan, and Lori Culbert. "Oppal Rules Out Trying Pickton on 20 Other Charges Unless Appeal Succeeds." *Vancouver Sun*, February 27, 2008.

Gibson, Kate, Raven Bowen, et al. *Evaluation of the Mobile Access Project (MAP): Report to the Vancouver Agreement Women's Strategy Task Team*. Vancouver: WISH and PACE, May 2006.

Hall, Neal, and Lori Culbert. "Pickton's 'Senseless and Despicable Crimes'; Judge's Decision Met with Screams of 'Yes, Yes!'" *Vancouver Sun*, December 12, 2007.

Hennig, Jana, et al. *Draft Report: Trafficking in Human Beings and the 2006 World Cup in Germany*. Geneva: International Organization for Migration, September 2006.

Pacey, Katrina, et al. *Voices for Dignity: A Call to End the Harms Caused by Canada's Sex Trade Laws*. Vancouver: Pivot Legal Society, March 2004.

Piche, Danica, et al. *Beyond Decriminalization: Sex Work, Human Rights and a New Framework for Law Reform*. Vancouver: Pivot Legal Society, June 2006.

Pivot Legal Society. "Sex Worker Charter Challenge Denied" (press release) Vancouver, December 16, 2008. Available at www.pivotlegal.org/News/08-12-16--sexworkchallenge.html.

RainCity Housing and Support Society. *Vivian Grace Ash: 1933–1999*. Vancouver: RainCity Housing website. Available at www.raincityhousing.org/what-we-do/client-stories/vivian-grace-ash-1933-1999/.

RainCity Housing and Support Society. *Women's Housing*. Vancouver: RainCity Housing. Available at www.raincityhousing.org/what-we-do/womens-housing/.

Shannon, Kate, et al. *Community-Based* HIV *Prevention Research among Substance-Using Women in Survival Sex Work: The Maka Project Partnership.* Vancouver: B.C. Centre for Excellence in HIV/AIDS, 2007.

Shannon, Kate, et al. *Drug Sharing with Clients as a Risk Marker for Increased Violence and Sexual and Drug-Related Harms among Survival Sex Workers.* Vancouver: B.C. Centre for Excellence in HIV/AIDS, 2008.

Shannon, Kate, et al. *Social and Structural Violence and Power Relations in Mitigating* HIV *Risk among Drug-Using Women in Survival Sex Work.* Vancouver: B.C. Centre for Excellence in HIV/AIDS, 2007.

Street Crime Working Group. *Beyond the Revolving Door: A New Response to Chronic Offenders.* Vancouver: Commissioned by the B.C. Ministry of the Attorney-General, 2005.

Tebrake, Rebecca. "Sex Workers Lose All-Night Support System: Provincial Government Failed to Renew Funding for Van Carrying Clean Needles, Condoms." *Vancouver Sun,* June 15, 2009.

WISH Drop-in Centre Society. *Our History.* Vancouver: WISH website. Available at www.wish-vancouver.net/index.cfm?go=site.index&section=about&page=history.

CHAPTER 15: NAOMI and the Fight to Save Insite

Boyd, Neil, Brian Kinney, and Carla McLean. *Final Report: Public Order and Supervised Injection Facilities: Vancouver's Supervised Injection Site.* Health Canada, February 2008.

Boyd, Neil, Carla McLean, and Mark Huhn. *Final Report: North American Opiate Medications Initiative, Community Impact Study, Vancouver Site.* Health Canada, December 2008.

Brehmer, C., and P.X. Iten. "Medical Prescription of Heroin to Chronic Heroin Addicts in Switzerland—A Review." *Forensic Science International,* 2001.

Bula, Frances. "Addicts Nervous about Qualifying for Heroin Trial." *Vancouver Sun,* January 28, 2005.

Bula, Frances. "Judge Rules Vancouver Supervised-Injection Site Can Stay Open for a Year." *Vancouver Sun,* May 28, 2008.

Freeman, K., et al. "The impact of the Sydney Medically Supervised Injecting Centre (MSIC) on Crime." *Drug and Alcohol Review,* 2005.

Fry, C.L., S. Cvetkovski, and J. Cameron. "The Place of Supervised Injecting Facilities within Harm Reduction: Evidence, Ethics and Policy." *Addiction* 101, 2006, pp. 465–467.

Hansen, Darah. "City's Users Just Say No to Free Drugs: Distrust, Delay Discourage Downtown Eastside Addicts." *Vancouver Sun*, March 15, 2005.

Hedrich, D. *European Report on Drug Consumption Rooms*. Lisbon: European Monitoring Centre for Drugs and Drug Addiction, 2004. Retrieved September 2007 from www.emcdda.europa.eu/html.cfm/ index1327EN.html.

Hogben, David. "RCMP Attempted to Discredit Insite, Pivot Legal Society Says: Lawyer Contends Police Commissioned Research in an Effort to Disparage Supervised Injection Site." *Vancouver Sun*, October 9, 2008.

Independent Working Group on Drug Consumption Rooms. *The Report of the Independent Working Group on Drug Consumption Rooms*. United Kingdom: Joseph Rowntree Foundation. Retrieved September 2007 from www.yps-publishing.co.uk.

Kerr, T., et al. "Impact of a Medically Supervised Safer Injection Facility on Community Drug Use Patterns: A Before and After Study." *British Medical Journal*, pp. 332, 220–222.

Munro, Margaret. "Scientists Blast Tories for 'Mistreatment': 85 Prominent Researchers Call on Leaders to End the 'Politicization' of Science." *Vancouver Sun*, October 10, 2008.

Naber, D., and C. Haasen. *The German Model Project for Heroin Assisted Treatment of Opioid Dependent Patients—A Multi-Centre, Randomized, Controlled Treatment Study*. Hamburg, Germany: Centre for Interdisciplinary Addiction Research of Hamburg University, 2006. Retrieved February 2007 from www.heroinstudie.de/H-Report_P1_engl.pdf.

NAOMI Study Team. *Reaching the Hardest to Reach—Treating the Hardest-to-Treat*. Vancouver, October 2008.

National Centre in HIV Epidemiology and Clinical Research. *Sydney Medically Supervised Injecting Centre Interim Evaluation Report No. 2: Evaluation of Community Attitudes towards the Sydney MSIC*, March 2006. Retrieved September 2007 from www.sydneymsic.com/Bginfo.htm.

O'Neil, Peter. "Feds Weigh Risks of Pulling the Plug on Insite: International Opinion, Demand for Research Funding among Concerns." *Vancouver Sun*, March 26, 2007.

Petrar, S., et al. "Injection Drug Users' Perceptions Regarding Use of a Medically Supervised Injection Facility." *Addictive Behaviors* 32, 2007, pp. 1088–1093.

Rhodes, T., et al. "Public Injecting and the Need for 'Safer Environment
  Interventions' in the Reduction of Drug-Related Harm." *Addiction* 101,
  2006, pp. 1384–1393.

Skelton, Chad. "Painkiller Works for Heroin Addiction; Dilaudid as Effective
  as Heroin, and More Effective than Methadone, for Addicts, Study Shows."
  Vancouver Sun, October 18, 2008.

Skelton, Chad. "Sullivan Drug Stance 'Simplistic': Larry Campbell Blasts
  Mayor for his Support of Giving Drugs to Addicts." *Vancouver Sun,*
  April 22, 2006.

Strathdee, S.A., and R.A. Pollini. "A 21st-century Lazarus: The Role of the
  Safer Injection Sites in Harm Reduction." *Addiction* 102, pp. 848–849.

Thein, H.H., et al. "Public Opinion towards Supervised Injecting Centres and
  the Sydney Medically Supervised Injecting Centre." *International Journal of
  Drug Policy* 16, pp. 275–280.

Vancouver Coastal Health. *The Downtown Eastside: A Neighbourhood in Recovery.*
  Vancouver, 2008.

Ward, Doug. "Keep Insite Open, Premier Says; Campbell Addresses Concerns
  that New Federal Anti-Drug Strategy May Close Site." *Vancouver Sun,*
  October 2, 2007.

Wright, N.M., and C.N. Tompkins. "Supervised Injecting Centres."
  British Medical Journal 328(7431), 2004, pp. 100–102.

CHAPTER 16: Housing Vancouver's Poor

Birnie, Peter. "Play about Civic Response to Welfare Cuts Offers
  Performer a Way Up." *Vancouver Sun,* January 28, 2004.

Davidson, Jill. *2007 Survey of Low-Income Housing in the Downtown Core.*
  City of Vancouver Housing Centre, July 2007.

Diamond, David. *History of Headlines Theatre.* www.headlinestheatre.com.

Diamond, David. *Practicing Democracy: Final Report.* Vancouver: Headlines
  Theatre, 2004.

Fowlie, Jonathan. "Governments Spar over Cash: Raymond Louie Says
  Projects Held Up, Coleman Says Ball Is in City's Court." *Vancouver Sun,*
  June 18, 2009.

Lookout Emergency Aid Society. *Our History.* Available at
  www.lookoutsociety.bc.ca/Our-History.html.

McInnes, Craig, and Frances Bula. "Campbell Blasts Campbell over
  Vancouver's Homeless." *Vancouver Sun,* October 10, 2003.

Patterson, Michelle, Julian Somers, et al. *Housing and Support for Adults with Severe Addictions and/or Mental Illness in British Columbia.* Vancouver: Centre For Applied Research in Mental Health and Addiction, Simon Fraser University, February 2008.

Swanson, Jean, et al. *Disappearing Homes: The Loss of Affordable Housing in the DTES.* Vancouver: Carnegie Community Action Project, April 2008.

Swanson, Jean, et al. *Still Losing Hotel Rooms: CCAP's 2009 Hotel Survey and Report.* Vancouver: Carnegie Community Action Project, June 2009.

CHAPTER 17: The Road Ahead

Bellett, Gerry. "Umbrella Agency Urged for DTES Support Groups: VPD Chief Proposes Body with 'Director for Most Vulnerable.'" *Vancouver Sun,* February 5, 2009.

Culbert, Lori. "Act Now to Stop Sex Trade Boom, Group Says: Transition House Members Opposed to Initiative to Create Legal Brothel for Winter Games." *Vancouver Sun,* May 30, 2008.

Culbert, Lori. "Family Wrestles with Street's Death Grip: Advocates Struggle for Solutions to Help Women Conquer Demons of Downtown Eastside." *Vancouver Sun,* February 28, 2008.

Culbert, Lori. "Police Becoming De Facto Mental Health Workers of Our Society: Closing of mental health institutions, funding cutbacks for social housing, inadequate welfare rates and abundance of drugs causing crisis in Downtown Eastside, officer says." *Vancouver Sun,* February 2, 2008.

Culbert, Lori. "Treatment Available but Nowhere to Go Later: Odds Are Stacked against Women Trying to Turn Their Life Around after Years of Abuse." *Vancouver Sun,* February 27, 2008.

Davies, Libby. *Olympic Hopes Dashed for Homeless* (press release). Vancouver, March 20, 2009. Available at www.libbydavies.ca.

Davies, William, QC. *Alone and Cold: The Davies Commission Inquiry Into the Death of Frank Paul.* Vancouver, February 2009. Available at www.frankpaulinquiry.ca.

Greater Vancouver Regional Steering Committee on Homelessness. *Still on Our Street . . . Results of the 2008 Metro Vancouver Homeless Count.* Vancouver, September 16, 2008.

Lowman, John. "Prostitution Law Reform in Canada." In *Toward Comparative Law in the 21st Century*. Tokyo: Chuo University Press, 1998, pp. 919–946.

Mackie, John. "Lighting up the Downtown Eastside: Restored Hotel, Stunning Deco Sign a Beacon of Hope for a Troubled Area." *Vancouver Sun*, January 8, 2009.

Mental Health Policy Research Group. *Mental Illness and Pathways into Homelessness: Findings and Implications: Proceedings and Recommendations.* CMHA Ontario Division, Clarke Institute of Psychiatry, Ontario Mental Health Foundation, January 1998.

Paulsen, Monte. "Mayor Sullivan's Big Ambitions." *Tyee*, December 21, 2006.

Sinoski, Kelly, et al. "Fire Victim Refused Shelter: 'Tracey' likely worried about losing her belongings because shelters don't permit shopping carts." *Vancouver Sun*, December 20, 2008.

Rolfsen, Catherine. "Homeless Shelters to Stay Open Three More Months." *Vancouver Sun*, March 10, 2009.

Rolfsen, Catherine. "Police Propose Change to Drug Strategy: Plan Calls for Seizing Narcotics, but Not Prosecuting Low-level Offenders in Downtown Eastside." *Vancouver Sun*, March 19, 2009.

Terri Jean Bedford, Amy Lebovitch, and Valerie Scott v. Her Majesty the Queen, Ontario Superior Court of Justice, 2007, Court File No. 07-CV-329807PD1.

Wilson-Bates, Fiona. *Lost in Transition: How a Lack of Capacity in the Mental Health System is Failing Vancouver's Mentally Ill and Draining Police Resources.* Vancouver Police, Special Investigation Section, January 2008.

Vancouver Native Health Society. *2007 Annual Report*. Vancouver, 2008.

Acknowledgements

THERE ARE MANY GENEROUS PEOPLE who agreed to tell their stories to fill the pages of this book: residents and activists, artists and support workers, nurses and doctors, Native leaders and politicians, just to name a few. The vast majority of them share a passionate commitment to the Downtown Eastside. We are grateful for their wisdom and insight into the community and, while we pause to thank a few specific people, we remain indebted to everyone who took the time to speak to us about the neighbourhood.

Many thanks to Judy Graves, Vancouver city hall's tireless housing advocate, for her guided tours of the Downtown Eastside, and to Donald MacPherson, the city's drug policy coordinator, for his experience and expertise. Also to the Portland Hotel Society trio—Liz Evans, Mark Townsend, and Dan Small—for their generosity, as well as to the folks at RainCity Housing and Vancouver Native Health. John Atkin provided his encyclopedic knowledge about the community's history. We salute Bud Osborn for sharing his stories and his evocative poetry; the title of this book is borrowed from Osborn's poem "a thousand crosses in oppenheimer park," a portion of which is reproduced in Chapter 7. The final words in the book come from Osborn's poem "Down Here." Both excerpts are reprinted by permission of Arsenal Pulp Press. The quotes from *Da Vinci's Inquest,* © Chris Haddock, appear with Chris Haddock's permission.

Our appreciation, also, to the *Vancouver Sun* for providing access to the research articles quoted in this book and to the *Sun's* photographers for the images displayed within these pages. In particular, a special thanks goes to *Sun* librarian Kate Bird, who gathered a century's worth of photos. In addition, the Carnegie Centre library was invaluable, providing access to historical reports and documents about the Downtown Eastside.

Finally, we acknowledge loved ones who provided support while we wrote this book, as well as the Downtown Eastside residents who let us into their community to tell their stories.

Index

Neil Boyd, Lori Culbert, and Larry Campbell
PHOTO BY ANDREW NAIBERG

As mayor of Vancouver from 2002–2005, **LARRY CAMPBELL** championed the Four Pillars Drug Strategy and oversaw the establishment of North America's first legal injection site. Prior to that, he set up Vancouver's first district coroner's office after serving for several years in the RCMP. His high-profile career as chief coroner for British Columbia inspired the Gemini Award–winning TV series *Da Vinci's Inquest* and its spin-off, *Da Vinci's City Hall.* A Liberal senator since 2005, Campbell continues his work on drug policy, mental health, and Aboriginal issues.

NEIL BOYD is a professor and associate director of the School of Criminology at Simon Fraser University. Educated in psychology at the University of Western Ontario and in law at Osgoode Hall, he is the author of five previous books, two textbooks, and many academic articles. He is a media commentator on drug law, drug policy, and issues of criminal violence and has completed two community impact studies for Health Canada, focusing on the NAOMI heroin prescription trial and the supervised injection site in Vancouver's Downtown Eastside.

LORI CULBERT is an award-winning investigative journalist with the *Vancouver Sun.* She has spent years writing about the Downtown Eastside, as well as about the dozens of women who have vanished from the neighbourhood and the trial of accused serial killer Robert Pickton.